Arthur's Round

# Arthur's Round:
## *The Life and Times of Brewing Legend Arthur Guinness*

### PATRICK GUINNESS

PETER OWEN
London and Chester Springs

PETER OWEN PUBLISHERS
73 Kenway Road, London SW5 0RE

Peter Owen books are distributed in the USA by
Dufour Editions Inc., Chester Springs, PA 19425-0007

First published in Great Britain 2008 by
Peter Owen Publishers

ISBN 978 0 7206 1296 7

A catalogue record for this book is available from the British Library

Printed and bound in Great Britain by
Windsor Print Production Ltd, Tonbridge

Front cover and inside back cover 'A Pint of Guinness's Best' (1850s) by
Charles Wynne Nicholls. Back cover and inside front cover stamp design
after a portrait of Arthur Guinness (c. 1790), reproduced by kind permission
of An Post ©.

# Contents

# Illustrations

# *Preface*

ARTHUR GUINNESS (1725–1803) is one of those iconic Irishmen about whom very little is known by the public at large. Whether from family or brewery myth-making or from his keeping a low profile, certain key facts and myths have been repeated until a wheel-rut of anecdote has emerged that has become history. His name and signature are seen in and on nearly every Irish village and are widely known abroad. His business and its social off-shoots have formed an integral part of Dublin life for over two centuries. Two and a half centuries after his first brewing on his own account in 1755, it is time to consider him and the Ireland in which he lived. Very few biographies have been published about Irish people of his time who were not politicians, so, apart from being the first publication to consider Arthur himself in the round, it is also a tale of grey areas.

Since Howard and Henry Guinness's useful notes were assembled and typed up between 1922 and 1934, and one of family trees prepared in three editions by Brian Guinness between 1955 and 1985, a clutch of books has been written on the family and brewery in recent decades, focusing largely on the application of wealth over the last two centuries. These include a brief brewery history (1955) and works by George Martelli (1957), Desmond Moore (1959), P. Lynch and J. Vaizey (1960), Peter Walsh (1980), Frederic Mullally (1981), Jonathan Guinness (1997), Derek Wilson (1998) and Michele Guinness (1990, 1999), together with some general television documentaries in the past few years.

All these contain inaccuracies – that the brewery's water supply came from the River Liffey is a well-known one. To be fair, most of these studies deal with the whole history of the entire family and not just Arthur, and in spanning over two hundred years they rather rush on past him to the main focus of their sagas. The volume by Lynch and Vaizey was an official brewery history up to 1876, well prepared on the economic story but short on local and social history, and it has been heavily plagiarized. It should be read alongside L.M. Cullen's 1972 book on the Irish economy after 1660, which has a wider angle. Essays by the Trinity College Dublin lecturer Sean Dunne (2003) have some novel and interesting interpretations and were based perhaps on his sociology dissertation at University College Dublin, now lost. Unfortunately he has felt unable to share the notes and references that would support his views. Dr Tanya Cassidy could not be contacted by post or email about her research. Recent analyses by Frederick Aalen (1990), S.R. Dennison and Oliver MacDonagh (1998), Peter Malpass (1998), Al Byrne (1999), Dr Andrew Bielenberg (2003) and Tony Corcoran (2005) concentrate usefully on the brewery as a social and economic phenomenon. Brenda Murphy and Kerry Byrne are, at the time of writing, working separately on the history of the beer itself.

Details apart, none of these many writers on Guinness has looked at its creator in any depth; this is the first attempt. In the process of the story I have considered their analyses and disagree on some points; the reader must decide if I am reasonable or not. Naturally, I have had to avoid ancestor-worship. Other mistakes have arisen from modern advertising and television, which is generally amusing but which has its own priorities, and the internet, which has thrown up a host of notes. Having its commercial aspect the 'heritage industry' feeds off, but must not be confused with, history. It seemed right that some analysis and attempt at chronology should be done outside of the restrictions of commercial, academic or government sponsorship – perhaps via the internet – but the volume of new material suggested it be preserved in book form.

Today, school-examination papers in Ireland mention Arthur, and the Guinness website describes him as a 'magic ingredient'. But how much of what we know about him is based on publicity generated over the last century by my own family? If he is seen today as an icon of Georgian Dublin, how iconic would he have been in his own time? The book examines this issue.

Arthur's political views are also examined for the first time, and can been seen to have been aligned with those of Richard Brinsley Sheridan and Edmund Burke. All three had a better grasp of the relationship between Britain and Ireland than most of their contemporaries. They understood the need for cautious political progress without bloodshed. This aspect of Arthur's life has never been fully explored. Henry Grattan was his man. The world of the Protestant Ascendancy was a two-way street for an indigenous Irishman if he chose to play by the rules. In its Volunteer phase Arthur's political leanings may be linked to the Duke of Leinster's liberal stance. His patriot tendencies thus come into clearer focus, and I attempt to explain that unsuccessful formula for Irish political conciliation. Towards the end of his life his views on Catholic emancipation have been classified by Professor R.B. McDowell as 'extreme liberal', yet he would not support violent revolution to promote change. One aim of biography is to examine the subject as a man of his time; while the man can be described, every reader will have a different idea of the time.

The most useful sources on his parents' important and largely ignored years living in and near Celbridge (1690–1764) are the notes of the late Lena Boylan. A stalwart of the Kildare Archaeological Society, she had read hundreds of letters to and from local people of all backgrounds. She was a compendium of the entire history of Celbridge and its recorded inhabitants from the earliest times up to date. Living on the Main Street and knowing every inch of the village, she could correlate all the names and mapless plots of land mentioned in old title deeds. She copied her notes to me in 1997 and assembled details on the local members of Arthur's dining club, the Friendly Brothers of St Patrick. The club's minute book for the years 1777 to 1791 was kindly made available for the first time in 2000, unlocking a wealth of material. This unknown local history colours and enlarges the better-known story of the city brewer.

In 1997 County Kildare historian Colonel Con Costello invited me to give the county's Heritage Day speech at Arthur's grave. In preparing for it I realized how much had been ignored and forgotten by the family, how little I knew of its origins and how many contradictory stories there were. In 2000 I supplied Leixlip Town Council with a millennium essay, and in 2001 the Kildare Archaeological Society kindly published my research on the Friendly Brothers of St Patrick. Since then I have been asked to speak to a number of other groups, while some novel and relevant genetic research has accumulated and was prepared for a thesis by Brian McEvoy published in 2004. The known facts are here, with considerable analysis of the many myths. Devoid of heroics, this is largely a family story of several generations of people of low or middling status who progress by small steps.

The genetic networks of County Down surnames included here comprise another new element and are designed to show degrees of relatedness of male ancestries at a glance, without scientific jargon or strings of numbers. I particularly thank Dr Brian McEvoy of Trinity College Dublin for preparing and lending them from his recent publications. I want to thank his 315 volunteer donors, of whom all bar four are unknown to me. Arthur's life was a continuation of a gradual cultural process of moving from the Gaelic polity to the commercial world, an acclimatization to be appreciated as slowly as a pint.

For those wanting more on the background of life in the Georgian city, the best source is still *Dublin 1660–1860* by Dr Maurice Craig and *Dr Johnson's London* by Liza Picard. For erudite comments on the Dublin street scene in 1760, the *Cries of Dublin* (2003), edited by William Laffan, is indispensable. Looking back at life before electricity, modern hygiene, aircraft, cars, telephones or the ideas of Darwin, Edison, Ford, Einstein and Gandhi requires a great leap of imagination. The background setting of Dublin and Kildare in Arthur's day is explored, and his family, business, political, social and charitable interests provide his main round. His life was also a round, returning with deliberate emotion to his place of origin – and of course he created the ideal material for innumerable liquid rounds.

Most of the Irish population have successfully adapted to urban life over the last century, and now seek a higher education and greater wealth. Ireland has changed from the inward-looking place of my youth to a more confident and realistic country, especially in the economic and financial fields. Its confident ability to raise employment, skills, inward investment and morale in the last decade would have had Arthur's full blessing, and, in return, today's Irish readership can better understand his and his family's commercial activities and priorities.

For anyone truly interested in Arthur's creation, the Storehouse Museum at the Guinness brewery in Dublin must be seen and smelt, having a wonderful system of vents to allow visitors to sense the brew at its various stages. In 2000 it hosted a reception by the Irish Taoiseach Bertie Ahern for President Bill Clinton of the USA, at which Mr Ahern said:

We're gathered in St James's Gate in the heart of the Liberties of the greatest city in the world. The Liberties are one of Dublin's great communities, and it's here that a great Irish businessman, Arthur Guinness, started the brew Guinness over 250 years ago, which in time became a global brand with strong links to Ireland. And the Guinness story reminds us that innovation and trade are very much part and parcel of the heritage of Dublin and this community.

Arthur's story must also consider what it took to progress in the Ireland of his day, and a question emerges as to why so few of his fellow Irishmen applied themselves to the basic skills of writing and trade. Was this cultural or from habit, or a lack of encouragement, resources or opportunity? Why was Mr Ahern's 'innovation and trade' adopted by the Guinnesses but not by many others? It will be seen that he had an unsuspected head start, prepared by his parents and even his grandparents, inheriting money and skills, and their contributions have not been recorded until now. Their homes near to Dublin and his move to the city made the difference. Luck and steady hard work also played their part. Quiet consistency is a theme in his work and his politics. All my life I have been asked where Arthur brewed the first pint. The question is not as simple as it sounds. Depending on the beer in question, the many myths and the unusual facts, I have teased out the unexpected answer – or answers.

This book is a tribute to the man who made one drink virtually synonymous with the country of Ireland.

All opinions and any errors in this book are mine, but I must acknowledge my gratitude and large or small debts for advice, information and encouragement from the following individuals: Sir Richard Aylmer; Toby Barnard; Sergio Benedetti; Ursula Bond; the late Lena Boylan and her daughter Catherine; Liam Chambers; John Colgan; Maurice Craig; the late Colonel Con Costello; Grattan de Courcy Wheeler; John Deaton; William Dick; David Dickson; Antony Farrell; Alex Findlater; Raymond Gillespie; Paul Guinness; Robert Guinness; Enda Lee; Charles Lysaght; Philip Magennis; Brian McCabe; Seán McCartan; Harry McDowell; R.B. McDowell; Donald Mills; Kevin Nowlan; Harold O'Sullivan; David McConnell; Kay Muhr; Chris Pomery; Jim Tancred; Kevin Whelan. I am also indebted to to the helpful assistance of all at Peter Owen Publishers; the staff of the National Library of Ireland; Eibhlín Roche and everyone at the Guinness brewery archives; Daniel Bradley, Brian McEvoy and the staff at the Genetics Department at Trinity College Dublin; Fred Krehbiel and William Laffan; and, not least, my father Desmond, my sister Marina and the saintly patience of my wife Louise.

I have included maps – old ones where possible – and images for which I hope I have also given sufficient acknowledgement. Measurements are generally given in imperial/avoirdupois with metric conversions provided in an appendix.

*Patrick Guinness*
*2007*

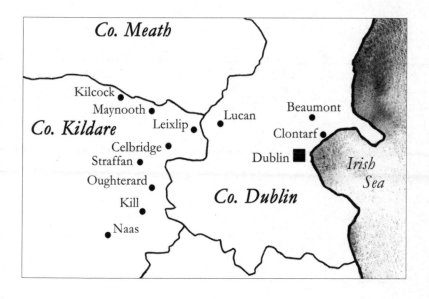

*CHAPTER ONE*

# Origins

*T*HE FAMILY FOUNDATIONS must first be laid down before we look at the man himself, and an understanding of Irish history will add some nuances to the facts. Arthur's parents – Richard Guinness (*c.* 1690–1766) and Elizabeth Read (1698–1742) – and their families emerged into the eighteenth century from the humblest of backgrounds, and he must often have reflected on this progress and how best to continue that momentum in his own life. He never denied his origins – rather the contrary – but he also did not allow them to limit him.

His mother Elizabeth's family, the Reads, lived five miles from his birthplace in Celbridge and must have been visited often in his childhood. Her parents were William and Catherine Read, tenant-farmers at Oughterard near Ardclough, in the north-east of County Kildare. The evidence is still there: today's visitor can drive out of Dublin on the Cork–Limerick main road and swing northwards at Junction 6, signed for Castlewarden, continuing for about a mile to the summit of a ridge and parking at a gate reading Oughterard Cemetery.

In Kildare, the anglicized surname Read derives from Mulready, or in the old Gaelic language Ó Maoil Bhríghde, a 'grandson of a servant of the cult of St Bridget'. At Oughterard – *uachtar ard* means upper height in Gaelic – stands a ruined church and round tower that were part of a monastery dedicated to St Bridget that was destroyed by the Dublin Vikings in 995 and again in 1094.[1] It also suggests that the Reads could have lived on or near the hilltop for centuries. The name Bridget, who was the patron saint of County Kildare (d. 520), derives from Bríd, or Brig, a pre-Christian fertility goddess associated with the druidic feast of Imbolc that took place in early February. It is also said that the St Bridget of Oughterard lived long after the original saint. The hilltop stands on a prehistoric ley line running from standing stones to its south northwards via other religious sites to a ford over the Liffey near Celbridge. Like many such places in Europe it was made Christian by building a church on the summit. In the Gaelic era, up to 1171, Oughterard was close to Liamhán (Lyons), the centre of the local kingdom of the Ó Dunnchada (Dunphy) family, who in turn were part of the Uí Faolain ruling dynasty in north Leinster.

When the Normans arrived after 1169 the area passed to Adam de Hereford, who willed it to a monastery in Dublin eighteen miles away. The Papal taxation of 1303 lists the annual value of 'Outherard' manor at twelve pounds, with a tithe of twelve shillings. A tower was built and the area was included in the defence of the 'Machery', the plain around Dublin where it was safe to use Norman law. In the 1530s all such monastic lands were seized by Henry VIII, and Oughterard was sold to the Alen family.[2] Such confiscations were ratified by the Papacy and Queen Mary in 1554 without local consultation. It then passed through marriages to the Anglo-Irish Ponsonbys from Tipperary, who lived there during Arthur's lifetime.

Up to the 1580s the Gaelic O'Toole clan, descendants of the Uí Faolain dynasty, would descend in armed raids from the eastern hills unless they were paid off by the locals with a 'black rent', which in 1574 came to £1. 6s. 8d. for Oughterard parish. This was costly, being about three times the nine shillings that the tenant-farmers paid to the landlord as their legal rent.[3] To everyone's relief, the clan was suppressed by 1600. In the civil wars of the 1640s the locals saw the armies march and counter-march on the main road far below, and royalists burnt Lyons manor in 1642. The parish was a war zone for eight years, being near the main road to the south-west out of Dublin. The Confederate Irish made incursions in the mid-1640s, burning crops and buildings, and finally whatever was left in the area was destroyed in 1650 by the English Cromwellian cavalry under Colonel Hewson.

In 1690 Arthur's farmer-grandfather, William Read, had bought a licence to sell ale in order to give himself some extra income, the first written proof of any link to beer in the family.[4] William would not have sold someone else's ale but would have brewed it himself, as many households did, as it was safer to drink than water. Living near the main Dublin–Cork road, it is likely that he sold his beer off a stall to passing traffic, most of which was on foot. Between 1689 and 1691 the road swarmed with the heavy passage of armies, officials, baggage and artillery trains, camp followers and refugees arising from the war between Kings James II and William III. Whichever of them won would make little difference to William Read. We can picture a regiment struggling into the foothills several hours' march south of Dublin on the rough, rutted, dusty main road and seeing a welcome ale tent with jugs of beer waiting to hit their thirsty palates. A later picture by Francis Wheatley, *An Ale Tent at Donnybrook Fair*, suggests the scene (Plate 2).[5]

Brewing ale was an ancient Irish skill, improved by the later addition of hops. Dioscorides – the first-century Greek physician and botanist – noted that the Hiberi (the Irish; usually Hiberni) drank a liquor called *courmi*, which appears similar to the Gaelic *coirm*, meaning ale. In the Irish *Táin* saga, King Conchubar (Conor) was said to spend a third of his time 'drinking ale until sleep overtakes him'. In the *Críth Gablach*, a law tract of the 700s, a king's weekly routine was considered: 'Sunday for drinking ale, for he is no rightful prince who does not promise ale for every Sunday.' The ancient Gaelic text, the *Senchas Mór*, refers to the testing of malt barley for ale-making. The former high kings of Ireland had to marry symbolically the goddess-queen Medb (Maeve), meaning 'the drunken' or 'she who makes drunk', at Tara by drinking ale and so acquiring sovereignty. St Patrick brought his personal brewer, Mescan, with him on his missionary tours, giving him status when visiting royal families whom he hoped to convert.

By William Read's day ale was the safest drink in everyday life, as running or well waters were often unclean. Compared with whiskey (*uisce beatha*, 'the water of life'), low-alcohol ale was safe for all the family and could be stored for a short time, as the alcohol killed any germs. The use of hops from the Middle Ages defined beer as distinct from ale, but eventually it was used in both. While hops imparted flavour and allowed the brew to be stored longer, they were not immediately popular and were seen in England as a German import. According to Andrew Boorde's *Dyetary of Helth* (1542):

> Bere is the naturall drynke for a Dutche man and nowe of late dayes it is moche used in Englande to the detryment of many Englysshe people ... If the bere be well served, and be fyned [clear], and not new, it doth gualyfy [reduce] the heat of the lyver.

People have always been particular about the quality of their beer.

William finally made it on to the Kildare electoral rolls in 1715 after the advent of the Hanoverians, proof that he had attained a certain level of wealth, and it is likely that he converted to Protestantism, the official denomination, around this time. William's involvement in beer-selling, the first known in the family, has generally been overlooked, but it was also a social turning point, the first sign that the Reads wanted to become involved in a non-farming income. Many myths about the origins of Arthur's famous black porter beer have arisen: Arthur's father burnt some malting barley by mistake, but it tasted fine; or the recipe came to the him from one place or another; most unlikely of all was the suggestion that it came to Arthur in his clergyman-employer's will, having been sat on, unused, for decades. As we shall see, Arthur first sold a dark beer in 1778 in response to imports from England. All the myths seem unlikely in the light of William's 1690 licence, and there is no evidence that Arthur's father ever brewed beer, although he must have understood the process and later married an inn-keeping widow.

Another local William Read of the previous generation may be found in the records.[6] He was listed in 1640 as a shepherd minding some three hundred-sheep for a 'New English' landlord, Sir Philip Perceval (1603–47), for the modest annual pay of 'diet and £2' in the townland of Castlewarden, which is adjacent to Oughterard. By contrast, Teige McShane, a cowherd, was paid six pounds; the gardener, Anthony Geffery, twelve pounds; and the bailiff, James Scully, eight pounds. It seems that Read was at the bottom of the heap. Sir Philip also paid the Alen family seventeen shillings and sixpence for the annual chief rent of Oughterard itself. He had arrived from England and started his career checking property titles in Dublin Castle as a humble administrator in the 1620s on a salary of thirteen pounds a year. By 1641 he had somehow legally acquired 99,900 statute acres in Ireland, which gave him an annual income of £6,000.[7]

This William Read was Elizabeth's grandfather, as no other Reads are mentioned at that time, and William remained a popular name in the Read family for more than a century. But how could he have risen from lowly shepherd to the relatively secure status of tenant-farmer between 1640 and 1690? The civil wars of 1641–50 and the Percevals' archives suggest the answer. Sir Philip had acquired sudden and great wealth in Ireland, typical of many unpopular 'New English' officials, which was lost for a time in the civil wars of the 1640s. Starting as a royalist, by 1644 he was swimming with the tide and had joined the English parliamentarians.

His land agent Valentine Savage, living in the safety of Dublin, complained in a stream of letters to Perceval in England in August 1647 about the state of his 396 acres and the lawlessness in north-east Kildare after nearly six years of warfare:

> I believe they will plunder me for want of linen and to buy them firing [firewood] &c. I might have prevented this and other inconveniences as the burning of your house and corn twice . . . I can neither preserve your things nor subsist longer myself . . . you have much more in arrears [of rent] due than will ever be paid.[8]

It was a litany of woe. The previous April he could not even find reliable English tenant-farmers 'that have stocks' [farm animals] to take the land free of rent 'until you come over'. Savage hoped that his patron would arrive with an English protective force, but Perceval died in London that November.

That long upheaval, followed by the Cromwellian raids, would have created an opening after 1650 for countrymen with local knowledge such as William Read the shepherd. The land had to be farmed by someone – anyone – at any rent or none, or it would have reverted to a wilderness. Famine and plague followed the wars, leaving fewer experienced, able-bodied peasants alive to keep things in order. In the Civil Survey of 1654–5 the main house at Castlewarden was said to have been worth £2,000 in 1640 but had 'decayed' to a value of £1,000. The next agent wrote to Perceval's son in 1655: 'Let Castlewarden building stand still awhile and erect nothing but little houses for tenants.'[9] It was the obvious opportunity for Read to step upwards on to the first rungs of the agricultural ladder. Although the area was close to Dublin, we must imagine a low level of civility, as the first printed but roadless map of Kildare was published as late as 1685. In the early 1720s Elizabeth Read, daughter of William the tenant-farmer – and granddaughter of the first William Read – married Richard Guinness, possibly in the church at Oughterard, and their first child, Arthur, was born in Celbridge in 1725.

Richard Guinness's immediate ancestry has been harder to trace and has been the subject of much speculation and lengthy research from many quarters. He appears from nowhere in 1722, working for a clergyman, Dr Arthur Price, in Celbridge, County Kildare. Price is a Welsh surname pronounced 'Preece'.[10] Price's father had been a local clergyman in Kildare, and his family came originally from Cardiganshire.

Richard's father was a Protestant tenant-farmer named Eoin (or Owen) 'Guinneas' or 'Guinis' of Dalkey and later of Simmonscourt just south-east of Dublin. This background is traceable in birth entries and a lease of 1726.[11] Owen Guinneas was a sidesman at Donnybrook Church in 1714, and Richard would therefore have been baptized as a Protestant. Farmer Guinneas had elder sons, and Richard had elder brothers named George and William. Richard's brother William was born in 1689, but Richard's birthdate around 1691 was unrecorded, evidently because another civil war was in progress or because the family moved to Simmonscourt that year. 'Owen Guinis of Symon Court, farmer' was a defendant in a 1714 debt recovery case.[12] Later, William and Richard Guinis were named in a lease-for-three-lives (a lease that lasted as long as one of the three men named in the document was still alive) granted by Joseph Leeson on 5 January 1726 for 'their brother' George, a dairyman who had moved to Milltown, then just a few fields away from Simmonscourt in the next parish. A later map shows how close they are (Plate 36). This is a feasible paper link, where the first lease had fallen in and the farm business moves to another tenancy near by. The name Owen – or Eoin – suggests a Gaelic-origin ancestry. He had another son named John, the anglicized version of Eoin, who had died in 1718.[13] The farm being so close to Dublin would have given Richard the opportunity to learn to read at the village school and to gain some experience of the varied realities and opportunities of life in the city and the countryside in his formative years.

Owen had no written lineage himself, but his family's oral tradition was made plain by his grandson. In 1761 Arthur Guinness assumed the arms of the Gaelic Magennis (Mac Aonghusa) clan from Iveagh (Uíbh Eachach), in west County Down in Ulster.[14] Their chiefs had been ennobled as Viscount Magennis of Iveagh between 1623 and 1693, in return for paying £2,000 to one of James I's favourites and subsequently as counts in the Spanish peerage. This suggests that he believed that he was related to these Magennises, also spelt MacGuinness, and that his forebears had anglicized their surname in the 1600s by 'dropping the Mac' – *mac* means 'son of' in Gaelic – as many others did. Several branches of the clan had also been Protestant since 1541, so to Arthur it must all have seemed a reasonable continuity. Besides, the Magennises had sold half of their 100,000 acres after 1610, rebelled in 1641 and were dispossessed, even the Protestant Magennises, of the rest in 1657 under Henry Cromwell's administration.[15] Many of the poorer Magennises then moved south to Dublin where we find Owen Guinneas from the 1680s.[16] To Arthur in 1761 such an origin would have spoken of ancient roots torn up by sudden loss from warfare, with new people moving in and displacing the original inhabitants.

Family historians such as Howard and Henry Guinness made much study of this possibility in the years 1900 to 1934 and usefully exploded a number of myths.[17] However, they also concentrated mainly on the senior Magennis viscounts of the Rathfriland branch who died out in the male line but ignored the other twelve branches of the clan with their varied histories. Nothing concrete was found, and Henry concluded that Richard Guinness or his father might also have come from a hamlet called St Gennys in Cornwall – although he omitted to mention that his source for this theory, his great-uncle, had been bankrupted and convicted of electoral fraud, so might not have been entirely reliable.[18] Further, this great-uncle had been an MP in Devon, next to Cornwall, in the 1850s, and may have wanted to portray himself to his electorate as having local origins. Others, such as Mullally, plagiarized this idea of a Cornish origin without a second thought, and this, in its turn, has become another myth based on hearsay.[19]

It would, in any case, have been most unlikely in the Ireland of 1761 – a time when the Penal Laws discriminated in favour of the Protestant Church of Ireland – for a young Cornish-origin Protestant merchant to assume the arms of a Gaelic-Irish Catholic Jacobite family that had been dispossessed of its lands in 1693. So what element of truth lay behind the assumption of arms in 1761 – an illegitimate descent from the chiefs, perhaps? In 1997 it seemed to me that a lack of a paper trail back to Ulster proved nothing more than that our ancestors had arrived poor in Dublin. Poor families escape the taxman and are seldom written about. A number of fires caused by revolutionaries in 1798, 1920 and 1922 had destroyed most Irish medieval parish records and many ancient legal documents – surely a twisted patriotism – but much research had already been done for the family by 1920, and yet little was found. Guinis/Guinneas/Ginnies is a rare and noticeable name in the records. However, a new type of historical record, DNA analysis, had become available by the time of my research, and this did reveal the truth.[20]

A recent male-ancestry genetic survey by Dan Bradley and Brian McEvoy at Trinity College Dublin on the Y-chromosomes of 315 men with Gaelic-clan East Ulster surnames added a considerable twist.[21] Like a surname, this chromosome passes only from father to son, with slow mutations over time. It was unlikely, but just possible, that we descended from the Genese family of Dublin-Jewish merchants, but no typically Middle-Eastern result was found. The reams of data threw several questions into sharp focus:

Was today's 'Guinness of Dublin' male DNA all the same, revealing our common ancestor Richard's own DNA pattern? Was Richard's pattern found in men alive today with Gaelic-era County Down surnames? Was the same pattern shared by the descendants of the former Magennis chiefs?

The answers to these were 'yes', 'yes' and 'no'. Richard's male-line ancestors did come from County Down, but our closest DNA cousins are not the Magennis chiefs but are now surnamed McCartan. In the McCartans' former barony of Kinelarty in central County Down there also happens to be a hilly townland and hamlet, variously spelt Guiness or Ginnies, which has been overlooked by the family's historians to date.[22] It derives from the place name Gion Ais, Gaelic for a wedge-shaped ridge, and not at all from the surname Mac Aonghusa or MacGuinness.

To explain the two networks of genetic results, the first looks at Magennises and McCartans, including derived names – *agnomina* – such as Neeson and McCreesh (Plate 37). Men with a similar DNA profile appear in clusters, each larger or smaller according to the number of men having that profile. The written cousinage of the Magennis and McCartan chiefs is confirmed, and their cluster is shown at A. The 'Guinness of Dublin' result is shown in green at B, and its closest cousins are seen to be those McCartans who were *not* chiefs. In a larger network of Gaelic surnames described by Brian McEvoy as the 'East Ulster genetic landscape', the same relatedness is seen (Plate 38). It took over a year for Dr McEvoy's findings to be peer-reviewed and published in the eminent journal *Human Genetics* in early 2006.

The once-ruling Magennis and McCartan chiefs had a listed mutual ancestor, Mongán, son of Sarán, who lived around 600 AD.[23] Finding their very distinct male-DNA profile in their descendants in 2003 and proving the oldest male lineage in Europe to be confirmed by genetics was a fascinating discovery. The cluster at A has star-shaped offshoots that show some normal, haphazard mutations of genetic code in Mongán's male descendants. Applying probability maths to find the age of the whole star-cluster gives a time-depth of some 1,500 years, exactly the century in which he and Sarán were alive. But this dynastic male DNA profile of the chiefs' *derbfine* – those cousins electable to the chieftainship – in the two clans is also thousands of years distant from today's

Guinnesses, 78 per cent of Magennises, however spelt today, and 50 per cent of the McCartans tested.

It is now apparent that in most Irish and Scottish clans many men took their chiefs' surname as a badge of identity, alliance or reward but could never be elected chiefs of their clan, having no shared male ancestry with the *derbfine*.[24] There is also a Guinness family living in County Down that is neither related to us nor to the chiefs. Just one man in the 120 Magennises tested was very close to the Guinness and to the plebeian-McCartan DNA profile. By using the clan chiefs' or viscounts' arms from 1761 Arthur made a mistake that is still common today, assuming that men of the same surname are all somehow descended from one man. This misreading of Arthur's exact County Down origin was understandable but led to continuing innocent errors. In 1814 his son Hosea applied to the Herald for a grant of the Magennis arms and was allowed an amended version, and in 1891 his great-grandson chose the title of Lord Iveagh.

In the 'Guinness of Dublin' tests, the male-DNA profiles of two men from Arthur's eldest sons' descents (born in 1765 and 1768) and one from his brother Samuel's (born *c.* 1727) were very similar, and therefore that commonly inherited profile was the profile of Richard, the common ancestor. It was a relief that these three lineages still shared the same profile after some fifty conceptions spread over 280 years. That profile, a string of numbers, was easily compared to those with Gaelic-era County Down surnames. The profile is also part of a much larger male-DNA group that is most found in Western Europe today, particularly in the Basque region and in Ireland where it is found in about 90 per cent of men.[25] (By way of comparison, it occurs in around 60 per cent of British men.) It is considered to have arisen in Asia before 20,000 BC and arrived with the hunter-gatherers of Western Europe before the last ice age, millennia before Ireland even became an island.

In sum, given the tiny population in Kinelarty in the 1600s, it seems more likely that the Guinness surname came from the place Gion Ais and definitely not from the grandees of the Magennis and McCartan clans. If the name came from Magennis, it was from a humble lineage, allied but not related to the chiefs. Either way, being outside the chiefs' electable *derbfine* cousinage meant that Richard's nameless refugee ancestor had lost nothing much before moving south towards Dublin in the 1600s. Under the patrilineal Gaelic system he could never have wielded any power nor gained much wealth as a peasant on what is still a bleak hillside. In 1640 Gion Ais still belonged, along with nearby townlands, to the clan chief Phelim McCartan. In much the same way, the Bohill surname from Kinelarty derived from a hill before they moved south to Dublin.[26] Others copied their chiefs' surname instead, although they were not male-line cousins, doubtless out of a sense of belonging.

Kinelarty is still a hilly, rocky, gorse-covered area in central County Down, east of Slieve Croob. It has a wild beauty but is less productive than the rolling drumlin country of Iveagh to the west or the coastal plains of Lecale to the east. Assigned to a Captain Malby from England in 1575, it was then described as 'all desolate and waste, full of thieves, outlaws and unreclaimed people'.[27] Malby didn't stay for long. But the barony has its considerable history, now augmented by the chiefs' genetically confirmed lineage back to at least 600 AD, and a beautiful lakeside religious centre at Loughinisland. The most famous descendant in recent years of the McCartan chiefs, through a female line, was General Charles de Gaulle, leader of the Free French in exile between 1940 and 1944 and later the President and founder of the Fifth Republic; he fondly recalled this ancestry when visiting Ireland in the 1960s.[28]

# CHAPTER TWO

# Transitions

GIVEN THEIR BACKGROUNDS, how did Arthur's grand-parents move up in the world? Like the Reads, it seems that the nameless refugee father of Owen Guinneas somehow managed to farm some land near Dublin and kept his head above water. Gion Ais/Ginnies/Guiness became a surname, and the family was told of an origin in County Down, but the next generation never went back to Gion Ais and forgot the exact origin of the name. The details were unimportant when compared with the everyday scrabble for survival. Such families were often described as 'mere Irish', which sounds pejorative in English, but mere derived from the Latin *merus*, meaning pure or unmixed. Either Owen or his father became Protestant, which would have made life much easier if one lived near Dublin, although this was less so for farmers who lived in settled rural communities further from the capital. A refugee can join any congregation and reinvent himself.

Socially, many Irishmen were adapting themselves towards Western European modernity, and the medieval period is said to have ended in Ireland only by 1660.[1] The Gaelic poets and bards, sponsored by the former chieftains, lamented by now that even the Irish poor were out of their kilts, were dressing as well as the Gaelic kings of old and were adopting English habits and language. The conclusion to the bitter poem 'Och Mo Chreachsa Faisean Chláir Éibhir' by Brian Mac Giolla Phádraig (*c.* 1675) was that the poor were getting above their proper station and were unlikely ever to sponsor him:

> Each beggarwoman's son has curled locks, bright cuffs about his paw, and a golden ring like any prince of the blood of Cas . . . each churl or his son is starched up around the chin, a scarf thrown around him and a garter on him, his tobacco-pipe in his gob . . . his hand from joint to joint bedecked with

bracelets . . . a churl in each house that is owned by a speaker of nasty English and no one paying any heed to a man of the poetic company, save for 'Get out, and take your precious Gaelic with you.'[2]

These despised churls sound typical of the likes of the Guinneas/Guinis and Read families, anglicized in both their dress and speech. They wanted to get on in life. They had nowhere to go but up, and by the last quarter of the seventeenth century they had already developed a taste for imported colonial consumer goods. Professor Kenneth Nicholls considers that 'the status of the great mass of the population in Gaelic Ireland, the actual cultivators and labourers – "churls" as they are referred to by contemporary English writers – was very low indeed'.[3] The Read and the Guinneas families had nothing to gain from a restoration of the former patrilineal Gaelic clan system. Clearly both families – Arthur's immediate ancestors in the 1600s – had been near or at the bottom of the Gaelic social world and were at best Gaelic-origin tenant-farmers in the new Anglo-Irish order.

Ireland was undergoing changes caused variously by the civil and Williamite wars as well as the impossible lurches of Stuart policy, but it was also, gradually, becoming more of a commercial nation. In the way that destructive volcanoes cause soils to become more fertile, the many social tremors in Ireland in the 1600s also threw up fresh soil that could be used to advantage, whatever one's origins, although most people remained poor. The historian Edmund Curtis (1950) described the Irish rural poor of the eighteenth century as 'helots', slaves to the system.[4] Why would anyone choose to remain a helot? Many preferred to remain in a tight, interrelated community in which they were well known than to be poor in a place where nobody knew them, but they could never gain much wealth in the long term. The underlying reason for this helotry is clear, yet it is seldom mentioned: it was the cycle of being born into a poor family in a poor place, something that was true all over Europe. Some, however, found ways to break that cycle.

Professor Luke Gibbons writes feelingly of the Irish peasantry's slavery and subjection, its servitude and ignominy, and of 'the eighteenth century, when the majority Catholic population was kept in bondage'.[5] If so, it was entirely logical for the Read and Guinneas families to move away from such a trap, and the question must be asked, why did so many others choose to remain in a rural system that offered them little or nothing? In that harsh world there was no legal restriction on Irish country folk moving away and bettering their lives. Religion and class might have hindered success but were not the principal obstacles. The worst difficulties were caused by the limited economic opportunities available in what had always been a relatively poor island and competition for land from a fast-growing potato-fed population.[6]

So the opportunities exploited by Arthur's ancestors, siblings and cousins depended on their lucky proximity to Dublin, as well as their adaptability. Being a tenant-farmer as distinct from an agricultural labourer – a churl or cottier – was already a big step upwards. Professor Cullen summed it up: 'The cottier afforded a sharp contrast with the tenant farmer. The latter knew real want only in the worst years . . . the former lived permanently at the subsistence line'.[7] Yet many still think of both groups as being in the same economic boat. Curtis and Gibbons did not consider to what extent the labouring cottiers – the majority of the poor – were actually in bondage to the tenant-farmers, who paid them by giving them the use of a small patch of land to grow potatoes. In turn, the tenant-farmers paid a rent to a landlord or middleman, as was usual across Europe, which, in the case of the Reads' parish, had been paid for centuries to a monastery in Dublin. Whenever a tenancy ended the tenant often had to bid for his land against others who needed to farm it – a traumatic moment but, again, common across Europe. The successful bidder could offer a rent that was uneconomically high. The important move was from cottier to tenant, but as far back as the Black Death of the 1340s many had moved from the countryside into Europe's growing cities.

Arthur's grandparents had somehow made that first move from the grim past, and he should be seen as standing on their shoulders. The Reads' progression from shepherds to tenant-farmers was augmented by some small cash-flow from beer-selling after 1690. Arthur's uncle James Read moved to Dublin and became a cutler from 1719, creating a new cash flow and new contacts, returning occasionally to Oughterard to describe new ideas and opportunities.[8] The Guinneas tenant-farmers had ended with 'dairyman' George, who died childless in 1731; his brother William was a gunsmith in Dublin by 1720, and Richard was an agent by 1722. The farm's dairy produce was sold in the city streets just a couple of miles away, and the boys had had a literate education of some sort. They had seen from childhood how the world went round, and they became small cogs in the machinery of commerce. At that time Elizabeth Read's understanding of her father's skill at brewing ale may have seemed unimportant.

Richard appeared in Celbridge, County Kildare, in 1722 working as the household agent for Dr Arthur Price (1678–1752), the Protestant Dean of Kildare, who finished building Celbridge House – now Oakley Park – in 1724, a fine seven-bay, three-storey house with a large garden on the edge of the village (Plate 3).[9] Within a couple of years Richard had met and married Elizabeth Read, a local farmer's daughter. The 'Richard Guinis' mentioned in the 1726 lease, son of Owen, fits his social profile – aged about thirty in 1720, a younger son leaving the home farm with a male-line Gaelic County Down origin. With his own background, and marrying a girl of the same status, understanding Gaelic as well as English, born Protestant, literate, he had all the ideal criteria for a wealthy clergyman's agent in the Ireland of the 1720s.

# CHAPTER THREE

# Childhood

*O*AKLEY PARK IS a fine house, and it appears that Dr Price did not want his agent's young family living under his roof. The date of the marriage of Richard and Elizabeth Guinness in the early 1720s is unknown, but in 1722 Price had bought James Carbery's two-storey, six-bay malting-house on a large plot about 100 yards away on the main street, and this is where they lived (Plate 4). That way the squalls and cries of his agent's children would not interrupt the prelate's meditations, study or entertainments. However, Dr Price did condescend to stand as godfather to Arthur, their first-born, in 1725, modestly giving his own name, and in 1727 he gave his father's name Samuel to the second baby.

The year of Arthur's birth is generally given as 1725. As he was described on his gravestone as '78 years of age' at his death in January 1803 it is possible that he was born in 1724. One source – the online reference Wikipedia – gives a very precise date of 25 September 1725, but then he would have been only seventy-seven at his death. It seems as if that source has pulled the third quarter-day of the year out of a hat. We can suggest January 1725, a season when newborn babies often died from the harsh winter cold unless they were sturdy.

The separate two-storey house would have been a boon for the newlyweds, a place to call their own so long as Richard kept his job. In terms of status it also put him a slight cut above any household staff that lived below stairs at Oakley Park. The house comprised 'the House Garden Malt house Stable Barn together with a little Park behind the House as formerly in the possession of Jas. Carbery'.[1] Carbery held on to a small brewery next door. Arthur's story has barely started, but already the myths accrue: Richard is assumed to have brewed in the malthouse and may have done so, but there is no proof – Carbery's separate brewhouse suggests not. Link a brewing family back to a malthouse and the convenient assumption is made. Probably Elizabeth brewed ale in the kitchen for her family, having learnt the skill from her father. Most likely the layout of the malthouse was such that it continued to be used only for making malted barley for the brewers in the village, so the infant Arthur would have inhaled the bracing smell of malt before he could walk. The open area at the back was about four acres, ideal for the children. Sean Dunne is not the first to imagine that 'one of Richard's duties was to supervise the brewing of beer for the workers on the estate', but, in fact, Dr Price had no estate in Celbridge, just a large house with walled gardens on twenty-one acres.[2] His 'workers' comprised his household staff, some of whom would have been part-timers and of whom we know little. Dunne has perhaps guessed on the basis that Price was relatively rich – rich people had estates, *ergo*, Price had an estate.

Richard first signed a proxy for Dr Price in the Kildare Chapter Book on 31 October 1722.[3] The prelate was the Dean of Kildare, based at the half-ruined cathedral where only the chancel was still roofed (Plate 5). Richard's main function was as an accountant, buying-and-selling agent and overseer for Dr Price, who, as a high-flying clergyman, could not be seen haggling and trading in the streets and markets for household items. As an agent Richard would have been entitled to a small percentage on goods bought and sold. He had plenty to supervise, taking into account the amount of care necessary to maintain a large house that was often empty, and his areas of responsibility would have included the garden, horses, a carriage of some sort, supervising the staff, a library, silverware, filing important papers and minding the priestly vestments and other such items of apparel. Dr Price never married, so it would have been usual for his housekeeper – and Richard as overseer – to keep things clean and tidy whether Price was at home or away, and to keep an eye out for damages or thefts, as would a wife.[4] It was a position involving an entire trust of Price's money and property that had to be observed to the letter. On one lease he is described as 'agent or receiver' for Price, a collector of rents and debts.[5] He would thus have needed the common touch.

We know from the records that Richard supervised Dr Price's accounts and the signing and wording of his leases, and returning them all to Price's lawyers in Dublin. These were all secretarial functions, some doubtless humdrum and too tedious for Price to want to be bothered with. Financially, Richard must have done well over the years from what might have been a modest wage and his percentages on purchases, as he had few overheads in terms of food, and his home was free with the job. Certainly, his legacy of £100 in Dr Price's will, proved in 1752, after an employment of thirty years, was modest without being stingy, and gives the impression that Price felt that he had earned quite enough.

The central streetscape of Celbridge today is almost unchanged from 1722, at least in terms of the size and outlines of house plots (Plate 39). Opposite Oakley Park, by the Liffey, stands Celbridge Abbey, improbably battlemented, the home of the van Homrighs, whose daughter Esther was courted by Jonathan Swift, Dean of St Patrick's Cathedral in Dublin and author of *Gulliver's Travels*.[6] The story of Swift and 'Vanessa' – by which nickname Esther was referred to by Swift – became a famous part of village lore, and he visited Celbridge towards the end of their courtship. It is perhaps not too fanciful to speculate that such a visitor may well have called on his fellow dean, Dr Price, just across the road. Later the Abbey was to be rebuilt by James, the father of the patriot Henry Grattan, whose political views matched Arthur's from 1780.

The sleepy place was becoming a commuter town for the rich and very rich, fourteen miles west of Dublin in a lovely wooded Liffeyside setting. Arthur's birthplace was also a place between places; near to Dublin but in the country, just as his uncle William's hilltop farm was on the last slope between the mountains and the Liffey plain. Both were places in between the old and the new, close to the county border, having rich and poor, traders and farmers, newcomers and long-established families. In a social sense, his parents' families were also between a harsh past and living in the hope of a better future – if they played their cards right.

At the other end of the main street, the Conollys, the richest commoners in Ireland, were building a vast, beautiful, winged Palladian mansion on their estate at Castletown, the first of its kind in Ireland.[7] Like Richard, they were born Protestant with an Ulster-Gaelic origin – Conolly deriving from Ó Conghaile, a name principally associated with that part of Ireland. As such, they had also been 'mere Irish'. Unlike Richard, but in a very Irish way, they had brought their trusted cousins down from County Donegal to help with their financial activities, men with anglicized Gaelic surnames, like Donnellan and Coane. To function easily in Ireland after 1690 it was helpful to be Protestant and to speak English, but that did not mean that one had to change a name completely or be unpleasant to anyone. There was a new dispensation, whether divinely ordained or not, and one could choose to go along with it if one wanted to get ahead in life.

This proximity of the Conollys to the start of the Guinness story has been ignored up till now, being considered much too grand and too far up the social scale for comparison.[8] And so they were, at the time, but they must at least have been an inspiration, proof that one could become rich and powerful, whatever one's origins, and yet be provident and well thought of at large. The lawyer William Conolly had prospered in land transfers in the late 1600s and married Katherine Conyngham, who came from a Scottish settler family in Donegal. Elected Speaker of the Irish House of Commons, he started building Castletown in 1722 but had not quite finished it by his death in 1728. It was hoped that every part of the house would be made from Irish materials and become a showcase of what was possible. Katherine kept up an occasional court-in-opposition there, being a childless widow and former political hostess, in contrast to the court at Dublin Castle, and entertained royally. She was, after all, one of the richest ladies in Ireland until her death in 1752.

Richard and the youthful Arthur would, therefore, have seen the wealthy traffic of every description – up to the viceroy himself – passing up the main street of Celbridge between Castletown and Dublin. (The road was busy enough to be rebuilt as a turnpike in the 1730s.) We can visualize them on foot in their inexpensive clothes gazing upon and wondering at smartly dressed, well-mounted messengers and laced, richly caparisoned, gilt-trimmed equipages, all jingling, rolling and clattering by on a regular basis. It must have seemed to the young boy that such wealth and confidence and its underlying system would last for ever – it was certainly a world away from the experiences of most Irish people at that time.

Back within doors Arthur was a clever and trusted youth, as Dr Price also employed him as a 'Registrar' in his late teens, a sort of secretary-copyist, and he first witnessed a lease in 1743. In 1742 Price had assigned a lease to Joseph Carter for named lives (a lease for the lifespans of all named lessees), including 'Arthur son of Richard Guinness ... all of the Town of Cellbridge [*sic*]', the first written mention of his name. It is possible that he attended the Charitable School established by the Conollys half a mile from his home, as well as learning the 'three Rs' from his father. Writing well and clearly was a passport to success for the children of the poor, and, to judge by his later neat copperplate script, Arthur must have practised diligently. Price must also have had a library at Oakley Park, which would have added literature to Arthur's literacy. All these opportunities gave him an extra advantage in comparison with many of his contemporaries in Celbridge and better shaped his mind for understanding the wider world.

Learning to write well was outside the experience of most other Irish children, but in part-compensation many oral traditions persisted. The former Gaelic and Norman-Irish systems had never provided a universal education, and writing was reserved for their élites. There was an informal 'hedge school' system, where Catholic farmers' sons would pay for a basic education from a self-appointed teacher, often using a barn as a schoolroom – although occasionally literally in the open next to a hedge.[9] Furthermore, in a close-knit rural community one could be teased for aiming too high or for 'getting above yourself'. The usual predictable rhythms of rural village life, with its comforting and natural patterns, also held very few opportunities for someone with writing talents, but in Celbridge and the Dublin area such skills were valued and encouraged. Illiteracy and not speaking good English limited many to manual work, with its discomforts, low pay and insecurities. For Arthur's forebears, embracing change was essential. Being poor, the third son of a tenant-farmer, Richard grasped the opportunity to be Dr Price's agent and to fly under his master's wing, and such a position primarily required literacy.

In his wider family in the 1730s and 1740s Arthur would also have experienced the pastoral life led by his Read cousins near by. Still farming five miles away at Oughterard, his uncle, William Read (1683–1773) had married Elizabeth Pretious, who came from a local tenant-farming family, and her sister had married the son of George West (d. 1716), a tenant-farmer at Blessington, eight miles to the south-east.[10] In terms of social status, these Read marriages with other tenant-farming families after 1700 underlines that Richard Guinness – who used the form Guinness, and not Guinneas from 1722– had come from the same kind of background.

Arthur must also have met Richard's Dublin-based brother William Guinness, Guinis or Guines, who had been apprenticed to a Dublin blacksmith, Laurence Quin, until 1719. Uncle William worked all his life as a gunsmith at the Rainsford family's shop in Dame Street, became a Freeman of Dublin, married in 1720 and died in 1767. Like Richard, William was working for someone else and had a skill-based urban profession. The difference was that an agent was paid in part on commission, but William would have received a set weekly wage. In turn, his son Richard worked for another gunsmith. That Guinness family, with its interfaith marriages, died out in the male line before

1900.[11] Metalworkers, merchant tailors and engineers, they provided another urban link, and we shall meet the Rainsfords again later on. Uncle 'George Guinis' of Milltown, the last farmer, was unmarried when he died in 1731, and the remaining term of his 1726 lease must have been worth something to his brothers Richard and William, but the value is unknown as no will survives. William and Richard were by then established in their careers, homes and marriages, and, being urbanized, neither wanted to take on the family farm.

James Read, another uncle, had moved to Dublin before Arthur was born. He was apprenticed to James Fox in 1712 and set up in the cutlery trade on joining their guild in 1719. In April 1733 his aunt Mary Read married Benjamin Clarke, a chandler in Dublin. The Wests' son John, an in-law of the Reads, became a Dublin goldsmith and was later elected Master of the Goldsmiths' Guild in 1776–7.[12] With Mary and James Read and William Guinness we see several family links in the Dublin commercial world, less than a day's travel from Celbridge, links that were maintained by Richard whenever he was in Dublin on business for Dr Price. Long before Arthur's famous move to St James's Gate in Dublin in 1759–60, his rural cousins had saved for years and had planned to make that move, had then gained skills and contacts and were trading successfully. Compared with the majority of the rural Irish population the family network in the city gave Arthur yet another unusual advantage.

A brief spat was recorded in a Court of Exchequer Bill of November 1743, between Arthur's uncles William Guinness, the gunsmith, and James Read, cutler, over a debt owed by a third party that was quickly resolved.[13] Here William's surname was spelt 'Guines' – halfway between Guinis and Guinness – and he was described as a 'man of very weak capacity', that is, weak in his capacity to pay. This is not surprising, given his lifelong status as an employee with a family to keep. Read and he were described as 'cousins', in the old sense of 'related', being in-laws. The case confirms that they were in mutual contact in Dublin, just a street apart, metalworkers joined socially by Richard's marriage.

What else must have been apparent to a child in the 1730s? Learning of the gradations between rich and poor, literate and illiterate, there was also the sensitive area of religion, as Ireland's Christians had been divided on sectarian grounds for nearly two centuries. The doctrinal divisions between Catholics, Anglicans and Presbyterians were not the major issues for the poor; what really mattered were the political, social and economic effects. From the 1690s the Protestant land-owning élite engineered a system of further control by enacting the Penal Laws, so as to make it harder for rich Catholics to hold on to their lands, at that time the principal guarantee of wealth and status. Priests had to be registered, bishops were forbidden and a host of unpleasant and unworkable restrictions followed. Some rich Catholics did convert, some converted on paper for form's sake, and a dwindling number of Catholic landlords held on to their faith. Since 1555 the formula across Europe had been *cuius regio, eius religio* – you must take your ruler's religion – and consequently many chose to leave Ireland to serve under Catholic monarchs in the 1700s.

Arthur's later opposition to these Penal Laws was regarded by the economic historians Lynch and Vaizey to be merely an interest in 'penal reform'. This normally means prison reform, and without linking it to the oppressive system in Ireland these authors have misrepresented Arthur's opinion, no doubt unintentionally. But they have been much plagiarized since their work was published in 1960, and this misunderstanding has persisted. Born Episcopalian Protestants, Richard and Arthur had no input into the creation of this harsh system, and we shall find that Arthur and his sons helped in the first instance to mitigate its worst aspects and later to eliminate it.

In the background, the Papacy and many of the Catholic Irish gentry recognized James III, son of James II, as the legitimate monarch of Ireland and Great Britain until 1766. This provided the political excuse for the continuation of the Penal Laws, and the system was slowly dismantled only from the 1770s. Had the Papacy abandoned its support for the Jacobites in the 1720s, the Penal Law system would have been unwound earlier. This Catholic loyalty was not reciprocated; the Jacobite heir Charles Stuart, 'Bonnie Prince Charlie', had converted to English Protestantism in 1750, making a hazardous secret journey to London to do so. In any case, the bulk of the Irish population of every religion had no means of influencing the policies either of the Irish Parliament or the Papacy.

However, the Reads of Oughterard must have noticed that their landlord neighbours – the Aylmers of Lyons, the Clinches of Newcastle and the Locks of Athgoe Castle – all in place since the Middle Ages, remained Catholic and were quite untouched by the Penal Laws as well as being popular locally. Although it was a harsh system on paper, and a continuous worry and insult, such landlords survived its provisions. The poorer Protestants were largely ignored by the new ruling oligarchy, and, if religion was really so important, no sustained effort was made to convert the poorer Catholics. By 1735 the non-Catholic part of the

Irish population had reached about 30 per cent, in hindsight its high point, and at that time it may have seemed that eventually most Catholics would conform.[14] In the minds of practical men the worst effect of the Penal Laws was to remove clever, useful Catholics from public life and most professions, and this made no sense on a small island that needed to make the best use of its slender resources. Although Protestant and Catholic are social markers much used in Irish history, there was nothing monolithic about either. As with Arthur, people usually followed their parents' religion out of habit.

Richard's pay came indirectly from Dr Price's partial income from church tithes, which were assessed on the value of crops in a parish. The tithing system known as 'Peter's Pence' had first been imposed on Ireland with the blessings of Rome on the advent of the Norman regime from 1171. By the 1730s a Protestant prelate such as Dr Price was entitled to his percentage by law regardless of the payers' religion. This was unfair to many and very unpopular from 1600, but in the Catholic kingdoms of Europe a Protestant would be expected to pay to his ruler's Church, so it was not unique to Ireland. Under this system the payments would be collected locally by tithe proctors who usually worked part time for a fee and which were then sent on by them and receipted by a personal agent, such as Richard. Dr Price would have been removed from his benefices if he had ever objected to the Penal Laws, but he also appreciated the history of the Gaelic Church. This is borne out by the fact that the first print of the famous and beautiful ancient stonework at Clonmacnoise monastery was dedicated to him in 1738 as 'Arthurus Episcopus Midensis' – Arthur, Bishop of Meath.

The tithing system was unfair to Catholics, Presbyterians and other dissenters, but certainly someone in Richard's position could do nothing about it. Like most Protestants he was too poor to have the vote, a right denied to all Catholics from 1728 to 1793. He had little money, and his ever-growing family had to be provided for. Richard was like the butler Thady Quirke in the novel *Castle Rackrent*, watching everything, tucking his savings away, listening to all, learning much but keeping his thoughts to himself. Knowing of the awful past, hoping for a better future, conversant with everyone in his job, he seems to have been another of the 'amphibian' types identified by Fintan O'Toole, men who understood and who had to live with the duality of Irish life.[15]

Regarding the colonial aspect of life in Ireland, Celbridge was proof that it could be a two-way street. A family with a Gaelic surname was at the social summit. William Conolly, the son of an innkeeper, had played his cards cleverly, buying large estates in his native Donegal.[16] His local and ancestral knowledge there had to be a big help, understanding the people, local markets, shipping and ports, soil fertility, farm products, the weather, allowing Conolly and his band of cousin-agents to take informed risks – and so, perhaps, hardly risks at all – in making investments and improvements. This pragmatic aspect, blending old local knowledge into a modern system, has not been fully examined by many historians. It would be ridiculous to consider a man like Conolly to be a colonialist in his ancestors' county of origin, yet he was applying new methods that would be described in other countries as 'colonial'. Despite his great wealth, he and his successors modestly refused to take a title in the Irish House of Lords, preferring to remain the richest commoners in the country.

After 1500 modernity in Ireland was going to be mediated by England, France or Spain. The English had a foothold around Dublin that was expanded at great cost, and between 1500 and 1800 the other two countries were happy to use Ireland as a sideshow, an irritant, but made few serious efforts to conquer the island as it had little wealth. By 1725 the top colonial administrators were born in England and the Irish Parliament mainly represented the aristocratic oligarchy. But all the Irish had taken to the fruits of colonialism, even the lowly churls in the 1600s. The potato, which allowed the whole population to increase rapidly, and then unsustainably so, was a colonial import. Slave-harvested tobacco, sugar, spices, coffee and tea were all popular. Silver or gold coins from the Americas were not refused because of their origin. Even the émigré Jacobite 'Wild Geese', who had flocked from Ireland to France, Spain and Austria after 1691, often served in those countries' colonies and were not noticeably concerned about the treatment of the Bretons, Basques or Czechs whose cultures were being erased. The power centres in Europe were increasingly civilizing, homogenizing and taxing the periphery, including Ireland. To the young Arthur, any exciting new goods introduced from abroad to Celbridge or Dublin could be compared with their absence on the unchanged, quiet rural hilltop where his mother's family farmed. What we can disparage as colonialism today might have appeared then as a series of opportunities to be grasped as part of the process of adapting to the evolving modern world. Foreign or newly introduced elements in everyday life would also have seemed less alien and intrusive in the Dublin area than elsewhere.

Ireland in the 1730s was at a disadvantage to England in terms of trade and taxation, reduced opportunity and in initiating legislation, but this was reflected by the market in the form of lower land prices and rents. We will see later how Arthur and his grander colleagues succeeded in moving to repeal the trade restrictions and some onerous links with Britain in the 1770s and 1780s. Some parts of Britain were economically worse off than the Dublin region, and this has often been forgotten by historians focusing solely on Ireland. Celbridge itself had been under Norman and then English control since 1169. In a sense, Richard with his Ulster origin via County Dublin was just as much an opportunist colonist in the village as any other arrival, a new and unfamiliar face looking for contacts and finding his feet. In contrast, Dr Price's father, Samuel, had been the local vicar before 1700 and so had a memory of the locality that went back a generation before the Conollys and van Homrighs arrived. Europe and the Levant were then almost entirely divided into eight large empires; that was the inescapable reality of the continent at that time. The ultimate centre for the Irish and British markets and anti-markets was the City of London, which invested to exploit parts of England just as readily as any overseas possessions. These differing aspects of colonialism are often interpreted today by modern standards, with academics currently shaping the trendy and subjective area of 'post-colonialism'.

Raised on the edge of this Anglo-Irish world, yet having Irish parents and having heard of the poverty and the dark history of the 1600s, it is likely that the young Arthur came to realize that there were good and bad people from every background, religion and social class. This assumption will become clearer when we examine Arthur's later life, but in many ways he and his family were in a liminal situation, a grey area, having contact with people of diverse backgrounds and creeds. Had his family been closer to the top or bottom of the social tree, its opinions would have been more clear cut. I suggest that an exclusive or sectarian view is easier to hold if one has little knowledge of differing social realities, whereas Arthur experienced plenty of variety in and around Celbridge.

# *Youth*

$S$UCH WAS THE setting of Arthur's childhood. With so much evidence that having a Gaelic origin need not necessarily be a drawback, he was reared in an untypical but not unique pocket of wealth near Dublin.

By the time Arthur was in his teens, and very luckily for Richard, the ambitious Dr Price had been advanced from Dean of Kildare to Bishop of Clonfert (1724), of Ferns (1730), of Meath (1734) and finally was appointed Archbishop of Cashel in 1744.[1] The vice-chancellorship of Trinity College Dublin completed his honours in 1747. In the nature of things, Richard's earnings, which were based on Price's spending, must have increased considerably, and he presumably had some resources to fall back on by now if things went wrong. Also the family had their Read cousins living near by.

When all was going well, a lengthy disaster struck Ireland. Between 1739 and 1741 Europe endured the severest weather since 1709. With hindsight we know that this was the worst part of the end of the mini ice age that lasted from around 1400 to 1800. Birds froze in mid-flight, crops failed, food shortages occurred and diseases followed, primarily in urban centres such as Celbridge.[2] The wealthy widowed chatelaine Katherine Conolly did her best for the people. First, in 1740 she built an arched and spired folly 140 feet high on the gentle summit two miles directly behind Castletown to 'answer the view'. Never mind that the field on which it was built belonged to her neighbours; it gave employment that allowed the poor to buy food. Then, in 1743 she built a corkscrew-shaped grain store near Leixlip called the Wonderful Barn, on the eastern axis of her house, to ensure supplies for the locality. Arthur saw these philanthropic works being built, and both still stand today.[3] Famine and disease killed up to a third of the population in places, but because this disaster caused little emigration it has largely been forgotten, and many now think that the equally horrible losses in the 1840s were the only famine to have beset the country.

Maybe from a famine-provoked disease contracted from their urban life in Celbridge or from a busy lifestyle, smallpox or possibly from a late childbirth, Elizabeth died in late August 1742, aged forty-four, and was buried at Oughterard graveyard alongside her parents. It would have been much simpler to bury her at the church in Tea Lane, Celbridge, where she had prayed for nearly twenty years, just two or three hundred yards to the west of the malthouse, and much easier to visit her grave.[4] As an Irishman, Richard understood that she did not belong there. Proper recognition had to be made of the family plot where her parents lay and her descent from the servants of St Bridget, the Ó Maoil Bhríghde. Her brother William must not be insulted by breaking such an important tradition. So the widower led off a sad little procession towards the hills to the south, some five miles away, following her coffin on a jolting cart with Arthur, now aged about seventeen, Samuel, Benjamin, Richard, Frances and Elizabeth. By traversing the wetland commons of Lyons they would have joined her Read siblings and cousins after an hour or two. We can picture her six children standing around the open grave in the late summer on the familiar rural hilltop, their fondest memories pierced by the wails of the keeners, the black-clad professional mourners who were employed with dread and discordant effect at Irish country funerals until 1900. Their lives were shattered, just as the ancient church and round tower beside the grave were by now falling, crumbling ruins. Only the view was uplifting: to the west lay the Liffey plain and to the east the hills and peaks of the Wicklow Mountains.

As a respectful husband and son-in-law, Richard placed a headstone for her and her parents:

> This is the burial place of Wm Read Senr where he and his wife Catherine Lyeth & also Elizabeth Guinness Daughter to Said Willm & Catherine & wife of Richd Guinness who departed this life ye 28 August 1742 aged 44 years. This stone erected by ye above Richd Guinness.

Some worn, stubby and uninscribed stones stand in an adjacent line, most likely placed there for other poorer Reads whose names are long forgotten. The children must have taken it badly, experiencing the traditional wake that would have been held at the Reads' cottage near by.[5] But a love of the place must have been strengthened in the impressionable young Arthur, listening again, no doubt, to long-forgotten local lore, and the sense of family belonging must now have been reinforced by their loss, as he and most of his family were to be buried there beside Elizabeth decades later. This side of eternity, he knew it was where he belonged.

A legend that may have some basis in fact says that Arthur may, in 1742, have briefly taken a household job as some sort of footman with the Ponsonby family at Bishopscourt House, just a mile away from the graveyard, between Oughterard and Kill.[6] There is no written proof, but proximity and his age make it feasible, and it would have reinforced his local links. As the person in charge of the household, the Ponsonbys' butler would have known of the Reads farming near by and of Dr Price in Celbridge. Richard may have wanted his son to learn how a grandee's 'big house' was run. The Ponsonbys were a family of political 'undertakers' – those who 'undertook' government business – political faction leaders in Parliament, described often as patriots when they disagreed with the Dublin administration, and it could be that Richard wanted to know what was being discussed around their table. As Earl of Bessborough, Ponsonby sat with Dr Price in the Irish House of Lords, before his death of a 'surfeit of fruit'. Solid proof is lacking, but the place, means and motives are all realistic. Whatever the truths of this, the legend extends to Arthur brewing a black beer for the household; if he did ever work there he would, at least, have seen them brewing the household ale every week or so.

Dr Price was Bishop of Meath between 1734 and 1744, living at Ard-braccan west of Navan, which he rebuilt, and from this another legend arose. He 'used to regale the Meath gentry with a delicious kind of black beer, which, since he is known to have employed one Richard Guinness . . . was doubtless the forerunner of Dublin stout'. So recalled Provost Mahaffy of Trinity College Dublin, a descendant of these gentry, who loved to repeat a good anecdote.[7] Myths arise thus: Mahaffy's ancestors knew Dr Price; Price's man was Arthur's father; Price entertained well; *ergo*, a tasty black beer must have been drunk. Michele Guinness (1999) was convinced enough to relay it: 'Richard Guinness, whose delicious home-made black brew had made the old ecclesiastic a favourite host with the local gentry'.[8] Mahaffy must have known that the gentry always preferred wine, ideally claret and port.

Another portent of change that would affect Arthur's future life occurred in 1739, when the 19th Earl of Kildare moved to Carton near Maynooth, north-west of Celbridge, and started rebuilding it as a winged Palladian mansion. The FitzGeralds had been created earls in 1316 and were based at Maynooth Castle; they had links going back to the Norman Conquest but also occasionally married the daughters of Gaelic chiefs. Ruling most of Ireland by persuasion from the 1470s, they lost much in an abortive revolt against Henry VIII in 1535 but were subsequently pardoned and had clawed back their prestige.[9]

In 1745 James FitzGerald, the 20th Earl, built Leinster House as his town house on the then unfashionable south-east side of Dublin, and in 1747 he married Emily, daughter of the 2nd Duke of Richmond. Emily (1731–1814) was a great-granddaughter of Charles II and so shared a distant cousinage with George II via his Stuart ancestors. This enabled James to be created Duke of Leinster in 1766. Owning over 60,000 acres in Kildare alone, he was one of Ireland's wealthiest men and was the premier peer in the Irish House of Lords. Emily's sister Louisa (1743–1821) later married Tom 'Squire' Conolly (1735–1803) in 1758; Conolly had inherited Castletown in Celbridge from his great-aunt Katherine.[10] (A television series, *Aristocrats*, was made about their lives in 1999.[11]) We shall link them all to the much humbler Arthur in the 1770s by an overlooked and most unusual route.

Despite the loss of his wife, Richard and his employer were prospering, and they must have come to appreciate the slow regrowth of the Irish economy up to 1750. In 1751 Ireland generated a tax surplus, which surprised everyone. As Lord Forster said in 1777: 'The kingdom [was] more improved in the last 20 years than in a century before. The great spirit began in 1749 and 1750.'[12] Dr Price was by this time an archbishop and at the summit of the episcopacy. A growing economy and a higher rank led to an increase in the good doctor's spending power, and Richard would have taken larger amounts on his purchases and sales. In Cashel, the main archdiocese in Munster, the southernmost province of Ireland, Price resided at what is now the delightful Cashel Palace Hotel, and Richard may have travelled there with him or on his behalf. But, considering all the evidence, Richard's main job in life was minding Oakley Park and all of Price's possessions and papers in Celbridge when he was away – he also had to watch over his own motherless children – and besides, the archdiocese had its own permanent and part-time assistants on the ground in Cashel.

Dr Price decided to take the roof off the ancient hilltop cathedral at Cashel and thereby created a spectacular and famous ruin. It was an important enough event for the Irish Privy Council to have to consider and then ratify this decision on 10 July 1749. His congregation had dwindled and he built a smaller cathedral near by. Today, those in the Tipperary tourist industry are too polite to criticize the archbishop's pragmatic decision – the ruins are a modern tour guide's romantic dream – and instead the Guinness connection to Dr Price is hailed, and some harmlessly comforting myths are relayed as well:

> It's said that the archbishop's brewmaster, a Mr Guinness, hit upon his recipe for dark brown stout in this building.
>
> Also in the gardens are hop plants . . . Richard's son Arthur helped to grow the hops and brew beer – which led to the establishment of his now world famous brewery in Dublin in 1759.
>
> As a young man Arthur planted hops here and made his first porter.[13]

In 1744 and then in 1746 Arthur witnessed other leases as 'Registrar' on Dr Price's behalf. Clearly he was already trusted and clever enough to become Richard's assistant and understudy. The various leases, contracts and accounts may have made tedious reading, but he had Richard looking over his shoulder and explaining the texts, the amounts and the realities on the ground. Arthur was now, in the eight years up to Price's death in 1752 – during which time he was described as Price's 'servant' – being given the best possible hands-on training for his future business career, and this gave him yet another unusual and practical advantage over most of his contemporaries. It is possible that this employment came about because of Richard's occasional absences in Cashel and Dublin, or that Price's expanding wealth required greater management or, most likely, that Richard wanted Arthur to learn all about the paperwork of business. But, as far as is known, and much as I would like to be proved wrong, Arthur never visited the beautiful city of Cashel.

Samuel (c. 1727–95), Richard's second son, was moving in quite a different direction, creating the family's first international link while still in his teens. He was sent to London to serve as an apprentice goldbeater. As the family had no connections there, it may seem an unusual choice, but instead it reveals something of Richard's canny nature. Apprentices all over Europe were often left idle because their masters did not want them to set up in competition when they had finished, and so a Dublin goldsmith might have taught Samuel very little. Much better to send him away to learn his skills and see what others were doing in what was then the richest and largest city in Europe, all on the understanding that he would eventually return to Dublin and be no threat to his master's business.

So, a proud father must have read this breathless advertisement placed in the *Dublin Courant* of 10 February 1750:

SAMUEL GUINNESS, Gold-Beater, just arrived from London, where he has been some Time for Improvement in his Business, has opened Shop at the Hand and Hammer, opposite Christ-Church Yard in Fishamble-street, Dublin, and intends to make and sell Leaf-Gold and Silver for Gilders, Painters, Book-binders and Japaners, etc., also Plate, Gold and Silver-Leaf Lead, superfine Gold Beater's Leaf and Lacker, at the most reasonable Rates – as he used the most diligent Application whilst in London, to acquire the beste Methods of working the above Materials to the nicest Perfection, he hop for Encouragement, and will take the greatest Pains to please those who shall be so kind as to favour him with their Custom.

N.B. As he learned the Method in London, of beating Gold proper for Lace, Party-Gold, and Button-Silver, which were never yet done in this Kingdom, he proposes (if encouraged) to prepare the said Goods in the best Manner which will be of considerable Advantage to those who are at the Trouble of importing them.

Not bad for a Celbridge lad aged about twenty-three and rather putting Arthur in the shade for a time. A central-Dublin premises was expensive then, as it is now, and the apprenticeship and living expenses in London must have cost Richard a good sum over several years. This opportunity sought, bought and gained by these Irishmen at the heart of colonial power gives today's 'post-colonialist' academics some food for thought. Perhaps the introduction was made by Dr Price. Samuel was a precursor of today's Irish students who learn a skill abroad – perhaps in electronics, finance or programming – and then come back to use that skill at home. Richard and Samuel probably saw it only in financial terms, as an opportunity to plan and pay for what would ultimately provide a handsome return, and so it proved.

The advertisement was repeated in the following three issues so that his name and new business could be seen widely until the end of the month in his new city home. There is even the suggestion of import substitution.

Having lived in London the transition to Dublin cannot have been hard. If it was smaller and more backward, its oligarchy was aiming for greater civility. On Saturday 24 February the *Courant* noted that 'a Proclamation was issued by the Right Hon. the Lord Mayor to prohibit the barbarous Custom of throwing [stones] at Cocks in the public-streets on Shrove-Tuesday'. Disaster had befallen one of his neighbours: 'Sunday last a Man in Wine-Tavern-street, who was putting a Fowling-piece [shotgun] in Order, imprudently snapped it over a box of Gun-Powder, which taking Fire by a Spark's falling into it, blew the Window out, the Door almost off the Hinges, and scorched his Face so terribly that he lies now in a miserable Condition in the Infirmary.' But some improving entertainment was just around the corner, as tickets were selling for a recital of *Ioshua: An Oratorio* by Friedrich Handel on 15 March.

It is significant that Samuel returned to Dublin – where the market was better known to him and his family, where he had contacts – and did not stay in Britain. Such a commercial reality was essential if the family was to plan to reduce its risks. Also he was not describing himself in 1750 as a silversmith or goldsmith, indicating that he may have served a shorter, more affordable apprenticeship as a goldbeater and not the full term for a goldsmith. However, decorative gold, followed by refining and safe-deposit services, ultimately led him and his descendants into banking.

Gold was then the primary store of wealth, so beyond Samuel's use of it for finery and decoration he had to understand how it was bought, stored and refined as well as the different grades of purity. As his siblings entered cash-flow businesses it made sense to have someone in the family who would learn about banking, money and the preservation of wealth. An underlying and almost invisible benefit of the Irish connection to Britain was the stability of the currency – while Ireland's currency had a slightly discounted fixed value to sterling, it was linked to the most reliable currency in the world. Unlike all other countries in Europe, Britain had always paid its debts on time, the country's finances being managed by the Bank of England, which had been established in 1694. The value of the pound sterling was fixed at four ounces of silver from 1570 to 1931 – except for a brief hiatus in 1797 – which was unique in Europe. This underlying stability helped the Irish commercial world in the 1700s and can easily be forgotten today. Such a benefit would have been of much greater value to a merchant than to a farmer, as the latter saw little cash, often having to barter his produce at a discount.

As we shall see, Richard set all his children up in or arranged their marriages into urban cash-flow businesses in the Dublin area. It was a vital judgement. This general commercial sense was also adopted by some wealthier Irish Catholics, who, unable to buy farming leases for over thirty years, were often engaged in trade instead, with some importing wine from France and even owning slave plantations in the Caribbean. The difference was that Richard could choose this urban commercial course for his family, but his Catholic fellow Irishmen were pushed into it by their legal disabilities as landowners until the 1770s.[14]

At the European level, De Landa considers Fernand Braudel's overview on this European transition from the static-rural existence to the urban-commercial potential, finding three layers.[15] Peasants had:

> the know-how and tools, the inherited recipes and customs, with which human beings interact with plants to generate the flow of biomass that sustains villages and towns. This . . . knowledge resists innovations and hence changes very slowly, as if history barely flowed through it . . . The peasant masses are . . . like an immobile engine that creates the energy which makes everything around them move. Next comes the world of markets and commercial life, where the flow of history becomes less viscous . . . we may say that towns fed on [the peasants], much as a herbivore does . . . here a degree of automatic coordination usually links supply, demand and prices. Then . . . above this layer comes the zone of the anti-market, where the great predators roam and the law of the jungle operates. This . . . is the real zone of capitalism.

Academics often ignore the untidy areas of overlap. Richard's children never reached the top layer of the predators, but he was certainly moving them into the middle layer where 'the flow of history becomes less viscous'. As a brewer, Arthur still had to 'interact with plants' intimately when choosing and buying his barley, wheat and hops throughout his life. He had to understand grains and the annual harvest yield from the farmer's viewpoint, even though he was a processor-buyer.

Many people in Ireland, from all backgrounds, from tenant-farmers up to landlords, preferred to invest their spare cash in land, but Richard had decided that agriculture held too many risks. It was a clever analysis of the Irish economy at the time, and he knew the realities on the ground, being the son and son-in-law of farmers. Furthermore, even if he never visited them, he would have learnt much over decades about the local economies in the far-flung parts of Ireland where Price had served as Bishop – Ferns in Wexford, Clonfert in Galway, Meath, Cashel in Tipperary – but there was nothing better elsewhere in the country.

For those who stayed behind on a farm the struggle for land ownership and land hunger remained a central theme of Irish history until the 1920s, although in hindsight it proved to be an economic dead end for most. The degree of hardship varied from place to place, but there was just so much less opportunity and room for manoeuvre in the countryside. Yet, despite being urbanized and a cog in the Protestant Anglo-Irish commercial world for decades, Richard had respected Elizabeth's humble but longstanding rural-Gaelic family background when it came to her burial. A very Irish affinity for origins in Counties Kildare and Down survived, along with an understanding of the unhappy past, but not so far as to limit or embitter his children in their new commercial lives, and this gradually separated his family from the everyday experience of the majority of the population.

# CHAPTER FIVE

# The Start

*T*HE FAMILY'S LAUNCH into the world in the 1750s establishes Richard Guinness as a saver, a planner and an investor who moved his offspring cleverly out of their motherless nest. He was their paterfamilias in much more than the biological sense, yet he has been seen largely as the latter and as an accountant-butler-agent. While little is known about him, the facts indicate that his clever decisions for his children were generous and very effective and thus reveal his priorities and wealth to us.

The next key date was the death of the family's patron, Dr Price, on 17 July 1752, who was laid to rest under the flagged floor of Leixlip church – about three miles from Celbridge – because Leixlip was the senior church in the parish union. Soon Leixlip would became a big part of the Guinness family story. In his will devolving an estate of £8,850, Price bequeathed £100 each to Richard and to his 'servant' and godson Arthur, far down the list of legatees.[1] Again, the myth-makers have seized upon this as the only known capital in the family's hands at the time, but we shall see that this was not the case. The myth even extends to Arthur moving to Dublin in late 1759 with the selfsame £100 in his pocket, having done nothing with it in the meantime, which makes his eventual achievement seem all the greater. Let us tease out the fibres.

Dr Price also left £4,400 to his Travers cousins, £1,000 each to his Vigors and Dean cousins, £1,000 to the school in Celbridge (the Charitable School set up by the Conollys that is now the Setanta Hotel), £100 'to my poor relatives in Cardiganshire', £100 to the poor of Celbridge and £100 to his butler John Earsum.[2] Another six servants shared £300. The £200 bequeathed to the Guinnesses has to be seen as an understandably modest coda to Richard's thirty and Arthur's eight years of service. In the slightly more inflated prices of the 1770s Arthur Young considered that £200, but better £500, was the minimum realistic working capital for a tenant-farmer setting up in Kildare.[3] It was a safety net and no more.

Unusually and tellingly, all his sermons were to be burnt, suggesting that he was open-minded and was not overly concerned about matters of Protestant doctrine when facing his God in the next life. Price's estate at death was not large for such a senior prelate, and as he had never married it could have been very much larger, all in all giving the impression that he had spent most of his income as it had arisen. As Richard took a percentage of Price's purchases and expenses and had low overheads, his saved commission on a fairly heavy expenditure over three decades could have added up to a good amount by 1752. Were one to add up Price's church income and subtract his estate at death, a rough idea of his spending over his lifetime could be made, but as no record survives of Richard's percentage of this, nor of his earnings, it would not be very informative.[4] Price knew that Richard had already put by a tidy sum.

Richard soon bought a sublease on 'George Viney's house' on the Main Street in Celbridge, which was built in 1724. George Finey – or Viney – had arrived in Celbridge in the 1720s, renting the large Killadoon estate near by, but he and his son John became bankrupt in 1751. It is still an end-of-terrace house of three bays on two storeys, considerably smaller than Carbery's malthouse (Plate 6). Viney died in 1751, and John had sold a long lease in 1752 to one Richard Nelson, who sublet it to the Guinnesses.[5] It was the family's main base from 1752 to 1764, when Richard sold the sublease back to Mr Nelson. In Dublin, on 19 October 1752, he married again, aged about sixty-two, to Elizabeth Clare, and was described as 'of Celbridge Co. Kildare gent'.[6] Elizabeth was the widow of his friend Benjamin Clare, and she ran the White Hart Inn, a public house – with a lease running to 1770 – which is now a Londis supermarket, across the street from the bridge in Celbridge. In due course her son Benjamin would marry Richard's daughter Elizabeth, and so a second child had been provided for.[7] Nothing is known of the Clares' origins.

It is telling that Richard did not want to move his family into the White Hart Inn and live above the shop, although he must have slept there himself. With his own door on the street at last, having lived in Celbridge for thirty years – a whole generation – and described or self-described as a 'gent' on his remarriage, we see the first real steps into the minefield of social respectability. Besides, his maturing family was too big for the inn, with Arthur now aged twenty-seven, as well as Benjamin, Richard junior, Elizabeth and Frances. Probably rather squashed into the Viney House, they all had a reason to leave and move on in life. Richard and his family must have reflected that Viney had arrived in Celbridge with money and connections at the same time as he, had farmed locally on a large scale, but had still lost everything by his death. Richard, who had arrived with nothing, and must have known the Vineys well for decades, was now living in his house. A financial lesson of some sort must have followed. Across the street, in the very centre of the village, stood the Catholic 'chaple' shown on Jean Rocque's map, which is still a church today (Plate 40).[8] This was technically illegal under the Penal Laws, but the Conollys as landlords and magistrates were happy to allow it to flourish – there was a lesson in tolerance. The Viney House sublease was the only document surviving by 1900 that connected Richard, Arthur and Samuel together as a family, proof of what little paperwork exists from that time; however, the recent genetics survey reconfirms the link.[9]

Arthur's brewing skills were honed between 1752 and 1755 at the back of the White Hart Inn, less than two hundred paces from his home at the Viney House. Many familiar local faces would have appeared in front of and behind the bar, along with all sorts of agents and merchants on their way to the Conollys and the neighbouring gentry. Such an inn would have occasionally employed Irish traditional musicians as well, still the most accessible and pleasing part of Gaelic culture and which is now popular around the world thanks considerably to Garech Browne, one of Arthur's descendants.[10] The complexity and spirit of the music itself was proof enough that there was nothing backward in the old-Irish psyche.

The young brewer had a background knowledge from his Read grandfather, mother and uncle, from his childhood next door to James Carbery, and Price's household would also have brewed. Bishopscourt may have used a different method in about 1742, if he did work there, and now his new stepmother was running a busy inn in a prosperous village. Failure in the brewhouse was not an option, and so it is likely that he was assisting whoever did the brewing there. There are many variables in the brewing process. Water, grain, malt, hops and yeast could all be brewed together well or badly, and the aim was always to create a consistently good product. At some point he mastered this. Unlike Samuel, there was no need to serve an apprenticeship, but there was the unspoken duty to do his best for his stepmother.

Naturally he would have known Mrs Clare in the village for some time before her remarriage to his father. When she took on the White Hart Inn lease for twenty-one years on 11 October 1749, Arthur signed as a witness, and he also registered the deed for her in Dublin on 24 November 1753.[11] A question arises: surely this level of literacy and savoir-faire would have been much better employed if he had become an accountant or a lawyer instead of a brewer? His choice of this very manual profession suggests that he had some prior knowledge of brewing or that, by 1752, he had a strong desire to become a brewer. He was at least in the fortunate position of having a choice.

One new element of civility had arrived in Kildare in 1752: the printing of a large and handsome map of the county by Noble and Keenan (Plate 41). This time the roads were shown, along with aspects of terrain such as the bogs in the west of the county. But Arthur's north-east corner of the county received particular attention, as the map was bordered with engravings of the classical buildings of the Conollys around Celbridge and of the Earl of Kildare at Carton near Maynooth.

Beer had taken on almost a moral quality of its own at this time. Starting in London, where many of the very poor had become dangerously addicted to cheap gin, a mixture of tax policy and encouragement in the 1740s had led to beer being seen as the weaker, healthier, safer alternative. This is seen in Hogarth's famous and popular prints published in February 1751 showing the imaginary Gin Lane and Beer Street. The underlying message supported Arthur throughout his career.

In Gin Lane only the pawnbroker's house is in good repair. Scenes of death, depravity, violence, neglect, suicide and hunger abound. The distillery belongs to a Mr Kilman. Over an arch at the left is written 'Drunk for a penny. Dead drunk for two pence. Clean straw for nothing' (Plate 22). Beer Street, in contrast, is clean and orderly, and only the pawnbroker's is in ruins (Plate 23). Fishwives learn a ballad; even they are literate and musical. A basket of improving books lies at the right. Two sturdy, jolly men quaff beer to the left. At the top a signwriter is painting 'Health to the Barley Mow' (the harvest). He alone wears a ragged coat, a jest from Hogarth that all artists are poor. In England the Gin Act of 1751 succeeded in reducing annual distilling from 11 million gallons down gradually to 3.6 million gallons by 1767. Beer could also be overconsumed; when in London the tiresome, if clever, Benjamin Franklin was so shocked to find his printing colleagues drinking six pints each during the working day that he weaned them on to tea. While the English brewers managed to reduce the gin trade, they also lobbied successfully to maintain high taxes on tea to keep it out of the reach of their poorer customers.

In Ireland these prints would have been seen in the cities and towns, but elsewhere the affection for whiskey and homemade poteen was a normal part of popular culture until the reforms led by Father Mathew's temperance movement in the 1830s. As Arthur's career developed we shall also find him and his fellow brewers banging this new moral drum, knowing that the underlying message of personal improvement had been planted in the minds of officialdom by new laws and these popular prints. But in a sincere sense it must have been apparent that the numerous and visible poor whiskey drinkers in Ireland were slowly throwing away any chances of betterment and self-improvement.

The English economist Arthur Young would have agreed. He employed between twenty and fifty farm labourers in the 1770s at Mitchelstown, County Cork, for several months and sought a reason for their general inertia:

> Is this owing to habit or food? . . . When they are encouraged, or animate them-selves to work hard, it is all by whisky, which although it has a notable effect in giving a perpetual motion to their tongues, can have but little of that invigorat-ing substance which is found in strong beer or porter, probably it has an effect as pernicious, as the other is beneficial . . . I have known the Irish reapers in Hertfordshire work as laboriously as any of our own men, and living on potatoes which they procured from London, but drinking nothing but ale.[12]

In their smartest clothes the family must have journeyed for the best part of a day from Celbridge out to the coast south of Dublin to attend Samuel's wedding on 6 August 1753.[13] First to go abroad, first to set up in trade, first to advertise and now the first to marry, Samuel, aged about twenty-six, was setting the pace within the family (Plate 29). His betrothed was Sarah Jago (1732–94), the beautiful 21-year-old daughter of Henry Jago, a Dublin carpenter who had died a widower in 1745 (Plate 30). Her uncle Robert Calderwood was her guardian, a Dublin goldsmith who had married her aunt Elinor Jago in 1736. In a sense, Samuel was marrying within his trade. The event was noted in *Faulkner's Dublin Journal* of 7 August 1753:

> Yesterday Mr Samuel Guinness, of Sycamore Alley, Goldbeater, was married to Miss Sally Jago, niece to Mr Robert Calderwood, a most agreeable and

accomplished young Lady with a handsome Fortune. The Ceremony was performed at Mr Calderwood's country House at Dunlary.

Samuel and Sarah's six offspring – of whom only three survived – followed in quick succession. Richard – the third Richard, his name reflecting Samuel's dutiful appreciation for his supportive father – was born on 6 September 1755 and was the only one to have a family. He became a cultivated barrister and then a judge. Mary, baptized on 9 December 1759 was next, followed by Samuel junior in January 1761, who also became a barrister. From the essentially skilled-manual trades of Sarah Jago's forebears we see a progression into the cerebral world of paperwork.

Henry Jago (1693–1745), Freeman of Dublin in 1714, 'of the Poddle, Joiner' in 1716, was the son of Ellenor and her husband Henry Jago, a 'gab-bardman' of Wood Quay who had died in 1703.[14] (A gabbard was a sailing skiff that plied up and down the river to and from visiting ships when the tide was in or moved people and goods across the lower Liffey.) At that time the last bridge before the sea was Essex Bridge, connecting Capel Street to Wood Quay. Here we see the humbler folk of the city acquiring a trade and improving their lives. A skill such as joinery led to membership of a guild, which led to the status of freeman and so the vote. Henry Jago's wife also showed signs of upward mobility. She was born Sarah Taylor (1691–1741), married a Mr Doughty, was widowed at twenty-five and then remarried and had at least four children. Not content just to be a joiner's wife, by 1737 she was in the interesting position of being Deputy Wardrobe Keeper at Dublin Castle, a supervisory role involving the storage, cleaning and mending of the vice-regal household's apparel, a job she held until her death in 1741. Other than Sarah, the marriages of at least two more of her offspring are known, one to a jeweller and another to a weaver.

The surnames around this marriage are English, and their circumstances are a reminder that moving from Britain to Dublin did not guarantee instant wealth. Jago may derive from the Spanish Iago or the Cornish Jagoe, but, whatever their origins, by 1753 we can only describe them all as Dubliners. They had made their lives in the city, which was the main interface between Ireland and Britain. Politically, Henry Jago had the vote but could change nothing. Economically, the link to Britain was essential, although they were disadvantaged in some respects. Socially, there was no problem in marrying the orphaned Sarah to an Irishman from Kildare, given that he had a trade and was ambitious. They had not prised ancestral lands away from any indigenous Irish, unlike some other settlers, and the trading settlement by the 'black pool' (*dubh linn*) had been founded and developed by Vikings, Gaels, Normans and English long before their lifetimes. Status and wealth still had to be striven for – particularly that position in Dublin Castle – and yet one of Samuel's in-laws was a weaver, one of the humblest trades in the city. Sarah's guardian and uncle Robert Calderwood died in 1766, apparently without children, so perhaps a legacy accrued from him to the couple on top of her 'handsome Fortune'. But his business experience was no doubt most useful to Samuel, who had moved in late 1750 to Sycamore Alley off Dame Street.

Note how close together they all were. The streets south of Essex Bridge – which had been rebuilt and widened by George Semple from 1751, and its much-vandalized statue of King George I moved to safety – were like a miniature family village. Adjacent were Dublin Castle, the old Customs House (now the site of the Morrison Hotel) and the theatre in Smock Alley, so it was the centre of town. Three hundred yards up and across the river stood the law courts. Samuel's addresses at Sycamore Alley and later Crow Street were near by. Uncle William Guinness, the gunsmith, worked in Dame Street. Wood Quay, where some may just have remembered gabbardman Jago, is on the river by the bridge. The Read cousins' cutlery business, which moved from Blind Quay via Exchange Street to the newly built Parliament Street in the 1760s, was adjacent. Benjamin Guinness, Samuel's younger brother, would set up before 1760 as a grocer at nearby 22 Werbergh Street. It was a mutual-support system, able to watch out for children, to recommend customers and to warn of any trouble. Easy to visit in the evening for a chat, they were all within a couple of minutes' walk from each other. Multiply their number by their now-unknown neighbouring friends and the Jagos' contacts, and one senses a supportive inter-related community of cousins in the heart of the city (Plate 42).

From the Kildare perspective, the Read cousins had led the way into Dublin. Samuel's uncle James Read, the cutler, had been elected to the city's Common Council in the years 1735–8 and died in 1744, but his nephews John and Edward Read, sons of farmer William Read junior, were apprentice cutlers and took on the business. Both died in 1776 and were buried on Oughterard Hill near their aunt Elizabeth Guinness, although they lived in the city for three decades. (A funeral eighteen miles out in the countryside was unusual and hard to arrange then.) The business continued under Thomas and John, sons of

John, until 1833. Having a foothold in the city, the Read family would not let that opportunity go, and yet their continued burials on the ancestral hilltop decades after the move to Dublin and their change of religion are proof of where they felt their spiritual home to have been. Their very surname reflected the ancient local religious cult of Bridget, and it was where they would all be resurrected together on the Last Day. This confirms their sense of a longstanding and typically Irish identity with an ancestral place, while in their everyday lives they were glad to engage in the modern, urban commercial world. So it was to be with their cousin Arthur.

The link to the modern pub and coffee-shop chain called Thomas Read, with an ornate red seal-shaped logo circumscribed 'Thomas Read & Co., Parliament Street, Estd. 1670' underlines the difference between history and heritage. This was the name of the Reads' Dublin cutlery shop, not a pub, and the original business *had* started elsewhere in 1670, long before the Reads owned it. When they moved to 4 Parliament Street, the Reads put up a proud boast by its new door: 'Dublin's oldest shop'. But, as the street itself was only built in 1753 and as today's pub chain bought the shop within the last decade, the boast and the attractive modern logo must be seen as a marketing exercise and not as historically accurate. The amusingly faux-Gaelic rendering of his name today in the 'Tomas O Riada Bar' only confirms that he never used the Gaelic version for today's marketing wizards to copy. 'Tomás Ó Maoil Bhrígdhe' would have been difficult for Thomas's anglophone clients in 1700s Dublin to pronounce or spell, and one must be identifiable to one's customers. Such are the marketing realities of past and present, but at least the Read surname and the link to Parliament Street live on today, even if only through the creative world of modern advertising.

Central as it was, this area around Essex Street and Temple Bar was also crowded and smelly. According to Warburton:

> of these streets a few are the residence of shopkeepers and others engaged in trade, but a far greater proportion of them, with their numerous lanes and alleys, are occupied by working manufacturers, by petty shopkeepers, the labouring poor and beggars, crowded together to a degree distressing to humanity.[15]

Some of the latter must have come from the countryside to try their luck in the modern city, but, unlike the Reads, they had perhaps not saved up much cash beforehand and had no plan, contacts nor any skills on their arrival in the capital to remove luck from the equation. This analysis sounds harsh today but reflects why the Reads succeeded in a harsh world while many others from the countryside did not. In turn, the Reads inspired their in-laws the Wests, who farmed near Blessington, to set up their famous goldsmith's shop. By the time of the arrival of Samuel and Arthur in Dublin, a proven formula of success by small, cautious, sensible steps was in place, and their cousins and uncle were there to give advice. A way forward was available for countrymen with savings, and arguably this engagement with modernity and urban trade would have been much the same whether Ireland was self-governing or run by any of the European colonial powers. At an individual level, one's attitude, adaptability, contacts and resources were all much more important than who was running Dublin.

Another advertisement appeared on 3 March 1753 in *Faulkner's Dublin Journal*, and Samuel was still not describing himself as a goldsmith. By now he was edging sideways from the personal finery of gold lace and silver buttons into the smoky business of smelting and refining with its unhealthy fumes:

Samuel Guinness, Goldbeater, at the Hand and Hammer in Sycamore Alley, Dublin, gives the highest Prices for Quadruples and their subdenominations, light Guineas, and all impassable [low grade] and broken Gold. Said Guinness makes and sells the best Leaf Gold and Silver for Gilders, Painters, and Japanners, Gold of a peculiar sort for Book-Binders, Edge Gilding Gold-beaters Leaf and Lacker.

Some of the broken gold offered to him may have been stolen, so it was a grey area where good judgement was essential if he was to avoid prosecution. Quality control, secure transport and the first use of the surname as a sort of trademark follow: 'As said Goods are liable to Damage by Carriage, unless securely packed, he will engage to supply all Country Customers with the greatest Safety. To prevent Imposition [copying] his Gold Books are Stampt Guinness's Gold.'

Arthur now made his first real move in life at the age of thirty, taking on a brewery in Leixlip in 1755. The date and the property are still frequently confused with a lease for other Leixlip properties that he bought in 1756.[16] Lynch and Vaizey missed this evidence by not spending time on local history and have since been plagiarized by other researchers. To be fair, their main focus was on the Dublin brewery from 1759. However, Arthur was named in a Chancery Bill of September 1755 as 'of Leixlip, Co. Kildare, brewer'; a map of family properties shows the 1756 properties excluding the known brewery site; and the 1756 lease describes Arthur as a Leixlip brewer already. Also, Arthur was described in 1773 as a brewer of eighteen years' standing, not seventeen, and a Guinness signboard that was found and then lost again at the brewery site in the 1950s all provide further confirmation that he had started up there in 1755.[17] The 1756 lease document is the only original survivor, and the properties are adjacent, so it is an unsurprising mistake.[18] A modern wall plaque marks the correct site today but has the wrong year, and I have prepared a map showing which properties were acquired when (Plate 43).

The brewery site was to the east of Ralph Square, and ran from the street to the Liffey. A handsome three-storey detached house stood back from the street with two principle rooms on each floor. The brewery sheds were at the back. Water from a riverside well and barley from the farmland around were in easy supply. Hops could be had in bales from Dublin, and power could be drawn from the river's current. While Leixlip was a small market in itself it was also on the main Dublin–Galway road and had acquired a number of small country houses of the type known as 'gentlemen's boxes' and was, like Celbridge, a popular place for the wealthy to live, being eleven miles west of Dublin. Such moneyed households might need and appreciate ale of a consistent quality. As many households and inns made their own ale, it is apparent that a brewer had to be consistently good at his trade. Simply by staying in his trade is enough proof that Arthur knew his business.

One invisible but vital ingredient for the future was also working for him, an ingredient much too humdrum for historians to consider. Brewers' yeast is unlike that used in bread, which dies at a certain heat. The brewing type grows in the process and can be skimmed off and used again and again. So miraculous did this seem that it was nicknamed God-is-good. A gram of yeast holds some three billion single cells. Arthur's yeast must have been a Kildare strain, very likely from the White Hart Inn, as he knew its capacity. It moved with him to Leixlip and Dublin, and his descendants moved its myriad descendant cells abroad to Guinness breweries worldwide over the subsequent two centuries, to countries as far apart as Malaysia, Trinidad and Nigeria, where it is still used today. In the industrial era of the nineteenth century many brewing yeasts could not withstand the higher temperatures and pressures of large-scale brewing, but by a lucky chance Arthur's strain held up well and has been described to me by a yeast geneticist as uniquely hardy.[19] In a process with many variables, not least in temperature, knowing how your yeast would react and how quickly it would turn sugars from the malted-barley-and-hops mixture (known as wort) into alcohol was essential in those days when beer was still handmade and much sniffed over. That is what makes it probable that he brought the strain he knew best to Dublin. So unscientific was brewing that the use of thermometers to check and measure the brewing process was first suggested only in 1758, in Michael Combrune's *Essay on Brewing*. As well as creating alcohol, yeast imparts flavour, adds vitamin B and stops the development of lactobacilli that can turn beer into acid. Arthur knew how best to use it only from endless testing and experience.

Coming from a different angle, Sean Dunne gives the principle reason as a matter of religion and not dependent on savings, skills and materials. 'Therefore, it was Arthur's privileged social position, as part of the wealthy Protestant minority, which granted him the opportunity to become a brewer.'[20] However, the records show that most Irish brewers were actually Catholics. The opportunity was really based on Arthur's hands-on experience gained in the White Hart Inn, and the move to Leixlip was assisted by his father Richard only because he knew that Arthur had the right brewing and business skills. A privileged social position could not of itself create the ability to brew and to sell beer – indeed, most privileged people of all religions did not want to get their hands dirty in trade – and his Church would not provide him with a safety net if he failed. In the Dublin area of the 1750s, people in the Guinnesses' social position were plentiful. If his father had some wealth, it was only because he had worked and saved his wages for years. Saving one's earnings was the usual way to finance a new business, regardless of one's faith.

Leixlip demesne and much of the village had been bought in 1734 by the Conollys of Castletown – there was no escape from their long shadow. They still lived at Castletown and rented the castle out, often to prelates or English administrators. On fine weekends Leixlip was visited by Dubliners coming to look at the Salmon Leap, a spectacular waterfall across the Liffey. It is from the Norse name for this, Lax Laup, that Leixlip took its name. The Latin version used by the Normans was Saltus Salmonis, and the adjacent parts of

County Kildare down to Naas are still divided into the baronies of North and South Salt. The passing trade on the road west out of Dublin towards Galway – at a time when road traffic in Ireland was still mostly on foot – and these weekend day-trippers from the city would all provide a thirsty market for Arthur's ale.

In a 1745 mezzotint (Plate 8), we see a gentleman promenading by the Salmon Leap with a fashionably dressed black servant boy and a dog by his side.[21] He looks across to the north bank, in the castle demesne, where another gent is escorting two smartly dressed ladies. The remains of a bridge arch and a millrace decorate the waterfall, which was a source of easily caught fish for the village. By chance, in the middle distance, the hills of Oughterard and Lyons stand before the Wicklow Mountains. Locals and horned cattle along the tree-lined riverside complete the rural idyll, miles away from the smells of Dublin. For those interested in colonial markers, the idea of leaving a city for a day's fashionable recreation, the smart clothes, the black servant and the mezzotint itself were all fairly new elements to Ireland. However, these would have been seen at the time as normal throughout Western Europe: colonialism and modernity marched in step. Founded by Vikings and rebuilt by the Normans, the village had always adapted to modern and foreign ways.[22] Today it is home to the vast Intel and Hewlett Packard electronics plants.

Some feeling about Leixlip's potential on the old main road west from Dublin to Galway spurred Arthur on to buy his well-known long lease on another property south of the Main Street and west of Ralph Square from 29 September 1756. His signature on the lease is underlined by a series of very confident whirls: this man could wield a quill pen (Plate 15). He had recently arrived, and he was still supposed by the myth-historians to have only £100 capital, yet he paid a premium of £264. 7s. 8d. just for these properties. The seller was an American, 'George Bryan of Philadelphia in the Province of Pennsylvania, merchant', and his lessee described as 'Arthur Guinness of Leixlip, brewer'. Arthur's object would have been to build more houses and sub-let each house at a profit while keeping an eye on them for necessary repairs. He would have hoped that the underlying land value would also rise over time. In the event of late payments of rent he was on the spot to determine if the excuses were reasonable or not. It is a sign that he did not intend to sink all his money into brewing but was already spreading his investment risks, just as many people today buy a second property to rent out. He went on to buy a long lease on another range of houses, 'The Mall', on the north side of the street in 1775, years after he had left Leixlip.[23]

Also, one Sarah Bryan, 'widow of Dublin', perhaps related to George Bryan, let a house, cabin and field 'lately held by Thomas Kelly' to Arthur in September 1756 for £4. 10s. annually, at Newtown, which is now in the Confey part of Leixlip. Presumably this was for grazing a horse or a cow or two. They would have been near to 'Gazebo Park' (now the Leixlip House Hotel), a house built by Captain William Brady on what is still called the Captain's Hill.[24] Brady would, as we shall see, become a part of Arthur's life through a local dining club.

John Hinton's famous print of Leixlip was engraved in the mid-1750s, looking down on the village from the Captain's Hill with the Salmon Leap upstream in the distance (Plate 7). In the background to the right stands the Conollys' castle, shorn of its battlements, and in the centre-right is Brady's domed hexagonal summer house built for its wonderful view at the edge of his garden. On the left over the Liffey bridge stands the Salmon Leap Inn. On the near side of it is the original brewery. The Main Street, the main road west out of Dublin, runs from the bridge to the church tower on the right. The buildings were all detached.

The Leixlip map (Plate 43) tells us that Arthur's 1756 property was on the far side of the street from Hinton's view, lying on each side of the buildings at the centre. The Mall, his 1775 property, was on the near side of the street, slightly to the right, below Brady's picturesque summer house. The conclusion must be that over three decades or so he built most of the central main street at a cost of several thousand pounds, which today still mainly consists of two-storey houses similar to those in Celbridge. No records survive of this development of several dozen houses. They are absent on maps of the 1750s, such as Jean Rocque's, and are not seen in Hinton's and other prints. Their presence by 1800, when the street was fully built on both sides, leaves Arthur as the only possible developer, a little-known fact.

Leixlip's medieval church had just been rebuilt in the 1750s with a large gallery on classical pillars.[25] It already had a clock from 1720, with a bell to give the hour to the village. Newly fitted Chinese Chippendale rails gave an exotic touch, and the schoolroom has the Ten Commandments on the wall in gold letters on black tablets. The windows were redone in the then fashionable pointed Gothick style. These features were not found in most Irish villages, but they hinted at civility and a wider world beyond Kildare. As well as meeting some of the local gentry and tradesmen there every Sunday, every time he walked up the aisle Arthur could not avoid stepping on a newly carved grave-slab, reading: 'Here are deposited the Remains of Doctor Arthur Price Lord Archbishop of Cashell who died the 17th of July 1752 Aged 74'. His godfather, benefactor and employer was still close by, and the stone was an immediate and very solid reference for anyone in the village who needed to know whether the newcomer and his wider family were trustworthy and respectable. 'Yes, he was my godfather . . . I worked for him for eight years and my father for thirty . . . we lived beside him in Celbridge' – we can hear the words tying the living young brewer to the dead prelate.

It would have been difficult for Arthur to set up in Leixlip as a householder and brewer in 1755 and to buy the 1756 property without a starting capital of at least £400. Richard must have subsidized this, along with the costs of establishing Samuel in Dublin in 1750 and then Benjamin as a grocer in Dublin. Some form of dowry would have to be paid when his daughters married, Elizabeth to Benjamin Clare in Celbridge and then Frances in 1763. From my guesswork at the costs involved, it would seem unlikely for Richard and Arthur to have saved less than £600 by the mid-1750s, to which we can add Dr Price's bequests to the family of £200 in 1752, along with any income or savings from the cash-flow at the White Hart Inn. That indicates that Richard might have saved an average of £20 to £30 each year during his employment between 1722 and 1752. Whatever the overall sum available, perhaps even approaching £1,000, Richard's roles as adviser, supervisor and investor in his children's largely successful futures cannot be in doubt.

In the background, the Seven Years War of 1756–63 had started, with Britain and Prussia fighting an alliance of almost every country in Europe. This caused economic upsets in Ireland, leading to the collapse of several Dublin banks in 1759 and a fall in land values, so making it a good time to buy property.[26] The British had just won a remarkable series of victories in Germany, the West Indies, Canada, India and at sea over the more numerous French, making a favourable peace very likely, at which point land values would probably rise again.[27] Arthur's acquisitions in Leixlip (1756) and Dublin (late 1759), his brother Benjamin's establishment as a Dublin grocer by 1760 and Samuel's move of premises in 1761 were all well timed. As with the apparent progress of the Read family after 1650, this fortuitous timing was based on a depression caused by war, and the family was responding intelligently to what was going on in the outside world. In the light of the 1759 financial crisis it is most unlikely that they could have easily borrowed money, given their status, and so would have paid in cash.

In 1992 the Leixlip Town Commissioners adopted a coat of arms that kindly includes a harp in memory of Arthur's links with the town, along with porter-coloured black-and-cream signs at the edge of town, reading 'The Original Home of Guinness'. Even if he had only brewed ale and lived there for four or five years, he had built much of the central main street, and his and his brother's involvement lasted until 1803; his eldest son's descendants owned the rental properties in the town until the twentieth century. Although the right-facing harp is still the beer's main trademark, and has recently been starkly redesigned, it was first adopted only in 1876, long after Guinness's Ale was last brewed.[28] It was so indubitably Irish that it was copied by the Irish Free State from 1922, facing left. The heraldry speaks of the kind local feeling for Arthur that has lasted until today. His shade would probably have been flattered to think that he would be remembered at all in Leixlip two centuries later and also glad that his family would adopt an Irish harp and his 'Arth: Guinneſs' signature as trademarks.

In 1758 Arthur joined a new Kildare dining club – the membership, politics and ethos of which has also been ignored by the family historians – that was to have a far-reaching impact on his life. In 1751 an anti-duelling order called the Friendly Brothers of St Patrick had been set up in Dublin; it was said to have been originally started fairly informally by a group of gentlemen in Athenry, County Galway, in the 1640s.[29] This set up 'knots', or groups, of men around Ireland who swore to observe its rules, including one never to duel (described as 'the barbarous practice of duelling' in their rule book), and the general purpose was to promote 'brotherly love'. When they met and dined they collected money for charitable causes such as schools and hospitals. To be identified, they had to wear some green ribbon through a buttonhole, 'on pain of a fine'. Although the anti-Catholic and anti-Dissenter Penal Laws were still in full statutory force, the membership was to be non-sectarian.[30]

Lawyers James Glasscock and Nehemiah Donnellan of Leixlip established the County of Kildare Knot on 20 October 1758. Glasscock was descended from Katherine Conolly's sister and lived at the Music Hall. Donnellan's family were at Ravensdale; they had come down from Donegal to Kildare with their cousin Speaker Conolly when Castletown was being built. Arthur would have known these men in Celbridge for years and was invited to join as the third 'Brother' on 9 December. On 26 December a further three men joined: George Tyrrell, a landlord in north-west Kildare, and local merchants Matthew Bathurst and William Donaldson. In 1759 six more joined: another Bathurst, another Tyrrell, landlord Mark Tew of Roddanstown, Kilcock, Richard Cooke, the lawyer Graves Chamney and Hugh Wilson, who was land agent for the Catholic landowner Lord Fingall at Killeen Castle in County Meath.

Today it is hard for us to understand the need for such a group and the underlying mentality of the duel. All over Europe in the 1750s, if one had wealth one had a status that was quite distinct from a moral status. Men were graded into many ranks that had meanings that are now lost. In a public dispute of 'honour', which had different meanings to different ranks, backing down would create a loss of status, and so men would duel with swords or pistols and 'resolve' their dispute by drawing blood or killing each other. It was a relic of the cult of chivalric honour or the trial by battle of the Middle Ages. In the film *Barry Lyndon*, directed by Stanley Kubrick (1976), we see the dashing protagonist duelling over his infatuation for a girl, then collecting gambling debts and finally he and his stepson duel over their perceptions of public insults. The macabre sequence from the challenge through the cold-blooded courtly procedure with seconds and a doctor and leading to a sudden dénouement is well represented.

For Arthur, an upwardly mobile merchant of middling status, but not quite a gentleman, joining such a group indicated his social aspirations and also his moral sense that duelling was wrong, being reflexive and bloodthirsty. His recent ancestry could not be described as anything but humble, and this lowly background might be insultingly referred to in public at any time, provoking him into a challenge to protect his newly gained status. Membership of the Friendly Brothers gave him an oath-bound reason to ignore such an insult. The humanist notion of brotherly love was a modern idea, and from a practical point of view there was always a dueller's widow and children to consider. The non-sectarian aspect must have appealed to a brewer who bought his materials from and sold his product to everyone.

The order's 'device', as described and engraved in the rules of 1763, has an interesting symbolism (Plate 13). At the centre are hearts bound together under a star-tipped 'celestial Crown' (a heavenly, not a royal, crown) surrounded by a

Celtic-style endless knot, set with 'shamrogue' leaves. These are flanked by heraldic dolphins, symbols of brotherly love. At the top stands a 'Wolf-Dog' on a helmet, looking more like a greyhound to us; the helmet is symbolic of the gentry. At the bottom, a heart on a Maltese-shaped St Patrick's Cross is surrounded by the motto *Fidelis et Constans* (Faithful and Reliable). The cross also bears a celestial crown. Above that is the motto *Quis Separabit* (Who Will Divide Us?), which enjoined the members to stay together in their order. The whole design is attractively embellished with swags and flourishes. Several of these elements were also engraved on each member's medal, surmounted by a Maltese cross with a red heart at its centre, which was worn to each meeting and which hung from a second green ribbon.

The rules started with a preamble that was in tune with the Age of Enlightenment, the philosophy of progress and reason that was emerging across Europe:

> Man being in his natural State, the most naked and helpless of all Creatures, is forced to fly to Society for Assistance; where, by Means of the Benefits mutually paid and received, his Weakness is protected, his Infirmities relieved, and all his Wants comfortably supplied: He therefore, that is the best Member of Society is consequently the best Man. But as no one can justly be said to extend his benevolent regard to a Million, who never loved an Individual of the Number, it is hoped it may prove somewhat conducive to the Good of Society in general to promote and encourage among men the just Observance of private and singular friendships; whence, growing more humane, their Hearts inlarge, taking in at first particular Societies and Ranks of Men, till, dilated by insensible gradations, at length they overflow with generous Sentiments of Candor, Benevolence and Friendship for all Mankind. A Heart thus tempered is prepared for the easy Reception of all other Virtues. For this divine and glorious Purpose, the ancient and most benevolent Order of the Friendly Brothers, diffused throughout the Universe, was first instituted.

The humanist sensibility is apparent: 'all Mankind' is to benefit, and the 'Universe' was Ireland.

Quite unforeseeably in 1758, by 1783 the Kildare Knot had gathered into its membership some two hundred of the merchants, gentry, professionals and nobility of Kildare, with a patriot political tinge and with Arthur elected as its

# CHAPTER SIX

# St James's Gate and Marriage

*T*HE NEXT COUPLE of years see Arthur settled in Dublin, married and in a new home. This is understandably where his career starts at St James's Gate, as mythologized in the usual histories and modern advertising, arriving on his own in the big city, rather like a Dick Whittington, still clutching that £100 in his hand. His premises are still the core of today's brewery, and this enables historians to overlook the deeper past. But a large amount of water had already passed under the bridge for him by the age of thirty-four. He had worked in a secretarial position for eight years, brewed in his stepmother's inn for three years and had been running his own brewery for nearly five years. He also had several cousins, an uncle and a brother who had been trading in Dublin for decades and who were now only about thirty minutes' walk away. He owned other property, his father had some capital, and he had joined a new humanist club.

Dublin had probably been in his sights for some time, as his community of cousins around Essex Bridge and Dame Street must have been visited often. In April 1759 he had his name added to his new guild, the Corporation of Brewers, paying the sum of two guineas (£2. 2s.), and this membership automatically added him to the list of Freemen of the City at Easter 'by Grace Especial', so enabling him to vote. This indicates that his negotiations to buy the Rainsfords' brewery at St James's Gate were already well under way. It had been disused since 1750, and they may have been anxious to sell their lease for any cash, given that the 1759 Dublin financial crisis was in full swing. That, in turn, may have caused Arthur to delay the final closure and assignment of the lease until 31 December. By 1 December he was already sure enough of the deal to list the property's brewing facilities with his new guild. In the background, his uncle William Guinness, still working in the Rainsfords' gun-shop in Dame Street, was able to cast some light on their financial position, and he had probably mentioned the vacant property to Arthur and Richard in the first place.

Another event in March 1759 catches the eye. Given the networking opportunities and his new presence in the city, it is most likely that Arthur was part of a procession of the Friendly Brothers – the order that he had joined barely three months earlier in Leixlip – that was described in *Owen's Weekly Chronicle* of 20 March:

> On Saturday last, being St Patrick's day, the Order of the Friendly Brothers of St Patrick went in procession to St Patrick's Cathedral . . . after which they proceeded to Sackville Street [now O'Connell Street] where the fine brass statue of Lord Blakeney, erected by them and cast by Mr Van Nost, was uncovered in the presence of that society, and of innumerable spectators.

Naturally, 17 March was the order's annual big day, and Lord Blakeney was an Irish officer whose continuous defence of Minorca in the Mediterranean against Spanish and French sea-borne assaults was heroic in a war that was still being fought. It was said to be the first statue erected in Dublin to a distinguished native. Subsequently replaced in 1808 by Nelson's Pillar, it stood near the site of the awesome steel 'Spike' seen today. Given the company present, many being unknown and unmet residents of his new home, it seems unlikely that Arthur would have missed the event.[1]

The public procession reminds us that the Order of the Friendly Brothers was not a secret society; such open publicity would help to spread their message about the evils of duelling. By contrast, other Age of Enlightenment groups such as the Freemasons and the Illuminati were secretive about their aims and membership. Given that the Friendly Brothers' green ribbons, their 'device', their emblems and their homage to St Patrick were all quintessentially Irish, and that they were opposed to needless bloodshed at home, they also wanted to be seen to support the war effort and to recognize bravery and success.

Still brewing at Leixlip and negotiating his lease for the disused brewery at St James's Gate in 1759, we can see from its terms that it had potential, but, despite a modest fixed annual rent of £45 and a tiny premium of one peppercorn for a term of 9,000 years, Arthur was almost starting from scratch.[2] The buildings on the four-acre site were itemized in the scrivener's legalese as 'the dwelling house, Brew house two Malt houses out houses and stables'. These can be made out on the edge of the city on Jean Rocque's map of Dublin published in 1756 (Plate 45).

By Dublin's main defensive gate in its late-medieval western walls, the site in St James's parish was bought from James, son of John Lock, by Giles Mee, MP, and he had built its first brewery in 1670. He also negotiated a second 99-year lease for the adjacent 'Ground called the Pipes', taking water from the city corporation, 'he payeing the yearly rent of forty shillings'. By 1693 Sir Mark Rainsford (also spelt Ransford) owned both and was brewing 'beer and fine ales' before becoming Lord Mayor of Dublin in 1701. Rainsford's son had married Miss Mee and leased the brewery in 1715 for ninety-nine years to Paul Espinasse, who ran it until his death in a riding accident at Drogheda in 1750. The lease reverted to the Rainsfords, but the brewery had lain empty since then.

Most historians have been surprised at Arthur's move, ignoring his Leixlip investments, his experience and his cousins in Dublin, and even today they are fixated instead on his £100 bequest from Dr Price back in 1752.[3] Michele Guinness added in 1990 that Arthur 'founded a small brewery on the banks of the Liffey', when, of course, it was high up the hill well away from the riverbank and had been there for decades. By contrast, Dunne rightly recognizes that he must have had somehow 'a substantial amount of money', but '[the] literature that celebrates Guinness [does] not stress Arthur's elite social position, but instead describes him as a daring entrepreneur'. The reality lay somewhere between these two views. He and Richard had more than £100, but his real capital at this stage was his practical experience. His social position was barely noteworthy in 1759 and was irrelevant to his skill as a brewer and his sales of ale. It was an entrepreneurial move, given the financial situation in Dublin at the time and the long-unused brewery, and there were considerable risks, but it also seems to have been cautiously delayed over many months, so it was not impulsively daring. Nor was the premium of one peppercorn for a property of four acres beside the city exactly a gamble. But it is also well known that starting up or running a second premises often makes or breaks a business. These were the real pros and cons of the move, not the £100.

The first item of importance was a water supply, and most of Dublin's breweries and distilleries were on the western side because of the proximity of a tree-lined reservoir, the City Bason, finished in 1721, four hundred yards west of St James's Gate. This was topped up by part of the flow of the Poddle river on its way to join the Liffey. The Poddle was divided by the stonework Tongue of Kimmage, and part flowed by Dolphin's Barn through a man-made open culvert towards the reservoir. Arthur's lease terms were very clear on this: 'together with the full and free use Liberty and privilidge of the said Pipe water or City Water Course Lying on the west of the premisses gratis and without any Consideration to be paid for the same'.

This clause, it transpired, was inaccurate, and a dispute arose with the city corporation from 1764 over a demand for payment for this water, which took two decades to resolve. The main brewery lease of 1759 simply ignored Giles Mee's agreement to pay forty shillings a year under the second lease of 1670, which related to the adjacent 'ground called the pipes', where the freeholder was the corporation and not the Rainsfords. Before 1750, having and paying for this water under the 'pipes' lease, the adjacent brewery property did technically take its supply from the tiny culvert property at no extra cost. By Arthur's time the two leases had become intermingled or were thought of as one, and the city corporation had not sought payment when the brewery was disused between 1750 and 1759. By 1759 it seems that everyone had forgotten the exact legal basis for the supply, and Arthur could rely only on the text before him that had been drafted by a supposedly expert lawyer.

As at Leixlip, a dwelling-house stood in the Dublin brewery buildings, convenient for overseeing the rebuilding and brewing. When he started his family he moved several miles out of the city, so it cannot have been an ideal home for children. The house included a garden with a summerhouse, a pond and 'also two small Necessary houses of Ease over the Glibb water', so that any bodily effluents could be washed away by the underground stream into his neighbour's property, as was normal then. Most likely one of these 'houses of Ease' was reserved for the brewing staff.

Looking inside the buildings, the charms of the 'Three Marble Chimney Pieces' in the empty house were greatly offset by the state of the brewing equipment in the sheds at the back. As the scrivener put it:

> Eleven troughs; One float very bad; One Kieve very bad and two Brass Cocks; One underbank quite [completely] decayed; One Copper; seventy Barrels with a large brass Cock; Two Underbank pumps; Two old Coolers quite

decayed; One Tunn; Six Oars [for stirring the brew]; One Shute; One Horse Mill one Hopper and pair of Stoves; Box [chest] of Drawers and Desk in the Office.

If he ever quit the premises, all these had to be returned to Rainsford 'in Like good Order repair and Condition Stiff staunch and tenantable'. Stabling for twelve horses and a loft for two hundred cartloads of hay were included. Finally, the lease reminded him of his parish social obligations in the days before income taxes and state welfare, being paid up and assigned to him free of 'all Manner of Taxes Subsidies assessments Church Parish and Ministers dues Work house money and all other Charges and Impositions whatsoever'.

One can imagine an inspection visit by Richard, with the old man scratching his head and wondering what the final cost would be and whether all the estimates been double checked. They took the plunge, which indicates that Richard approved of Arthur's management record in Leixlip. Richard must have been involved, as the Leixlip brewery and investment properties were not sold to pay for the Dublin brewery, as is often assumed. The investment properties remained Arthur's, and Richard junior (c. 1730–1806) took on the Leixlip brewery and its house. Thus a second Guinness brewing business was established, distant enough to avoid mutual competition.

Dunne says that successful trading at Leixlip enabled the move: 'The brewery prospered and it provided Arthur with the financial capability to purchase St James's Gate Brewery in Dublin.' While one hopes that Arthur had saved more than the value of one peppercorn between 1755 and 1759, the start-up working capital required would have been very much higher and must have come, at least in part, from Richard. Legal fees, travel and food on inspections, the repair or replacement of all that 'decayed' equipment, the selection and hire of brewery staff, horses and hay, cleaning, the buying of grains and hops, firewood and coal, inks, wax and paper, repairs to buildings, the establishment of trade accounts and even some bachelor furnishing for the house, all had to be added to the tiny premium.

In 1760 came the first mention of Arthur in print – a fact that has been generally overlooked – advertising the sale of a lease of land at Oldtown, west of Celbridge. The family was already moving on from its first Liffeyside cradle and would be gone by 1764. *Faulkner's Dublin Journal* of 22–5 March stated:

For 31 Years from the first Day of May, the Lands of Oldtown near the Town of Cellbridge in the County of Kildare, seventy Acres, all Meadow and Pasture and fit for Dairy or Grazing. Enquiries to be received by Mrs. Dunn in Cellbridge, or Mr. Arthur Guinness in James's Street, Dublin.

I wondered if this sale of a farm might have raised the money Arthur needed to reassemble his new brewery in Dublin. However, the deeds are clear that this property was bought by Dr Price in 1736 and passed as a legacy in 1752 to his nieces. Of these, Mrs Dean moved into Oakley Park (still known as Celbridge House) until her death in 1774. So the press notice tells us instead of Arthur's continuing link to Dr Price's family long after his estate had been distributed, and it was an opportunity for him to earn a fee when the property was sold, acting in his turn as agent for Price's family, taking on his father's role. Given the financial crisis, it was a bad time to sell, and Price's nieces held on to the land for several decades.[4]

So far we've focused on Arthur's purchase of the premises at a very good price. However, viewing the brewery as a going concern, we can see now that he had taken on a potentially serious business risk. Competition from England and the excise (tax) system were slowly working against the Dublin brewers. The latter had cheaper materials, but some English brewers had already developed large-scale production, reducing their unit costs and selling a better-quality product. Lynch and Vaizey (1960) comment that Irish duties were raised in 1741, when English imports were just 5,000 barrels, and again in 1789 when imports were much larger. The move from village to city brewer brought Arthur head on with competition that was unknown in Kildare. This was his biggest worry for the next thirty-five years.

Shipping was the backbone of Dublin's business, and in Arthur's youthful visits to the city the forest of masts along the Liffey and the smell of salt air must have been a novel and exciting element, Kildare being an inland county. However, his emotion is more likely to have been one of anxiety over his decades as a brewer, as each newly arrived ship might carry hundreds of hogsheads of beer brewed in Britain, often used as ballast, which competed on his doorstep. On the flip side of the coin, ships also carried English hops, barley and malt, which were needed by the Dublin brewers. These growing imports reflect the growth and increasing wealth of Dublin from 1750 and were, of course, unforeseeable in 1760, but, in fact, until reforms in the 1790s Arthur had entered a very competitive arena skewed in part by the excise laws. Was that entrepreneurial or foolish? Would one take that step if one were half-hearted or inexperienced? The assumption must be that he felt that his youthful energy and attentive management would make up the difference and that he had found some way to keep his production costs down.

It is feasible that on his start-up in 1760 Arthur carted barrels of his ale the eleven miles from Leixlip to Dublin and gave free samples to inns and taverns to get orders. His cousins living in the city were there to make introductions to innkeepers and publicans. This pre-marketing process could have started in 1758 or 1759, and it would seem careless for him not to have done this. He knew the quality and capacity of his yeast. Barley and malt could be had from Britain, Kildare or Dublin. In terms of logistics and materials handling, there seems to have been no major obstacle; the main tasks were to rebuild the internal brewery equipment and to hire a reliable workforce. This in turn may have been done affordably given the economic recession. All should go well if properly planned; he had spent months in closing the acquisition, months in which to plan, and he had the experience of starting from scratch in Leixlip.

On the political front, in late 1759 *Faulkner's Dublin Journal* was optimistic about peace in Europe, and this must have been encouraging to Dublin's businessmen. Captured letters sent from Spain to its French ally indicated that the French strategy of denying support to its colonies by assembling troops in northern France for a knock-out invasion of England had been abandoned: 'It appears that our intended Descent upon Great Britain is given up at least for this year [1760].' In hindsight, this strategy proved to be the very last chance for Bonnie Prince Charlie and his father James III to reign over the British Isles, and the 'descent' never happened. The British forces had had a fortunate year, and 'letters from The Hague of 16th instant [December] say positively that the Congress for a general Peace will be opened there the latter End of next Month'. However, peace was not finally concluded until 1763.[5]

*Faulkner's* went on to castigate the antisocial behaviour of both the rich and poor in its next issue:

It were much to be wished, that the Nobility and Gentry would be so kind . . . as to caution the Footmen who carry Flambeaus [flaming tar torches] behind their Carriages . . . from beating them against the Rails of Houses (a thing much practised by them), as many Accidents have happened by pieces of the Flambeau sticking to Rails, and falling into Kitchen Windows.

Perhaps Mrs Faulkner had left her basement windows open after dark. As for the capital's poor:

Within a few Days we have had many Riots and Robberies . . . owing to the Custom of giving Christmas Boxes and New Year's Gifts to the lower kind of People, who never apply the money to good Purposes, but quite the contrary, in strong Liquors and intoxicating Drams [whiskey], which set them outrageously mad . . . If this money was laid out in Cloaths and Food, it might be of Use . . . poisonous Drams and Spirits have been the cause of more Murders and Quarrels . . . than all other Liquors in the World put together.

Given the year-end weather, the poor needed a slug of whiskey to keep the cold out of their bones. For the censorious George Faulkner, giving them holiday money in the season of goodwill could all too easily lead on to mayhem, riot and murder.[6] Ale was the unmentioned but civilized alternative.

The next step for Arthur, while reassembling his new brewery in 1760 and starting to sell ale into a new market, was to find a wife, preferably from a good family and with a dowry of some sort, like his sister-in-law Sarah. Aged thirty-five that year, it was time for him to start a family. He chose well, his offer being accepted by Olivia Whitmore, and they married on 14 June 1761.

The wedding required a financial splash, and a silver cup was made that included the arms of the Magennis viscounts of County Down – namely a rampant Milesian lion surmounted by the red hand of Ulster, with a wild boar as a crest (Plate 16). Beside it was a crosshatch to represent the Whitmores. As we saw in Chapter 1, this was incorrect, as the evidence points only to a plebeian Gaelic County Down origin. His father Richard must have relayed this half-jumbled past, and both he and his brother William were still very much alive in 1761. We think of Richard as a quiet man, and this myth may have been nursed quietly in his heart for decades, just as he had saved his money quietly, finally to emerge with pride on this cup. By 1795 Arthur would also have the arms on the wax seal with which he completed legal documents and sealed letters. It was his badge of identity.

With the anti-Jacobite and anti-Catholic Penal Laws still current in 1761, this adoption and display of the arms of a Gaelic Catholic clan – one that had finally been dispossessed for its Jacobite loyalty a mere sixty-eight years earlier and with the Scottish Jacobite rising of 1745 just sixteen years in the past – was unusual. It was an assertion of his Gaelic-Irish identity, and, given the politics of the time, I believe it reveals a great self-confidence. Shortly afterwards the trans-lation of the Gaelic saga of Ossian (*Oisín*) was published by James McPherson, a Scot, which became a success throughout the British Isles, depicting the former Gaelic culture as romantic and closer to nature. While it made the old culture more fashionable, the book was later proved to be largely a fake, although based on an ancient legend.[7]

John Locker, goldsmith of Parliament Street, made this silver cup. On 6 April 1760 he had married Catherine Read, daughter of William Read junior of Oughterard. As such, she was Arthur's first cousin, and we note that she and John were living and working beside her brothers John and Edward, the cutlers, and near to Samuel Guinness. On making the wedding cup, Locker only included his personal mark, leaving off the hallmark, indicating that it was a gift and therefore untaxable.[8] This claimed Magennis link seems to have been believed also by his Read cousins, and there was no sense of embarrassment about a claim of Gaelic Milesian origin in the wider family, which may be sur-prising as Locker sounds like an English surname and Arthur's new in-laws, the Whitmores and the longer-established Grattans, were Anglo-Irish.

It could also be that the vague and misremembered County Down origin was revived in 1760 when Arthur saw the tombs of some of the Magennis viscounts who had been buried in St Catherine's Church in the 1680s, just two hundred yards from his new brewery, as suggested by Derek Wilson.[9] The train of thought might have been: We came from County Down, which was ruled by these Magennises, also spelt MacGuinness; drop the Mac as many have – Guinness. If so, it was a logical assumption, but some County Down origin-leg-end must also have been passed down verbally, given his male-DNA profile. The interesting point is that he would not have recalled it so publicly if he had wanted to anglicize himself completely. Despite these apparent contradictions – identifying with the losing side in the Williamite conquest of 1691 versus his status as a city merchant and the Protestantism of his birth; the land-owning, titled Milesians versus his life in the urban Anglo-Irish world; and the tenor of the Penal Laws – it was an origin to be proud to claim. He was the precursor of his family's refusal to accept other peoples' ever-changing definitions of what it was, or is, to be Irish.

Like Sarah Jago, Olivia was fatherless but was well provided for by her mother's family. William Whitmore had been a grocer in Essex Street, Dublin, and we can see his signature on a bill signed a few months before his death for 'Brazil Sugar, Green Tea and Eating [olive] Oyl', all of which were imported luxury goods (Plate 14). He had married Mary Grattan from Carbury, County Kildare, in 1735, and their daughter Olivia was baptized in May 1742, so at the time of her wedding she was just nineteen.

Mary Grattan's rather grand settler family had bought lands at Carbury in north-west Kildare in the late 1600s, and the first family will was that of 'Symon' Grattan, proved in 1697.[10] His son John inherited several thousand acres, married Martha Mason and was the father of Mary. Another oft-repeated myth links them to the famous Irish parliamentarian Henry Grattan, whose forebear was at Trinity College Dublin in 1655, but this cannot be established. The Grattans pursued a lengthy legal dispute concerning lands with the local Colley family who changed their name in 1728 to Wesley, then Wellesley, and were the forebears of the dukes of Wellington. John Grattan built a windmill with carved date-stones in 1738, which still stands at the 'windmill crossroads' near Derrinturn, surrounded by his grain fields. Long a ruin, it clearly did not work well, and one wonders why it was not built on Carbury Hill near by.

How did he meet Olivia? Most likely because the Whitmores' shop in Essex Street was so close to Arthur's community of cousins by Essex Bridge. It could also be that Arthur was introduced to the Grattans by George Tyrrell, his Friendly Brother, as they were near-neighbours around Carbury. His social network of contacts had already developed to the extent that either avenue of introduction was possible. My guess is that the introduction was made in Dublin, with Tyrrell available if required to confirm to his rural neighbours that Arthur was a solid citizen. As with Samuel Guinness and Mr Calderwood in 1753, there was no social problem for the Whitmores and Grattans in marrying Olivia to a Kildareman from outside their Anglo-Irish milieu, given his desire to succeed.

Arthur's in-laws were gentry, so in social terms the marriage was a move up in the world for him and also recognition by them of his worth or potential. Olivia's grandmother, Martha Mason, was the daughter of Robert Mason of

Knock, County Offaly, of a seventeenth-century English settler family, and had a descent from the family of William of Wykeham, Chancellor of England in the 1380s.[11] This enabled her male descendants to be educated for greatly reduced fees at Winchester College and at New College Oxford, as Founder's Kin. In time, Arthur would take advantage of this unusual tradition when educating his eldest son. Olivia's maternal lines were interesting and well recorded, but little is known about the Whitmores, her father's ancestors.

Whether from the Grattans or the Whitmores, Olivia's dowry of £1,000 was quite an amount. A source in London at that time considered that £122 per annum was 'an Estimate of the Necessary Charge [cost] of a family in the middling Station of life, consisting of a Man, his Wife, four Children and one maidservant, the Station in Life of a Tradesman who sets up Business on £1,000, a very substantial Start in Life'.[12] In his dictionary Dr Johnson wryly described those in the 'middling station', his own rank, as 'within reach of those conveniences which the lower orders of mankind must necessarily want, and yet without the embarrassment of greatness'.

But, as we know, Arthur already had his new brewery and a range of houses that he was building or renting out in Leixlip, all paid for with cash. Living costs in Ireland were lower than in London. On top of these assets he now had enough in Olivia's dowry alone for a 'very substantial start in life'. He was a rich man if he played his cards right. Another way of quantifying the dowry is to compare it with the £10,000 that came with Jane Conolly of Castletown, sister of the very wealthy Squire Tom, when she married George Fitzgerald from Mayo in 1770. So £1,000 was a lot of money for Arthur in 1761 but was just a tenth of a grandee's dowry, reminding us that he and Olivia were far from the top of the social tree. Unfortunately for the Conollys, Fitzgerald became a wastrel duellist who blew the money in his vagrant life between Paris, London and Dublin.[13] On his return to Mayo he even manacled his father to a bear and imprisoned him in a cellar. Clearly psychotic, he was hanged for murder in 1786 after surviving twelve duels – an uncomfortably close moral example for Arthur's Friendly Brothers to recall.

Samuel also moved in 1759, first to Castle Street and then on to Crow Street, off Dame Street, in 1761. He was still close by his community of cousins. He and Sarah were also diversifying by branching into fashionable clothing and aiming to sell to the nobility. In another breathless splash, seen in *Faulkner's Dublin Journal* of 26 June 1759, we find:

John Wetherell, Haberdasher, from London, having entered into Partnership with Samuel and Sarah Guinness, who have opened Shop at the Sign of the Dove in Castle Street . . . intend to carry on a Haberdashery and Millinery Business by Wholesale and Retail in the most extensive manner. As said Wetherell was bred to the Haberdashery Business in all its Branches in the most eminent Shops in London, to which Place he intends to go four or five Times a year to lay in fresh Assortments of Goods, and bring over the newest Fashions, the Nobility and Gentry, also City and Country Shop-keepers, may depend upon being supplied with the best Goods on the most reasonable Terms –

N.B. Said Wetherell is just returned from London with a large Quantity of Goods, viz., Plain and figured [decorated] Gauzes and Cat guts [stockings], plain and figured modes, Sattins and Sarsenets, with all kinds of Silks for Cloaks, Hats and Bonnets, Minionet, Blond and Black Laces, Trollies, Coxcombs, Footings and Edgings, Silk Gloves, Mitts and Ribbons, Silk Stockings, Web for Breeches, Chip [straw] Hats, Fans, Pendants, Necklaces, Ear rings, Italian Flowers and Pompadores, Gause handkerchiefs, Muslin and Cambricks, Silk, Cotton and Thread Stockings of the Nottingham Manufacture, with all other goods in the Millinery and Haberdashery Way – Said Guinness will give the highest prices for unpassable and old Gold.

We note that Samuel could not resist adding a reminder about his own business in the last line. While the text demonstrates the popular adoption of London fashions, London was in its turn copying Paris. It is interesting that Sarah was involved and was probably managing this enterprise, knowing no doubt what might sell to other merchants' wives. Considering her late mother's position in Dublin Castle in the 1730s it is likely that Sarah had fond childhood memories, associating her mother – who had died when Sarah was aged nine – with finery and had perhaps always dreamt of working on or selling smart clothes herself. This could explain why she married a man who could make gold lace. The Seven Years War was unresolved, and so the English manufacturers had given easier credit terms for sales into Ireland, as most of their Continental market was still enemy territory. Yet again, the centre of trade was extending an opportunity that could be grasped if one was ready to take it.

While Arthur was still brewing at Leixlip, we see Samuel and Sarah already diversifying into a second line of business. Although the 'Guinness and Wetherell' partnership was listed in the 1760 Dublin almanac, it was gone by 1761. Stock control may have been difficult and clothing customers often paid late or not at all, particularly the nobility. Sarah was said to have had quite a temper on occasion, once hurling a coffee-pot at her husband 'to clinch an argument', so let us hope that Mr Wetherell got back to England in one piece.[14]

# CHAPTER SEVEN

# Beaumont and Dublin

*T*HE NEXT STEP for a man such as Arthur was to buy a 'gentle-man's box' on the edge of the city. No doubt Olivia's £1,000 dowry was used for this as well as for further brewery improvements. Clearly the house at St James's Gate was rebuilt in the 1760s but evidently had some fault. Perhaps it was too noisy for the baby – their first child, Elizabeth, was born on 28 February 1763; Samuel had named his first-born after their father and Arthur repeated the compliment to their late mother. Maybe it was in too poor a part of the city, and its location might put off the better sort of guest – the entire neighbourhood, the Liberties, suffered from an unsanitary poverty that was legendary. Or per-haps a part of the house was needed for the brewery, so giving rise to unhealthy smells and taking up living space that made it too cramped for a family with ser-vants. Whatever the reason, they bought or built Beaumont House on high ground several miles north of the city, near the main north road, in 1764 (Plate 10). It is still identifiable today, although surrounded by necessary additions for the hospital convalescent home of which it is now a part. A listed building, it is, at the time of writing, being properly restored by the conservation architect John Deaton.

Concerning Beaumont, Lynch and Vaizey (1960) pronounced that 'after six years in business he could afford to live in the style of a gentleman'. This suggests, beyond the evidence, that Arthur's business was an instant success. More realistically, after some ten years as a brewer, or twenty-one years from his first employment as a secretary, he was able to afford Beaumont thanks entirely or in part to Olivia's dowry. Looking at Jean Rocque's 1760 map of the county of Dublin, the house is unidentifiable (Plate 46). Perhaps it had just been built in 1764 by Arthur himself or was shown as 'Moorfield' and was misplaced by Rocque a couple of fields to the east.

Beaumont became the family nest for Olivia and Arthur's twenty-one children, of whom only ten survived to maturity. The eleven that died young were buried at far-off Oughterard beside his mother's grave. Such a child-mortality rate was normal at the time but sounds terrifying today. With its large grounds but no estate, its icehouse and stables, quite near to the sea and with a panoramic view south towards the Wicklow Mountains from the front balcony on the first floor, with the city lying in between, it proved ideal for the family. On a clear day the view north from the roof just included the peaks of the Mourne Mountains in south County Down. That distant, undenied, unchanging, motionless past lay in one direction, and the ever-changing, rapidly growing city was his future in the other. Yet Beaumont has hardly been mentioned in the histories, and even my family admits that they have never visited it. Its plaster-work cornices and chimney pieces were redecorated in the Adam style that was popular from 1770, most likely chosen by Olivia, and it remained in the family until 1855.[1]

The first known portrait (Plate 24) of Arthur may date from around this time, possibly executed in 1765 when he was forty. It comes as a surprise to those who only know his famous and rather suave later portrait wearing black-cloth. Here a jowly, plump youngish man looks out confidently at the artist. Bewigged and laced in style, he sits on a damask chair and leans on an ornate table surrounded by a curtain, a quill pen and a book, the essentials of civility. The half-revealed leather bookend reads 'Led . . .', the start of 'Ledger'. But there can be no doubt of identity as he holds a letter addressed to him at Beaumont, County Dublin. He is not posing stylishly out of doors under a tree with a horse or a gun, as might the gentry, but is at a table about to reply to the letter, literacy and communication recognized as the keys to his success. Like the letter, he has recently arrived. The brewery and the historians have ignored this portrait, except for Henry Guinness whose cousin owned it, and they were descendants of Samuel, not Arthur. The better-known portrait done in the 1790s shows a man in modest garb with the same slight, confident smile and was the model for the bicentennial Irish stamp issued in 1959. Both portraits show large nostrils, essential for sniffing his corn and hop samples, his malt and his brews.

From Beaumont Arthur involved himself in the vestry of the local church at Raheny. As well as Richard, God had clearly provided in many ways since his move from Leixlip. John Wesley, the founder of the reforming Methodists, had put it well in 1748: 'We must exhort all Christians to gain all they can and to save all they can; that is, in effect, to grow rich.' Dr Samuel Johnson, who had suffered years of hardship before his literary success, agreed: 'Poverty is a great enemy to human happiness; it certainly destroys liberty, and it makes some virtues impracticable and others extremely difficult.'[2]

In January 1764 Arthur's uncle William Guinness's son Richard also married, to Anne Bourke.[3] Richard was an employee gunsmith, like his father, and was admitted to the Freedom of the City in June 1758, so allowing him the vote. He then worked at 107 James's Street, not far from Arthur's new brewery. Anne was a Catholic, and it seems to have been a successful mixed marriage. Of their four children, at least two would be Catholics, and Anne was buried in 1795 at St James's Catholic chapel. All Catholic churches were called chapels in the time of the Penal Laws. St James's had been built by the Very Reverend Canon Richard Fitzsimons in 1749 at what is now 85–6 Watling Street, just opposite Arthur's brewery gates (the present church to the west dates from the 1850s). The 1766 census listed 1,475 Catholics and 799 Protestants in the parish, with no record of serious intersectarian tension. Having this successful example of cousinly religious tolerance on his doorstep must have reconfirmed Arthur's own tolerant views on religion, but only Wilson (1998) and the book of family trees (1985) mention Richard and Anne at all.

In August 1764, newly elected as a warden in his guild, the Corporation of Brewers, Arthur took part in 'riding the franchise' around the city parishes, an ancient custom. The unlettered called it 'riding the fringes', which also made sense. It sounds like a quick formality, and few Dubliners today have any idea what it involved. From the Middle Ages onwards the Freemen of Dublin had walked around their boundaries every three years to remind themselves of their chartered 'franchise' within which they had rights. Tense stand-offs had occurred between the clergy from all the monasteries, the men of the Liberties and the nobility. By 1764 it was largely a peaceful affair, including a motley procession of all the twenty-five guilds of the city arranged on floats, each pulled by a team of large horses, cheered on and followed by crowds in the streets or watching from windows.[4] These processions were best described by Walsh in 1811:

> The weavers fabricated ribbons of various gay colours which were sent float-ing among the crowd; the printers struck off handbills with songs and odes

prepared for the occasion, which were also thrown about . . . the shoemakers had a person representing St Crispin with his last; the brewers St Andrew with his cross; the smiths . . . were accompanied by Vulcan and Venus, which last was the handsomest woman that could be procured for the occasion, and the most gaily attired. She was attended by a Cupid who shot numerous darts . . . at the ladies who crowded the windows.

The merchants processed with a huge shamrock in homage to St Patrick; all were led by the Lord Mayor and his officers and aldermen with their carriages, golden maces, swords and chains.

Barrington added in 1829 that:

the skinners and tanners seemed to undergo no slight penance . . . being dressed up close [tightly] in sheep and goat skins of different colours. . . . the butchers were enveloped in hides, with long towering horns, and rode with brandished knives and cleavers! The master tailors . . . were not accustomed to horseback . . . A tailor on a spirited horse has always been esteemed a curiosity, but a troop of 150 tailors, all decked with ribbons and lace and every species of finery . . . presented a spectacle outvying description.

It must have been quite a show.

The procession route ran from the old Customs House and ambled down-river towards Ringsend where the Lord Mayor threw a spear into the sea to mark the city's eastern boundary. Thence south to 'Clanskiagh', back up to 'Mr Leeson's house at Stephens-green' and then on to a regular stand-off. On approaching the Liberties and wanting to process down the Coombe, the Lord Mayor and his remaining followers had to contend with the poor but proud inhabitants who were jealous of their own boundaries, in a different form of street theatre:

They assembled in detachments in some places . . . and made a show of strongly opposing any invasion of their independence . . . They seized upon the sword-bearer of the Corporation, wrested from his hand the civic weapon, and having thus established their seeming right to resist encroachment, the sword was restored on condition of receiving a present as a tribute, and liberat-ing a prisoner from confinement. These demands being complied with, a formal permission was given for the procession to move on. The man who wrested the sword . . . had an achievement to boast of during the rest of his life.

The surviving marchers on foot and horseback went from the Coombe to Dolphin's Barn, then northward across fields to the 'Liffey-strand' near Island-bridge. By now the procession of floats must have fallen away, and the marchers could knock down any new fences barring their traditional route. Crossing the 'Deer Park' (Phoenix Park) they scrambled over its wall and on via Stonybatter, 'Broad-stone', 'Drumcondra road cross', Ballybough bridge, then along the coast road to 'the shades [sheds] of Clontarf' and the 'Mill at Rahenny and from the Mill northwards 130 perches [650m] to a little Brook which is the end of the Liberties of Dublin'. By then Arthur was conveniently close to his new home at Beaumont.

Various stops were made along the way for much-needed liquid refresh-ments and in order for the Lord Mayor to hold open court in the streets with numerous marchers gathered around. For example, he might summon 'Sir Michael Creagh! Sir Michael Creagh! Come and appear at the court or you will be outlawed.' Creagh had absconded with the Mayoral gold chain back in 1688, a new one had been made, and he had died an outlaw long before, but he was still summonsed in jest decades later. Ridiculous impromptu laws might be made; an elder warden had to find four trumpeters for a saint, but the saint him-self had to pay their wages, or another would be ordered to find 'a maiden to lead the dragon'. This was street theatre of a third kind, an attempt to show the human face of the guilds and corporation behind all their wealth and visible pomp.

Although Arthur was on horseback it must have been an exhausting day for all, a light-hearted rambling precursor of today's city marathon and at least as colourful as the revived modern St Patrick's Day parade. Being the brewers' man leading their float must have been a proud moment, his first minor but visible public role in the city, and taking part meant that he was now a Dubliners' Dubliner. It was a part of his city life every three years for the rest of his days. Barrington summed up that 'Nothing can better shew the high opinion enter-tained by the Irish of their own importance'; but, to be fair, this was a local Dublin urban tradition, untypical of the rest of the island. As with the colourful ancient Catholic patterns in the countryside, this charming ceremony was swept away by the civilizing 'improvers' of the nineteenth century.[5]

# CHAPTER EIGHT

# City Life

*S*OME TIME BEFORE 1760 Benjamin, the third and most invisible Guinness brother, had also moved from Celbridge to Dublin. It is again unimaginable that a man aged about twenty-eight could move to the centre of Dublin from Celbridge with no known assets, take on a premises at 22 Werbergh Street near the castle, and stock it as a grocer without considerable support from someone. Who else but his father Richard? Again we see that he was just several hundred yards from the familiar faces of his city cousins, he was not in competition with them, and Richard had set him up in an new urban trading business with the largest Irish market on his doorstep. It was said by Henry Guinness that Richard junior was in partnership with him for some time, taking on the family's Leixlip brewery only in 1763; if so, Arthur was supervising both breweries between 1760 and 1763, and this might explain his move to Beaumont in 1764.[1]

Benjamin's near twenty years in Dublin have scarcely been mentioned, neither has the context of his establishment been considered. Michele Guinness states: 'entrepreneurial skills were evidently in the genes. While Arthur was building his business . . . brother Benjamin became a well-to-do merchant . . . Samuel was a prosperous goldbeater, and Richard [junior] continued to thrive at . . . Leixlip.'[2] This was the case, but nobody just 'became' a merchant. They had used Richard's support and knowledge to good effect – the French would say that they were all *habile* – but there was nothing genetic about it, and they could not have started to trade without his ready cash and advice. As Richard had arranged for Arthur to work as a secretary in the 1740s – learning about leases, property, buying and selling and accounting – he must have taught his other sons the same business skills. No arcane knowledge was required, just some savings, trading nous and steady application.

Benjamin never married and died aged about forty-six, his will being proved on 14 May 1778. But he did leave us a fine billhead designed by 'J. Debenham' in chinoiserie style (Plate 20). This style would have been immediately suggestive of tea, the luxury then pronounced 'tay', as it only came from China at that time. Tea boxes are shown labelled Bohea and Souchong. At the top, a bearded man leans on a barrel, holding a staff, with a sugar loaf at his feet, with scales and a tea-leaf scoop on each side. The text below reads: 'Benjamin Guinness At the Green Man and Sugar Loaf Werbergh Street next the Church sells Superfine Teas, Wines, Spirits and Groceries of every Denomination By Wholesale and Retail on the most Reasonable Terms. Dublin Bought of [from] Benjan. Guinne∫s 17—.' Such a business would have been impossible without other peoples' reliable trading links to the Chinese Empire, the 'Middle Kingdom', on the far side of the world. As with Samuel's partnership with Wetherell, Benjamin was a link on the already global chain of trade that gave this interesting opportunity to a Celbridge lad. We cannot say how successful Benjamin was, but by staying in business for about two decades he was not a failure. Arthur's fourth son born in 1777 was named after him.

Frances was the youngest and last child to leave home. At about the late age of thirty she left her father in Celbridge and was married on 25 June 1763 to John Darley (1733–85), a stonecutter, whose large family's business in Mercer Street was respectably busy.[3] Stonecutting was a mason's trade that involved squaring off and dressing large facing stones. Being based in Mercer Street, just west of St Stephen's Green in Dublin, Frances was just a few hundred yards south of her siblings and cousins. The urban setting, the skilled trade, the family near by, the steady cash-flow – it all fits the social pattern we've seen before. Sadly they had no children; John died in 1785 and Frances remarried again in 1788 to Michael Raye. He seems to have been comfortably off as he had two Dublin addresses, at Richmond and in Dorset Street. Both died in 1795.

What would be found on the city streets? The poorer hawkers and beggars of Dublin in 1760 can now be seen in the drawings of Hugh Douglas Hamilton, published recently in *Cries of Dublin*.[4] (The cries were the calls and shouts of the city's street traders.) Despite the prevailing poverty, even the poor wore torn greatcoats with wigs – perukes – breeches and quite good shoes with heels. People became accustomed to the disgusting smells of a city, with litter and ordure thrown into a channel – in Dublin, the 'kennel' – that ran down the middle of the larger streets. A daily scene from Samuel's life, almost on his doorstep, is

Hamilton's drawing No. 45, 'A Shoeboy at Customs House Gate', being, of course, the old Customs House beside Essex Bridge (Plate 18). In the background a single barrel is carried on a cart, in its turn a scene from Arthur's life.

This shambolic and smelly city was also run in a small way by Arthur. His guild, the Corporation of Brewers, elected him as a warden in 1763 and its master for the year 1767.[5] Founded by Royal Charter in 1696, the guild was a trade body selecting four men to sit on the city's Common Council, which led to Arthur's involvement in Dublin politics. Its other functions were protective; it could inspect premises and fine a non-members five shillings per barrel for brewing within two miles of the city boundary. Dublin had ninety-one small breweries in 1682, which had fallen to about forty by the time of Arthur's arrival. By 1720 the value of imported hops was a sizeable £40,681, but that trade was restricted to English hops by statute in 1732. By 1760 the guild's business was in general decline; Lynch and Vaizey consider that it was largely inactive, only holding occasional meetings. This inactivity explains why Arthur, a new member in 1759, could be elected master just eight years later – not from any unique skills but from his lifelong desire to join groups and to network. He had to join the guild, but the Common Council gave him a much broader canvas, and he was chosen as one of the brewers' four representatives for the rest of his life.

According to Michele Guinness (1999), on 12 March 1765 the *Freeman's Journal* regretted that it had misreported the death of the eminent brewer Mr Ennis of St James's Street as Mr Guinness.[6] Arthur was already important enough for them to apologize. She continues: 'His rise had been meteoric . . . he had acquired status . . . But eminence does not guarantee supremacy.' I found no such apology; the *Journal* reported on 9 March: 'Died . . . In James's-street, Mr Ennis an eminent brewer; and not Mr Arthur Guinnis, as mentioned in some of the Papers; that Gentleman being in perfect Health.' The interesting phonetic misspelling has been ignored and is an echo of 'Guinis' in the 1726 Milltown farm lease. Far from eminence or rising meteorically, the newspaper still could not spell his surname after his five years in the city, even if he was described gratifyingly as a gentleman.

The drunken sons of other gentlemen could be dangerous on the streets. In March 1760 'a Boy was killed and a Gentleman had his Back broken, by a Parcel of Young Bloods, or Choice Spirits, who assemble together in order (as they term it) to Slack people without any distinction whatsoever.'[7] Slacking involved knocking the victim to the ground and then picking him up and throwing him down repeatedly. Luckily for Arthur, Rocque's map of 1756 shows a watch house on the main street near the brewery, occupied by the City Watch, usually an inefficient police force. The brewery area had quietened down somewhat, as the raucous St James's Fair, held outside the city gate by St James's Well every 25 July, had been abolished in 1738. It was said to be 'a riotous and unedifying gathering' – no wonder a brewery was built alongside. Arthur was lucky enough to avoid personal violence, but there were other losses. Just after Christmas in 1765 a brewery backhouse of Arthur's burnt down, but fortunately the fire did not spread. The following August his garden was raided by his impoverished neighbours: 'some villians [sic.] . . . carried off a quantity of fruit and all the garden implements.'[8] The brewery property was still on the edge of the city, so having a garden and orchard there was not unusual.

The hungry Libertymen next door were as nothing compared with the gentlemen of the Excise. In October 1766 Robert Bray, a Surveyor of the Excise, broke into the brewery to see if any undeclared, untaxed barrels could be found. To motivate them, such men were often paid a commission on the value of any seizures, so it is hard to know if Bray had a tip-off or was 'surveying' by chance. He was imprisoned and fined £100 for forcible entry. Undaunted, he tried again in 1767, with the same result and the same conviction. In November 1768 he was back again – third time lucky? – and bringing some heavy artillery with him this time, in the person of Hugh Hughes, His Majesty's Inspector of Excise. Yet again the court found it to be an unlawful intrusion, both men were fined £170 and the harassment seems to have ended. Just to rub it in, Arthur asked for a part of the fine to defray his costs in the matter.

However, the Excise Returns of 1766 also give a useful idea of how Arthur was trading in terms of sales and volume after seven years in the city. He paid £1,498, just above halfway up the payments of the forty Dublin brewers assessed that year. The top three were paying over £4,000 each, way above his level. Mr Bray's persistent activities suggest that Arthur may already have been a little higher up the scale than halfway, perhaps quietly slipping untaxed barrels out a back gate to his customers after dark, and that the near-certainty of finding him at fault outweighed the risk of all those fines.

By late 1765 Richard had nearly completed his paternal role. Samuel and Arthur were trading in Dublin and had married better than he. His first grandchildren had been born. Richard junior had the house and brewery in

Leixlip. Elizabeth was with Benjamin Clare at the White Hart Inn in Celbridge. Frances had married a tradesman in 1763, and Benjamin was a grocer in Werbergh Street. In 1763 or 1764 Richard sold the lease on the Viney House in Celbridge, as land values had risen and no children remained at home, and he and his wife moved in with the still-unmarried Richard junior at the Leixlip brewery. Some more capital was now available for supporting his children. When at church, Dr Price's flagstone tomb was there to remind him of Celbridge and his career. In a life that had seen good and bad times, his family were provided for and his earthly duty was done.

# CHAPTER NINE

# Problems and Solutions

*A*RTHUR WAS NOW in his prime, with family and business as the mainstays in his life. The economy was slowly improving, land values and the population were rising and a sense of political independence developed in the 1770s. On Richard's death Arthur became the head of the family, but their father's plans had left his siblings well able to fend for themselves. How one copes with the inevitable problems of life is often a guide to personality, and some arose in this decade.

Richard, the grand old man, passed away in Leixlip in 1766, aged about seventy-five. Richard, his second wife Elizabeth and his son Richard junior were listed in a census as living together in Leixlip on 16 April 1766. On 7 April he also signed his last document, witnessing the execution of the will of John Barton, brewer of Leixlip.[1] Although Barton must have been a business rival of the Guinnesses' brewery in the village, he clearly trusted Richard to help pass on his property in a scrupulously honest fashion. He was evidently a very competent local brewer, as some bills show that he had been selling beer as much as two decades earlier to the Conollys, the richest possible clients in the neighbourhood (Plate 17).[2] This trust was a sign of Richard's standing in a community where he had been living for only two years. Celbridge is just three miles away, and no doubt his good reputation as a bishop's agent in the area had preceded his arrival. Barton may have given Arthur advice on brewing in the 1750s and evidently trusted Richard Guinness entirely; the Guinnesses must in turn have thought highly of a brewer who had the Conolly households as his clients. Barton was another local name, best known for the Bartons who built Straffan House, now the home of the world-famous K Club golf hotel, who made their fortune not from beer but by importing wines from France.

Yet in 1922 the family historian Henry Guinness was dismissive of the children's appreciation for Richard's achievements:

> It is most remarkable that so little is known of Richard Guinness and nothing whatsoever of his parentage. He was . . . in honourable employment . . . but for some reason or another there are no family records or traditions connected with him. His children appear to have deliberately destroyed or suppressed all reference to their father.[3]

When we see that there are few exact birth or death details for his wife and children, as the local church records were burnt in 1798, and only the 1752 lease for the Viney House connects Richard, Arthur and Samuel on paper, it is not 'remarkable' at all. The family was poor in the 1720s and not so grand before 1800 as to keep an archive, and the casual destruction of many legal and accounting documents has been a common practice until very recently. Only on the formal application for the Magennis coat of arms in 1814 did the past need to be examined. Richard was listed at the start of the family tree in 1814, so 'suppressed all reference' is an exaggeration, and his nephew and many of his descendants were given his name. It was, of course, unimaginable in 1922 that the male-line ancestry could be revealed by genetics. While Henry's research findings stand inspection, his analysis on this point does not.

Richard in his lifetime had no reason to keep papers; he had quite enough to do minding Dr Price's. From obligations to his employer and his family he had to stick quietly at his job. It could all go wrong – there could be other disastrous years like 1739–41. He obviously recalled some family origin from County Down, but it had no relevance in his everyday life. He kept his head down at his work, owned little property and therefore had no vote and was of no public consequence until 1752. The family properties bought with his help from then on are all known about. His executorship of John Barton's estate is telling, an implicit recognition of Richard's practical knowledge and trustworthiness. When we piece together Richard's evidently steady support in his arrangements for his children, no reason for destruction or suppression existed. This lack of paperwork is apparent in Arthur's life, too, as few of his personal writings are extant. Lynch and Vaizey regretted that as late as the 1950s the brewery archives had some 'extremely badly preserved' books of letters.[4] It is one of the facts of biography that family papers are burnt, before and after

**1.** The graveyard at Oughterard, County Kildare, the home of Arthur's mother's family. Arthur is buried here alongside his mother and many of his relations.

**2.** *An Ale Tent at Donnybrook Fair* by Francis Wheatley (1770s). Arthur's grandfather William Read (*c.* 1660s–1730s) most likely sold beer in this manner to passing traffic on the Dublin–Cork road from the 1690s.

**3.** Oakley Park – formerly Celbridge House – Celbridge, County Kildare, today. This was the home of Dr Arthur Price (1678–1752), Dean of Kildare, Arthur's father's employer and after whom Arthur was named.

**4.** James Carbery's malthouse in Celbridge, Arthur's first home, today the Mucky Duck pub. Owned by Dr Price, Arthur's parents Richard (*c.* 1690–1766) and Elizabeth (1698–1742) moved in after 1722.

**5.** Kildare Cathedral in 1738. In his role as Dean of Kildare, Dr Price's office was based in the semi-ruined building.

**6.** 'George Viney's house' in Celbridge today. Arthur's father subleased the property in 1752, and it became the family's main base until 1764.

**7** and **8.** Leixlip, Country Kildare, in an engraving by John Hinton from the mid-1750s (above). It was here in 1755 that Arthur took on his first brewery. The Salmon Leap at Leixlip in a detail from a mezzotint of 1745 (below). Leixlip was close enough to Dublin for the wealthy to go there for the day to take the country air, which is likely what the fashionably dressed man and his servant are doing in the foreground of this picture.

**9.** Inside a brewhouse, 1747, with brewers at the centre stirring the mash with oars. This is a scene that would have been familiar to Arthur.

**10.** Arthur's 'gentleman's box', Beaumont House, today. In the seventeenth century this stood just north of Dublin and is now part of a convalescent home. Arthur moved in with his family in 1764, and the house remained in the Guinness family until 1855.

**11 and 12.** The membership book of the 'Principal Knot of the County of Kildare 1777' (above left). The book, bound in red Morocco leather and decorated with gilt, was ordered by Arthur, by now the secretary of the society, in whose script (above right) we find the list of members and his notes on meetings.

**13.** The device of the Friendly Brothers of St Patrick (the Kildare Knot). The symbolism of the design includes Irish elements (the Celtic knot, the shamrock and the cross of St Patrick), symbols of brotherly love (dolphins and hearts), a helmet (for the gentry) and celestial crowns.

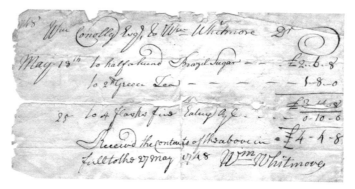

**14.** A bill signed by William Whitmore, the father of Arthur's wife Olivia, in 1748. Whitmore had been a grocer and purveyor of luxury foodstuffs in Essex Street, Dublin.

**15.** Arthur's elaborate signature (above) on a document for properties in Leixlip he leased for development in 1756.

**16.** The coat of arms of the Magennis chiefs (left), from whom Guinness family tradition claimed descent.

**17.** Bills signed by Leixlip brewer John Barton in 1748 (right). Although Barton would have been Arthur's brewing rival in Leixlip after 1755, Richard Guinness witnessed the execution of Barton's will, suggesting the Guinnesses and Barton were on good terms.

**18.** 'A Shoeboy at Customs House Gate', a 1760 drawing by Hugh Douglas Hamilton from the *Cries of Dublin* series, which depicted contemporary street traders and scenes from eighteenth-century Dublin life.

**19.** 'The Trusty Servant' of Winchester College, Hampshire, where Arthur's eldest son Hosea was schooled. Later in life Hosea, by then a churchman, was on the committee of the Society for the Encouragement of Servants, possibly inspired by this representation of the ideal serving man.

**20.** The billhead of Benjamin Guinness (*c.* 1730–78), grocer, the third son of Richard and Elizabeth Guinness. Arthur's brother had moved to Dublin before 1760 and established himself in business at 22 Werbergh Street.

**21.** Captioned 'Health, Peace and Prosperity', this 1794 illustration from the English *Gentleman's Magazine* depicts a man enjoying a drink in front of a barrel marked 'Guinneſs Porter'. This was the first public representation of Arthur's brew, published in London, the original home of porter.

**22.** *Gin Lane* (1751) by William Hogarth. Although the picture depicts the detrimental effects of cheap gin on the population of London – note that the pawnbroker is the only thriving business – the authorities in Ireland were equally concerned about the high consumption of spirits there.

Beer, happy Produce of our Isle
Can sinewy Strength impart,
And wearied with Fatigue and Toil

Labour and Art upheld by Thee
Successfully advance,
We quaff Thy balmy Juice with Glee

Genius of Health, thy grateful Taste
Rivals the Cup of Jove,
And warms each English generous Breast

**23.** *Beer Street* (1751), Hogarth's companion piece to *Gin Lane*, was a government-sponsored print designed to persuade the gin-drinking population in England that beer was the healthy option – a view the Irish brewers and their supporters would have endorsed.

**24.** The earliest known portrait of Arthur, possibly dating from around 1765. The confident and fashionably dressed businessman holds a letter addressed to him at Beaumont, County Dublin, to which he is about to reply. Literacy was the route to his success, a fact acknowledged here.

**25.** Arthur's wife Olivia (*née* Whitmore; *c.* 1742–1814) around the 1790s. She married Arthur in 1761 and bore twenty-one children, of whom ten survived to adulthood.

**26.** Arthur's eldest son Hosea (1765–1841). He became a prominent Dublin churchman and was involved in many good works to help alleviate the suffering of the poor.

**27.** Arthur's second son Arthur II (1768–1855) around 1800. He took over the management of the brewery and guaranteed the continuity of his father's work.

**28.** Arthur II's wife Ann (*née* Lee; 1774–1817) around 1800.

**29 and 30.** Arthur's brother Samuel (*c.* 1727–95; left) established himself as a goldbeater in Dublin in 1750 and later moved into banking. He was the first of the Guinnesses to be educated abroad, his apprenticeship being served in London. Samuel's wife Sarah (*née* Jago; 1732–94; below), whose uncle Robert Calderwood was a goldsmith like her husband.

**31.** Samuel junior (1761–1826), the younger son of Samuel and Sarah. He became a barrister.

**32 and 33.** Samuel's and Sarah's elder son Richard (1755–1829; above left) was, like his younger brother Samuel, a barrister, later becoming a judge. Above right, Richard's wife Mary (*née* Darley; died 1836), whom he married in 1783.

**34.** William FitzGerald (1748–1804), 2nd Duke of Leinster and 21st Earl of Kildare, by Sir Joshua Reynolds (*c.* 1775). The Duke was the premier peer in the Irish House of Lords as well as being one of Arthur's Friendly Brothers.

**35.** The well-known portrait of Arthur from around 1790 on which the 1959 commemorative Irish stamp marking the bicentenary of the opening of the Dublin brewery was based. The modest clothes contrast with the earlier portrait from the 1760s (Plate 24), but the confident smile is the same.

death, but Richard's vital, if unsung, role in arranging for his family is now clear.

In 1761, after the partnership with Wetherell had collapsed, Samuel moved to 4 Crow Street in Temple Bar on a 900-year lease. The property extended between Crow Street and Temple Lane, with underground vaults and room for a refinery at the back. It sounds more suitable and healthy for smelting metals than in a single house. Yet again he advertised in the *Freeman's Journal*, on 2 April 1768:

Whereas a Refinery for Gold and Silver, after the manner of those in London, is much wanted in Dublin. Samuel Guinness, Gold-beater, in Crow Street, is now preparing one, at a considerable Expence, where the Public may be assured of receiving the highest Prices for old Gold and Silver, and Gold and Silver Lace. In London the refiners are a distinct Trade and have the sole Market for those Articles, and, from their great Consumption, can afford to give higher Prices for them than those of any other Occupation, upon which Footing it is to be established by the said Guinness.

N.B. Proper persons will attend at all Hours to burn and clean [gold] Lace, at his House in Crow Street and at his Gold-beating Manufactory in Dirty Lane, at the Back of said House.

As well as his business ventures Samuel had an interest in the stage. Close by, in Smock Alley, stood the Theatre Royal, which was managed in the early 1760s by Thomas Sheridan, father of the famous playwright and Whig politician Richard Brinsley Sheridan. As with the Guinnesses the Sheridans had a male-line Gaelic ancestry – being formerly Ó Sioradan from County Cavan – which did not hinder their lives in Ascendancy Dublin in any way but gave them a sensitivity to the hardships of the past century. In 1764 Thomas was in financial difficulties and fled to Blois in France. In his letters from there to Samuel Whyte in Grafton Street, he asked for his best wishes to be passed on to Mr and Mrs Guinness 'and let them know I shall ever retain the most grateful sense of their civilities to me'.

This led on to business and indicates how a goldbeater such as Samuel could move into banking and deposit-taking. Naturally such a business would have a safe or strong-room, as higher-value coins were made then from precious metals. When people deposited coins with a goldsmith for safekeeping he became, in effect, their banker. On his return to Dublin in 1776, Sheridan appeared on stage for twenty-five nights at the Theatre Royal in Crow Street, a few doors away, and his receipts were handled by Samuel, as 'communicated to the author [Mr Whyte] by Samuel Guinness Esq., Mr Sheridan's confidential friend on the occasion, who received the money for him, and whose return [account], in his own handwriting, now lies before me'.[5]

Any of Sheridan's Dublin creditors from the 1760s had to be avoided, and the solution was to entrust his payments to Samuel. By now the Sheridans' star was back in the ascendant. Thomas's son Richard was suddenly famous throughout the British Isles for fighting and surviving two duels with a love rival named Thomas Mathews in 1772, and, best of all, the saga of the duels included a scandalous elopement to France with Miss Eliza Linley.[6] This friendship continued into the next generation; Samuel's son Richard visited the Sheridans in London in 1780, in particular dining with Thomas's daughter, Mrs Le Fanu, where he met the famous actress Mrs Siddons.

Arthur might well have disapproved of the company of such a family – unpaid debts, the stage being then almost an immoral career, the duels, an elopement – but Samuel seems to have been quite relaxed about doing a favour for an old friend and neighbour. It is an interesting link to a well-known name. Samuel's and Arthur's sons were educated at the same Mr Whyte's Classic Academy at what is now Bewley's in Grafton Street. Whyte's other alumni included R.B. Sheridan, Thomas Moore, Robert Emmet and Arthur Wesley – alias Wellesley – later the first Duke of Wellington.[7] Note that Samuel was described as Esq., short for Esquire, indicating an educated or cultivated man and rather grander than some merchants. While a vague term in itself, it could be equivalent to the equally indefinable but desirable status of gentleman, as best teased out by Dr Toby Barnard.[8]

Thomas Sheridan was interesting in another way, as at this time he was working on a system of universal English that could be accepted everywhere. Dr Johnson's successful dictionary was done, and so the next logical step was to deliver the words in an agreeable way that lessened the impact of the speaker's origin or home district. It may seem ironic, if you take the view of the Irish as a downtrodden people at the time, that a Gaelic-surnamed man would try to homogenize the use of English worldwide, but again, if one sees it as a sensible or practical idea and an opportunity to be grasped, then it was entirely logical. However, when he tutored wealthy Scots and then set up an academy at Bath in England to enable the new English monied merchant classes to lose their origins and regional dialects, it was not a financial success.[9] Unfortunately the

Sheridans' undoubted talents, bravura and cleverness were matched by an inability to manage money.

Richard junior, the fourth Guinness brother, continued to brew ale at Leixlip until 1803. Compared with Samuel and Arthur he is more of a shadowy figure, and no portrait survives. However, he kept in the business, helped originally by Arthur's time in Leixlip and his methods and marketing. One suspects that he had a good living but, given the size of his village market, could never earn as much as Arthur. At some point he bought an inn just across the Liffey, still called the Salmon Leap Inn today – or locally as 'the Lep' – which any tourists from Dublin had to pass on their way to see the eponymous waterfall; he was trying to corner that weekend seasonal market and gain the whole margin from his production cost to retail.[10] A feasible legend says that he also had some sort of pub or shebeen at the brewery property on the main street, where shops stand today.

On 23 May 1775 he married Ann, daughter of Thomas Forster of Roristown, County Meath, so he also had married into the minor gentry, and a dowry of some sort would have arrived with her.[11] Perhaps in light of this success, he joined Arthur in the Kildare Friendly Brothers in August 1776, which Samuel never did. Why did it take Arthur so long to propose him for membership? Was he concerned that Richard would let the side down in some way at the Knot meetings? Richard's recent marriage into the gentry would increase the likelihood of a duel. Some drunken squire might disparagingly mention his trade or his lowly origins in polite company, and so compel Richard into a duel to confirm his new status. We would call this solution a survival strategy, and Arthur was being cautiously protective at the right time in Richard's life.

By 1778 Richard had been brewing for over a decade on his own, and one senses that he was under Arthur's influence much more than Samuel ever was. Being in Leixlip he was usefully on the spot to keep an eye on Arthur's investment properties, those bought in 1756 and another range of houses across the street on the north side bought in 1775, now generally known as The Mall. Leixlip was still a big part of Arthur's life, and eventually all these investment properties were bequeathed to his eldest son Hosea. Richard also engaged in some local property trading in the 1780s, including deals with Archibald Hamilton Rowan, who was to become a revolutionary in the 1790s.[12]

This first Guinness brewery could also have become world famous, perhaps, but Richard and Ann had four daughters, and with no son to continue the business he sold up his Leixlip properties in 1803, after over three decades of brewing ale on his own account, and died in Portarlington in February 1806. Yet, even then, like a homing pigeon, he was brought back for burial at Oughterard, over thirty miles away. Aged only about ten when standing by his mother's open grave back in 1742, it was where he, too, knew he belonged.

On 10 November 1773 we find Arthur visiting the imposing classical Irish Parliament building with some fellow brewers, complaining to Dr Clement's committee about their problem with taxation that unfairly helped beer imports from England. There were two taxes, one on malt when it was made and one on each barrel of the finished product. This is the key record explaining why Arthur started to brew porter, but, again, historians have usually noted only that he was described as 'another considerable brewer' and had been brewing for eighteen years. Compared with many of today's inquiries, the report was a model of brevity.[13] Let us take a ringside seat.

First, the salient statistics concerning volume sold and money taxed were dealt with. The 'Examinator of the Excise' confirmed that the tax raised on beer had dropped steadily over the decade from £145,933 in 1762 to £93,998 in 1771 and £96,269 in 1772, 'and this not owing to any temporary Accident, but to a gradual Decay in the Trade'. Next the 'Examinator of the Customs' said that beer imports from England had increased in the same period from 28,935 to 58,675 barrels. He added that a recent corn scarcity in England, causing 'some Distress in the Brewery [trade] there', was the only reason why the imports had not reached 100,000 barrels. In volume terms, each barrel held thirty-six gallons or 288 pints (about 164 litres), and barrels of thirty-two gallons were also commonly assessed.

Next, the city brewers stepped forward with their tale of woe, led by 'Mr George Thwaites, Master of the Corporation of Brewers in the City of Dublin', who had been in the trade since 1739. Then, it 'was considered as one of the most lucrative in the City', but he had seen the number of Dublin breweries drop from seventy to 'not above thirty . . . he does not believe that any Brewer in Dublin has fairly made any considerable Profit for the last seven Years'. It must have seemed that Arthur, now aged forty-eight, had been in the wrong business all along. Thwaites made his points with hand-wringing pathos:

he believed that one fourth of the Brewers of this City, honest industrious Men, have failed within these last ten Years, owing to the increased Price of

Malt, Hops, Fire and Labour of all Kinds, while at the same Time the Brewer is prevented from raising the Price of his Liquor in the same proportion; and consequently to save himself, is obliged to lessen the Quantity of Malt and Hops; from whence the Liquor is less agreeable and nourishing for the People. That this has thrown them into the excessive Use of spiritous Liquors, the Consequence of which is a total Depravation of the Manners of the lower Class.

Then, Thwaites averred sadly to the social and moral cost of this decline, hoping that the committee would subconsciously recall Hogarth's famous prints of Gin Lane and Beer Street:

> he remembers when he went into Trade the Journeymen [day labourers] of Dublin were a sober, industrious, thriving People, who of an Evening used to content themselves with a Pot of comfortable Ale; that at present they are the most enfeebled, wretched Set of Creatures he ever saw, almost always intoxicated with Dram-drinking.

A new and competitive product, porter beer, had arrived from England as well. From the Dublin brewers' perspective, 'if they raised the Price of their Ale, in the smallest Degree, the Publicans would sell nothing but Porter . . . at present the Publicans had a greater Profit in selling Porter than in selling Ale'. They were now reduced to price discounting on their sales by over 5 per cent, having already paid excise duty on the full value of a barrel. The publicans were the brewers' marketplace, of course, and porter was what they wanted; in turn, it was what their customers preferred. The demand was there, yet nobody was brewing porter beer in Dublin.

The committee must have quietly pondered how all these dram-drinkers were able to afford so much imported English beer as well. And why would you pay more for your labourers now, if they were all so 'enfeebled'? Was Mr Thwaites not over-egging the cake? Worse was to come: 'He apprehends, that if some Steps be not taken to encourage the Brewing Trade of this Kingdom, so long on the decline, that the Trade, and the Agriculture, and Revenue, are in Danger of Ruin . . .'

Next, Thwaites disarmingly admitted to importing English porter beer himself as a wholesaler, but as such he knew of the relative tax and price advantages and of an export grant available in England. Looking at it from the English exporter's point of view:

> on Importation into this Kingdom he pays something less than fifteen pence Irish, per Barrel, from whence deducting the [English export] bounty of one Shilling, English, a Barrel, the remainder is about Two Pence a Barrel, which is the whole of what imported Porter pays [in tax] in England and Ireland, while, on the other Hand, the Irish Brewer pays near five Shillings and six Pence per Barrel, a Difference under which no Trade can subsist. The Consequence is, that by this means the English Brewer can afford to sell his Porter cheaper here than in England . . .

Mr Andrews, 'a Considerable Brewer', spoke next. He had 'minded himself to have set up a Brewery at Holyhead [in Wales], for the Supply of the City of Dublin . . . [so] that he could undersel the Irish Brewers . . . but could not get a Brewery ready built at Holyhead'. He would like to pay to build one there, but the laws were now so evidently unfair that they must be reformed soon and so he would lose his investment. Arthur was the third and final brewer to speak, mentioned at the end of the report:

> Mr Arthur Guinness, another Considerable Brewer, confirmed the Evidence . . . and further said, that he also had intended to set up a Brewery in Carnarvon, or Holyhead, if he could get a Brewery ready built there. That he went to Wales in search of a Brewery, and that he would at this Day settle there, and build a Brewery, if he could be assured that the [tax] Laws would stand as they are, for seven Years.

Then on 28 February 1774 the brewers were back, this time to complain about a proposal to move the Customs House east towards Dublin Port. It was a long-standing issue in the city. We recall that the breweries were mostly based in the western part, near the essential water in the 'City Bason'. This proposal would add to their costs and could lower their property values, despite their major contribution to Ireland's tax revenues:

> the Brewery [trade] in this City has always paid more than one-half of the whole Revenue of Excise in the Kingdom at large. That the Petitioners

Breweries are situated in the upper [upstream] Part of this City, and a very great Part of the Petitioners Fortunes expended on them. That the Petitioners apprehend their Property will be greatly affected by the Removal of the Custom-house lower down the River; as also their Trade greatly distressed by an additional heavy Tax [cost] on the Carriage of Coals and Corn, as shipping must necessarily lie lower down the River.

Later that day a similar petition was received from the 'Manufacturers and other Inhabitants of the Earl of Meath's Liberties, and the adjacent Parts in the West End of the Town' – Arthur's neighbours. As the Customs House was conveniently right beside his community of cousins near Essex Bridge, they would also be affected.

The result of the brewers' excise-duty complaint in 1773 has also been ignored. The hand-wringings of Thwaites and the threats of a move to Wales by Mr Andrews and Arthur Guinness failed completely, and it was a quick decision.[14] Just twenty days later, on 30 November, the committee resolved:

> that an additional Duty of two Shillings the Barrel for and upon every 32 Gallons of Beer or Ale . . . brewed within this Kingdom by any common Brewer, or in his Vessels, or by any other Person . . . who doth or shall sell or tap out Beer or Ale publicly or privately . . .

A 'further additional Duty of four Pence the Barrel' was also imposed on the same basis.

How was Arthur expected to cope? All those 'ors' covered every angle. Even setting up in Wales and brewing for the Dublin market could be taxed under the clause 'or in his Vessels', meaning the brewing kieves, vats and tuns. We see that the venerable city guild was powerless before its Parliament, even though it was paying a sizeable percentage of Ireland's revenue, its members had the vote in what was then a small electorate, and their nominated men sat on the city's Common Council. The guild's motto, *Spes Mea in Deo* (My Hope Is in God), must now have seemed quite appropriate. Something radical was called for, and the recent popularity of this dark English porter beer in Dublin may hold the answer.

Historians have largely ignored Arthur's visit to Wales, as at face value it may have seemed in a sense disloyal to Dublin. As well as doing his sums to determine comparative advantage and finding that his investment would be covered in seven years, Arthur was saying that he had actually made the sixty-mile sea crossing to see what was available on the ground. The towns he said he had visited are close to Ireland, and obviously his intention was still to sell into the Dublin beer market that he knew so well. It may all have been a bluff pre-arranged by Mr Andrews and himself, as no amounts were mentioned.

But it could also have been true. Some Welsh historians, such as Carwyn Jones, believe that Arthur stayed in Llanfairfechan and visited Gwindy on Mount Road, a malthouse where a 'black wine' had been brewed since 1527, and copied their recipe. Jones's 'The famous brewer is thought to have been influenced by . . .' has the all makings of a tantalizing new myth.[15] The problem is that no source is quoted, no dated letters or bills exist and no date for his visit is mentioned, but around 1770 to 1773 would be convincing. Importantly, the Welsh did not know about his claim to have visited that part of north Wales. The historian Lloyd Hughes sadly died in 1993, but we are assured that he 'wouldn't have said something unless absolutely sure of his facts'. With a gleam in his eye, Jones cannot resist adding that 'Irish people may splutter into their pints on St Patrick's Day', prompting a gentle riposte from Guinness plc that 'The Welsh may have their porters, but only Guinness has its Guinness.' When Arthur was looking for breweries in that area he would at least have heard of Gwindy. He may have seen their process, but the main problem for him was the ever-increasing imports into Dublin from London and Bristol. He needed a large new brewery to be competitive, located with tax advantages relative to his Dublin market, and not just another recipe for a black wine.

Arthur had had an ongoing problem with the city since 1764 over his vital water supply. Giles Mee's water agreement for ninety-nine years with the corporation would apparently end in 1769. Despite the clear terms in his lease allowing him a free supply, the city now wanted him to pay for it after four years of taking it for free, and such a payment would rise over time. From the city's point of view, they had 'used all reasonable methods to induce Mr Guinness to become a tenant to the city for water, which he has hitherto declined, insisting upon a right thereto'.[16] He must have had a quiet word with his Friendly Brothers, the city aldermen Lightburne and Featherston, to resolve the matter but evidently without success.

By 1773 the dispute warmed up when the city's waterpipe committee discovered that Arthur had widened the waterpipe from the open culvert into the brewery, suggesting that at least his brewery's volume was not in decline, but possibly he was compensating for a drop in pressure. He and Messrs Foster and Greene had made unauthorized breaches in the culvert wall, 'all of which conveys of said water are very injurious and unjust . . . as the persons receiving the water do not pay for it nor have not for several years past'. They ordered him to restore the wall 'within a reasonable time', but he replied that he would 'defend it by force of arms' and rather overconfidently 'invited them to try how far their strength would prevail'. He had seen off the Excise men in the 1760s and felt that he would have less trouble from the corporation, given his place on its Common Council.

Despite this threat, in April 1775 the city fathers next decided to cover over the culvert where it adjoined the brewery and to lay down new pipes. Clearly, the tiny area of land under the culvert was not part of Arthur's brewery lease. On 10 May the pipe-water committee's men moved around the back of the brewery by the path beside the culvert, bringing along Sheriff Truelock and two of his men as reinforcements or witnesses in case of trouble. That was quite reasonable, as Arthur had warned them that he would forcefully defend his property. It sounds as though Arthur had been warned by an insider or saw them coming:

> The Committee met with obstruction, and on the arrival of Mr Guinness on the scene he violently rushed upon them, wrenched a pick-axe from one and, declaring with much improper language that they should not proceed, he stood with the pick-axe in their way and prevented them from working . . . if they filled up the watercourse from end to end he would immediately reopen it.[17]

With hindsight, Arthur should have had the free water supply mentioned in his lease double-checked and reconfirmed with the city before he took the brewery on. Such a confirmation is essential when a third party is effectively a part of a property transfer. It could be that he had not been told of Giles Mee's 99-year water lease, or that he had ignored it. Possibly the city had ignored the matter for many years before 1759, but widening his pipe from the culvert after the dispute had started was provocative. It all suggests an obstinate adherence to the exact wording of his lease, but in the fast-growing city the demand for water on the modest partial flow from the Poddle and the recently started canal was ever increasing, so the city fathers had to do something. The pickaxe and the improper language reveal his fear and anger, but, notably, he was not prosecuted; he had only threatened violence in defence of his business and nobody had been injured. With his brewers looking on he also had to be seen to lead and show his resolve to them. As with the Excise men, he had had no formal notice before the officials arrived and the prior involvement of the Sheriff was proof that some trouble was expected.

The Corporation was still patient: 'A proposal of accommodation was made when Mr Guinness promised on his word of honour that . . . he would submit his title to . . . examination.'[18] However, on examination no clear title was found to exist, and 'all the right he offered was ancient custom', just a claim to an easement, like a right of way or a right to light. Such an easement had to exceed twenty-one years, and the water lease had technically expired only in 1769; however, the £2 annual rent had not been paid since the 1740s, and Arthur could argue that more than twenty-five years of neglect should be sufficient. Just before this fruitless 'examination' was made, Arthur filed a legal bill against the corporation and luckily obtained an injunction in court, copies of which were served on the Lord Mayor and some of his officials on 22 May 1775, thereby kicking the matter into touch. The pipe-water committee could not interfere until the courts heard the case, perhaps a delay of several years. Within a fortnight of the stand-off he had defended himself proactively, but he still relied on an uncertain legal position. He was playing for time in the examination, knowing it probably would not work, while in the meantime he was instructing his lawyer to obtain the injunction, causing further delay. Surely it would have been more sensible for him to pay £5 or £10 annually instead of prolonging the matter? Lawyers' fortunes are made from obstinate litigants.

Being on the Common Council, Arthur was also on an internal committee of thirty councilmen that examined the Corporation's accounts on 19 January 1776 and which included a provision of £50 towards the city's legal costs to pursue him in this same water dispute. That way he could know at first hand what importance the officials of the pipe-water committee were giving to the matter – some but not a lot. One can imagine the embarrassed or smirking glances exchanged around the room: there he is, this awkward man, who has served an injunction on our Lord Mayor some months ago and is now here shamelessly in our midst while we are discussing his case. But the faces were not all hostile for, as it so happened, the City Treasurer's brother was in the Kildare

Knot, of which Arthur was by now the secretary, along with Friendly Brothers Aldermen Lightburne and Featherston.

This is the most likely explanation as to why Arthur was treated so patiently over the years. He was on the Common Council, was the secretary of that humanist gentry club in Kildare that had some grand members, was by now the treasurer of the Meath Hospital and had been the master and warden of his guild, so he had to be handled with respect, and he took advantage of that. He had acquitted himself in these other roles, he was in the city network and was the sort of person one might bump into anywhere. He had a dispute over his water supply, as did others. He was not apparently a uniquely large user, a vast new supply from the Grand Canal was coming soon, some lawyer had muddled up his lease – why turn a nuisance into a drama? This official lenience has been wondered about fruitlessly by historians, focusing on him with the pickaxe and ignoring the wider picture. But in the real city of the 1770s, the dispute itself still had to be resolved. The pipe-water committee men had just reported on 16 January 1776 that its members would henceforth to be guided by Giles Mee's expired water lease of 1670. To excuse any criticism for delay on their part in letting the matter run on for twelve years, '[we] have done everything in our power ... to give [all] the inhabitants an ample supply of water'.[19] On a further visit in 1779 Arthur was found to have bricked over the culvert, making impossible an inspection of his wider pipe into the brewery.

In the background the Grand Canal that would link Dublin with the River Shannon had been begun in 1755, starting at the city reservoir, and it was taken over by the corporation in 1763–72, from 1766 specifically as a water supply. As it continued to be slowly dug and lined ever-westwards it would carry an ever-increasing water supply into the city, so delaying a final settlement made sense for him. Delayed but not shelved – and in 1781 he proposed a settlement, 'to avoid expense', to the pipe-water committee's relief. The matter was finally resolved by arbitration in 1784.

Martelli fairly described this dispute as the 'Battle of the Poddle', and so a recent myth about the brewery's water supply should be laid to rest. Michele Guinness says that Liffey water was used, but this has always been a Dubliner's half-joke and half-insult, and she is based in England. Mullally, with an Irish-sounding name, is as bad: 'The River Liffey was the main source of fresh water for the burgeoning city ... This minor Battle of the Liffey was resolved ...' Wilson states: 'With good Liffey water ... Arthur doubted not that he could turn a handy profit.' Just a small part of Dublin's heritage of humour, this half-joke had become half-history.[20] How water from the Liffey could flow uphill to the city reservoir without pumps simply never occurred. Perhaps some leprechauns carried it up at night. The historical record and the facts were always clear, and in recent years Jonathan Guinness has saved the day, knowing his Dublin and being mystified by 'the rumour that it is brewed from the waters of the polluted Liffey'.[21] So it surprised me in 2005 to see an Irish Diageo – Guinness's parent company – supplier's advertisement reading: 'Just as Liffey water is a vital ingredient in Guinness, talented people are a critical ingredient in Diageo's success story.' Was it yet another advertising joke?[22] At least the latter phrase is true.

Although the intermingled Poddle and Grand Canal were the main supply from the 1770s onwards, it has led to a lesser myth, suggesting that the canal supply comes only or primarily from another suitably eponymous St James's Well in Kildare. The well's water, from the vast aquifer under the Curragh plain, does feed the canal, but by the time it reaches Dublin the canal has also collected water from a few other sources as well. It also passes under Oughter-ard Hill, Arthur's own maternal-ancestral source. Being exposed for miles it has always needed filtering and boiling before it can be used for brewing. As Moore (1960) put it best, the water has a 'medium hardness softened by boiling'.[23] By 1935 Dublin Corporation ran two low-key pumping stations at the canal's fifth and eighth locks, which delivered some 330 million gallons that year to the brewery through two enormous pipes. By then a well in the lower brewery was fed by the underground Camac river, which runs from Saggart, and there was another connection from Vartry reservoir in the Wicklow Mountains.

Some problems could not be resolved. Arthur's powerlessness concerning taxes, English imports and his water supply is apparent. So when Dunne refers to Arthur's 'elite social position', it can be put in context.[24] He was clearly wealthier than many Irishmen, and was in a élite in that narrow sense, but not when it came to influencing the decisions made by the authorities that impacted on his business. He could vote for them and approach them face to face, he could be intransigent, he might be treated patiently, but he could not in the end pull any strings. The recent books on the politics of the real Irish élite at this time by Malcolmson, Kelly, McDowell and Small reconfirm this – Arthur is mentioned in none of them.[25] It could be that Dunne followed Lynch and Vaizey, who said 'his family connections were the strength of his business'. This referred to his rather grand Anglo-Irish in-laws, but there is, again, no proof of any benefit from them beyond Olivia's sizeable dowry in 1761, and not one of them was a client-publican. His father had taught him about business paperwork and had helped fund the start of his career as a brewer, but the rest was down to him. Olivia's cousins and in-laws might well have invited the couple to dinners and parties at which they would have met interesting or important people, adding intangibly to their social respectability, but the foundations of his business, his skills, his premises and some of his networks of contacts were all largely in place before his marriage. The important family connections on the ground that launched him in Dublin were his humbler brothers, uncle and cousins who were working in the city in 1759.

At that time the social élite was the political élite. As a secretary from 1744 and a Dublin businessman from 1760, he had taken his opportunities over thirty years, but he was still boxed in by the power-brokers of the city and the kingdom and by the realities of the beer trade across the British Isles. Arthur had no MPs in his pocket, no lords or castle officials at his beck and call, and he controlled no political groups. Had he gambled away all his wealth at the races in, say, 1770, would the real élite have stepped in to support him? Of course not. He was just another Dublin 'common brewer', if described as 'considerable', along with several dozen others. Given the times in which he lived, he would aim for *respectability* in the eyes of the real élite, as this might help his business reputation, his creditworthiness and his children's marriage prospects. The only way up into the real élite would be to brew more consistently and trade ever more successfully, even perhaps some day across the British Isles. That would take decades to achieve and would clearly not come about by selling ale.

# CHAPTER TEN

# Porter Comes to Dublin

RTHUR'S SOLUTION WAS to copy the English porter brewers and beat them at their own game. This development was not based on an inherited porter recipe or he would have been brewing it since 1755; neither was it developed by him, nor was he the first to brew it in Dublin – so many legends have arisen around his best-known product – yet he was quick to adapt when a surprising opportunity arose. The saga of how porter brewing came to Dublin includes some unusual elements that have nothing to do with Arthur himself.

Ralph Harwood of Shoreditch in London was already brewing a dark beer in 1722, just before Arthur's birth. The porters of London liked to drink dark mixes of different beers called 'half-and-half' and 'three threads' (meaning three thirds), and Harwood developed a way of brewing the same liquor as the three-beer mixture which he sold as Mr Harwood's Entire Butt. A butt was a barrel, so the three parts were sold as one, or 'entire', in one barrel, which was easier and quicker for a publican to pour than tapping a glass of the drink from three barrels.[1] Some historians say that this was the first porter beer, others that it was only the first successful, well-known brand of porter. Mathias (1959) casts doubt on the exact origin. Harwood was canonized as the inventor long after his death, in an 1802 issue of the *Monthly Magazine*. Lisa Picard has described the Georgian licensed street porters, reliant on their hands and feet, as 'the taxis and vans and motorcycle couriers of London, without whom it could not have functioned'.[2] The thicker beer gave the porters a sense of extra strength to cope with their exhausting, dehydrating daily rounds, and it became an instant success.

Whatever its origin, by 1727 the Swiss traveller César de Saussure noted that in London:

The greater quantity of this beer is consumed by the working classes. It is a thick and strong beverage and the effect it produces, if drunk to excess, is that of wine. This 'porter' costs threepence a pot. In London there are a number of alehouses where nothing but this sort of beer is drunk.

These were soon renamed porterhouses, where one could also buy a meal of 'porterhouse steak'. In 1751 *The Student or Oxford Monthly Miscellany* urged: 'Let us not derogate from the merits of Porter, a Liquor entirely British, a Liquor that pleases equally the Mechanic and the Peer – a Liquor which is the Strength of our Nation, the Scourge of our Enemies, and which has given immortality to Aldermen.'

Dr Samuel Johnson's friend Henry Thrale was a wealthy London porter brewer, which the good doctor described in his dictionary as: 'a cant [slang] name for strong beer'. Thrale's new premises was inspected by the Irishman Thomas Campbell in 1775:

> The immensity of the Brewery astonished me. I was half-suffocated by letting in my nose on the working floor – for I cannot call it a vessel – its area was greater than many Irish castles. The reason assigned [given to] me that Porter is so much lighter on the stomach than other beer is that it ferments much more and is by that means more spiritualized.[3]

It seems that Campbell's brewery visit was made in hopes of meeting Dr Johnson, who was often the guest of Mrs Thrale, and who had been introduced to them by Anthony Murphy, another Irishman.[4] Mr Thrale had borrowed £2,000 to re-equip his brewery in 1772 and nearly went bankrupt as a result. Like Arthur, like Dr Johnson, he came from a humble background, with his grandfather described as a 'cottager', a farm labourer, yet by this time he lived in Grosvenor Square. Some of the grander gentry members of Dr Johnson's circle, such as James Boswell, resented Thrale's sudden rise in wealth and status, given that he was only a brewer. Dr Johnson was appointed an executor on Thrale's death in 1781, and when advising on the best way of describing the brewery for sale for £30,000 he coined a famous phrase: 'We are not here to sell a parcel of boilers and vats, but the potentiality of growing rich, beyond the dreams of avarice.' In the event it was sold to the Barclays for £135,000, a staggering return on £2,000 in a decade.[5] Was that down to the likely profits from porter or to the good doctor's skill with words?

The longer process was only a part of porter beer's secret. It used extra portions of charred malt and barley to give body and colour. More hops were added to help preserve the brew. The essence was more fully extracted from the raw materials by prolonged mashing, boiling and fermentation, resulting in a more stable product that could keep better in store and be exported to the tropics – and Ireland – without going off mid-voyage. For a country like Britain, with the largest navy and merchant fleet in Europe and a solid tradition of following the sea, it was the ideal beer to export around its expanding empire. Its bulk provided ballast in a ship's hold on the way out which could be filled with more profitable foreign goods on the way home. Hence the Dublin brewers' problems in 1773. There was one big drawback. The longer time spent in production tied up more of a brewer's working capital, and so it could only be undertaken by the larger brewers, but in the long run would make them even wealthier. The process could take up to nine months, depending on seasonal temperatures. This explains Mr Thrale's vast 'working floor'.

How best to copy such a beer in Dublin? Clearly it was selling well in the city, and so all that remained to do was to make it. Arthur would have known about the product and general process for years. But it must be made to taste as good as or better than any import and be brewed to a consistently high standard. Although the myth-historians think that Arthur had already been brewing a red-brown-black porter for some time, even since Celbridge or Cashel, some at least mention Harwood, and Dunne imagines that Arthur was 'inspired' by the Londoner. But the real inspiration lay much closer to home.

Certainly Arthur did not brew the first porter in Dublin. In 1776 James Farrell of Blackpits, south-west of St Patrick's Cathedral, hired or poached a London brewer, John Purser, to come to Dublin. Purser, 'knowing his Business as Porter Brewer as any other Person in London', moved from Reid's Brewery at Liquorpond Street – a great address for a brewery – and worked for Farrell and other Dublin brewers apparently on an informal consultancy basis. Corcoran (2005) says that Purser came originally from Tewkesbury, Gloucestershire. Arthur may have hired him on a freelance basis or, in his turn, simply copied what the others were brewing with this new skill. Competition from English porter was bad enough, and now his rivals in Dublin were starting to brew it as well. He had to keep up or fall behind, and those that fell behind could go bankrupt. Really he had no choice. Purser's acquaintance with Arthur at that time is suggested by a deed of 1780, where his son John Purser junior was a party and Arthur was grantor.

Henry Guinness (1925) went into greater detail.[6] Purser had set up as a brewer in London at Leather Lane and then in Hackney, but being short of capital he 'was compelled to become a working brewer' in the 1770s, working for someone else in a managerial position. James Farrell had sent his trusted agent Robert Barnewall to London to find such a man, and Barnewall confirmed this shortly after Purser's death in a brief testimonial dated July 1781: 'I ingaged Mr John Purser in London to come to Dublin to brew Porter for Mr Farrell and I was informed on a very strict enquiry that he was perfectly capable and was very able in that business.' Purser had died on his way south to see what was brewing in Cork City, and was buried at Rathcormac, County Cork. The prominent Dublin brewers George Thwaites, Edward Atkinson, Nathaniel Warren, James Farrell, Thomas Andrews and P.H. Sweetman also wrote testimonials to his prowess, which were kept by John's proud brewer-descendants.

Mr Purser had chafed at working for his employer in London, having been a self-employed entrepreneur, and preferred offering less restrictive consultancy services to these Irishmen. Farrell considered him as more of an employee:

> I certifie that Mr John Purser Brewed seven thousand five hundred barrels of Porter for me the last Season he lived in my employ which I think was extremely well manufactured and that he is as skilful in the Art of brewing porter as any person in London in my opinion.
>
> Blackpits 17 July 1781<br>James Farrell.

It seems odd that Arthur did not join in writing a testimonial in 1781 if he knew Purser's son by 1780, but perhaps he was away or busy. At any rate, Mr Purser arrived at Farrell's brewery in 1776, before Arthur's first tentative sales of porter in 1778. Given porter's longer production cycle, the run-up would have involved up to a year of costly experiments. It was a necessary decision but was still something of an expensive gamble unless, and even if, you really knew your business – Purser had run out of money when self-employed, and Thrale had nearly failed over a debt of £2,000.

There is a further twist, as the Thwaites family claimed to have brewed porter to perfection by 1763 and had asked the Irish Parliament to grant-aid its production. Nothing came of this, and as we have seen George Thwaites decided to import it from England as a wholesaler. So the eternal question that I have been asked all my life: 'Where did Arthur brew the first pint?' must be reconsidered in several parts. He brewed ale in Celbridge for his stepmother at the White Hart Inn in 1752 and definitely on his own account at Leixlip from 1755. As for porter: 'Who brewed it first in Dublin?' – seemingly the Thwaites family; or better: 'Who brewed it and sold it first?' – step forward James Farrell.

Farrell – anglicized from Ó Fearghail – was a clever and prosperous brewer who lived in North King Street and then in splendour at 37 Merrion Square (now the Goethe Institute). He was a member of the improving Dublin Society and had been in the drinks business since the 1750s. He was also one of the Knights of Tara, another anti-duelling group, which promoted public displays of fencing as a genteel antidote, wearing leather slippers and tying multi-coloured bunches of ribbons on their shins.[7] In 1790 Charles Bowden, an English visitor to Dublin, recorded that he had called on Farrell and his brother-in-law Mr Byrne, 'another eminent brewer', and was 'never more elegantly entertained in my life'.[8] He added that they were 'held in the highest estimation by all ranks for the most exalted virtues'. Both were Catholics, a reminder that Arthur's religion was of no help in his daily business of selling beer to publicans.

Indeed, brewing was a trade that included every background and origin. Peter, Thady and Patrick Grehan were brewing alongside Arthur in James's Street. While the other large Dublin brewers included Anglo-Protestants, such as the Leesons and the Pims, and in Cork the Beamishes; there were also many long-established famous Irish brewing names, including the Norman-origin Brownes, Sweetmans and the Smithwicks of Kilkenny, who were Catholic. Mr Barnewall, the key man who hired Mr Purser, came from a famous landed Norman family in County Meath that had remained Catholic. The final consumer was not at all interested in the social origins of any brewer, just in the quality and price of their products.

The employment of John's son, John Purser junior (1760–1830), as head bookkeeper at the Guinness brewery followed in 1799, much later. He was always called 'Mister John' at work, and his son, the next John Purser (1783–1858), also started at St James's Gate in 1799 as an apprentice brewer. Finally John Tertius Purser (1809–93) was general manager until he retired in

1886. This employment of the Pursers may have been an overdue form of thanks on Arthur's part, or it may just have reflected their undoubted skills. By 1900 John Tertius Purser's grand-nephews, William and Samuel Geoghegan, were respectively head brewer and chief engineer at St James's Gate, the last generation to assist.[9] Their family's long contribution to Dublin and its brewers has been unfairly overlooked.

The Pursers' adherence to the tiny Moravian sect was clearly irrelevant to Arthur – religious faith and skill in brewing were quite separate matters. Moravians were described as Dissenters, with a spiritual lineage back to Jan Hus in Bohemia, but a closer examination of them throws up a most compelling reason for Purser's move to Dublin. John Wesley had visited Count Nikolaus Zinzendorf (1700–60), 'the chief of the Moravians', at Hernhuth in Germany back in 1738 and translated one of his hymns. In the London of the 1770s they were considered even odder than the Quakers, and their number included the future wife of the visionary spiritual English artist William Blake. Still led by the next Count Zinzendorf, who was guided from 'Above' to move from frugal Hernhuth to prosperous London, they were linked, according to recent research by Dr Marsha Schuchard, to the ecstatic and esoteric Swedenborg, the Illuminati and the Freemasons. They meditated on Christ's penis and attempted to maintain respectful erections during times of prayer. In imagination, they penetrated Christ's body through the lance-hole made in his side during the crucifixion. The Count argued that the commandment against adultery was defunct, but he tutored newly married wives with special prayers for bedtime: 'When my dear husband lets his oil sizzle in me, this Grace is a sacrament.' He cohabited with a fourteen-year-old girl who was appointed an Eldress of the Church in Fetter Lane. Zinzendorf's son favoured rapturous 'love feasts' and concubinage.[10]

In their public lives outside church the Pursers were stern-faced, ascetic, buttoned-down and efficient managers. They remained Moravians in Dublin, so John was motivated to move elsewhere to follow the original teachings of Hus and not the Zinzendorfs' newfangled interpretations. Barnewall could not know that his offer of a position in Dublin was heaven sent. That way John's daughters would escape from the zealous attentions and wandering hands of the count and his son, rather as people extract their children from offbeat cults today. And why pay his hard-earned money to such a family? Being a clever man he must have felt that public masturbation was ridiculous and disrespectful to the Godhead. Professional porter brewing came to Dublin for religio-sexual reasons as much as for Mr Purser's desire to be more independent.

If porter brewing required capital and skill, at least Arthur's prowess was confirmed at this stage when he was appointed in 1779 as the supplier of beers to Dublin Castle, the main seat of administration. This did not change the family's liberal politics: one might expect that he would have adopted a more pro-British stance, but instead he embraced the growing patriot movement. A big customer is often a slow payer, particularly a government, so the appointment may have been more flattering than profitable for him. He was still not the biggest brewer in Dublin, and so the reliable good quality of his beers was the only consideration. I have looked for an inside contact in his networks of friends who might have arranged it, but without a definite result. A possible candidate was Friendly Brother Sir George Massey, who had the enviable-sounding position of Gentleman at Large at the castle, but the contract was probably arranged by a humbler official.

There is a recent mention of a historical liquid additive, which is eternal and which is nurtured daily and lives on in today's brew. Modern brewing experts in Dublin with their stainless-steel vessels run by banks of computerized equipment still apparently need to inject an extract of Arthur's original Georgian product into the modern pint of Guinness. As well as the yeast strain which is still used today after 250 years, and Arthur's skills passed down from his grandfather Read, this weird, sour extract festering away in the oldest tuns, dating from even before 1760, is all that remains of Arthur's beers, according to *Homebrew Digest*, attributed to Martin Lodahl:

> they have a series of huge oaken tuns dating back to the days before Arthur Guinness bought the brewery, which they still use as fermentors for a fraction of the beer. The tuns have an endemic population of Brettanomyces, lactic acid, bacteria and Lord knows what else, and beer fermented in it sours emphatically. They pasteurize this and blend small quantities of it with beer fermented in more modern vessels.[11]

If a secret ingredient has caused the success of the beer, this surely is it, Brettanomyces and all. It raises a colourful image of offspring germs exhaled by dead generations of Dubliners fermenting and multiplying in the ancient vats' liquid for ever, bio-city and bio-brew fused and immortalized together in a quiet corner of the modern brewery. Today's top brewers say that this is just an urban myth, but along with the other myths we have examined it begs the question: what is it about the unique and mysterious nature of Guinness that causes such legends to arise endlessly like the bubbles inside a pint?

In so far as Guinness-the-drink is a longstanding part of Irish culture, it must be clear why it could hardly have emerged as a world-famous product from *within* the popular rural Irish culture of the 1700s. If Arthur had not moved to Leixlip and Dublin then he would never have met John Purser. First, Guinness-the-family had had to disengage itself over several generations from the restrictions in the culture, while retaining the cultural goods that it wanted to keep. Over several generations in Dublin it was able to create by luck, accident, copying and effort a 'stout porter' from the 1820s that is known around the world as Irish, with the most famous Irish harp adopted as its trademark from 1876. Various types of the original porter were continued until 1974.[12] Thankfully the popular culture has moved a long way towards modernity and self-confidence since 1960.

We recall that back in 1750 Samuel proposed to make gold products in Dublin for 'those who are at the Trouble of importing them', effectively substituting imports from Britain. A generation later Arthur was now taking that same path, albeit under pressure. The apparent disabilities of the Kingdom of Ireland could be overcome. The London brewers and goldsmiths started ahead of the game. They were better capitalized to try out new products and had a large wealthy market on their doorsteps. Their surplus production reached the Continental mainland as well as Ireland, thanks to 10,000 well-financed and insured merchant ships protected by the strongest navy. They could only fail from a lack of consumer demand.

Non-English subjects, such as Samuel and Arthur, then copied them in a small way at home; but in the fullness of time Samuel's descendants would be banking successfully in London, and Arthur's descendants would sell more porter and stout in England than all the English brewers combined. The apparent colonial position on the map was reversed, and competitive trade was the key. One had to be determined enough to copy and improve upon what the colonial power was selling – and knowledge could be bought in. The obliging Mr Purser was quite the opposite of the archetypal colonial oppressor, being instead a man with valuable skills and good reasons to leave home. As a technician he would earn more in 1776 in Dublin than he could in London. Historians have too often concentrated on Ireland's undoubted past disabilities and have some-times ignored how such an opportunity was taken up or passed by.

Far from Arthur being considered the iconic founder of Dublin porter brewing, the credit really lies elsewhere. The heritage industry will have to decide whether a statue to James Farrell in Blackpits is more appropriate than a plaque to Mr Purser at his resting place in Rathcormac. Should Barnewall and the Zinzendorfs be forgotten? They all played their part. Arthur's lasting con-tribution to Dublin and to his family was to copy porter well and in volume, a process that he was to step up a gear in 1799.[13]

# CHAPTER ELEVEN

# Arthur's Patriot Politics – the Kildare Knot and the Volunteers

*I*N THE YEARS around 1780 the turmoil caused by the American Revolution enabled a limited political independence for Ireland, sought by 'patriot' politicians who were linked in turn to Arthur's Friendly Brothers in Kildare. While he was never rich enough to be a politician, the style and ethos of this group have not been fully examined by his historians. His support for the patriot leader Henry Grattan in the 1780s and 1790s was known about, without much analysis beyond Grattan's support for tax relief for Irish brewers.

Arthur's involvement in politics was as a member of Dublin's City Council and never in Parliament, but it was a long involvement, from the 1760s until his death. He has, therefore, been thought of as rather apolitical, an observer, too busy. As we have seen, he was effectively powerless in changing the areas of public life that mattered most to him. Had he ever been invited, he was not securely wealthy enough to leave his business and become an MP sponsored by some grandee.

A closer examination of his dining club in Kildare reveals his patriot sense of national politics. In the 1760s Britain's provinces in America were in turmoil over new taxes; it was not just over the expense but their lack of any say in how the money was spent by the government in London. This was considered demeaning, given their largely English ancestry with its perceived traditions from Magna Carta to the revolution of 1688. Assertive, self-reliant, two million strong, no longer worried about the French in Canada, and with a history of stable local government, many of the colonists launched a rebellion, and in 1776 their leaders signed a Declaration of Independence. Britain sent thousands of soldiers to try to re-establish control but had failed by 1781. This focus on America gave the Irish patriots in the Dublin Parliament a chance to reform some odious legislation.

Economic thought was also stimulated from 1776 by Adam Smith's support for free trade in *An Inquiry into the Nature and Causes of the Wealth of Nations*.[1] Smith proposed that 'it is not from the benevolence of the butcher, the brewer or the baker that we expect our dinner, but from their regard to their own interest'. This sense of enlightened self-interest also had an effect on every local economy, including Dublin's, in which 'every individual . . . endeavours . . . to employ his capital in support of domestic industry'. Smith suggested that an 'invisible hand' pushed and pulled a business into its most effective position. An Irish patriot would agree that by 'preferring the support of domestic to that of foreign industry, he intends only his own security'. As well as undue political control by the English Parliament and government, based on laws passed in 1494 and 1719, Hely Hutchinson criticized the restrictive Irish-English terms of trade imposed by London from the 1660s in his 1779 *Commercial Restraint of Ireland*.[2]

Furthermore, the long-standing and needless, if haphazard, oppression of the Penal Laws was weakening. The 1745 Jacobite revolt in Britain could have spread to Ireland but was ignored, partly because of the effect of the 1739–41 famine and partly from the suspension of the Penal Laws by the viceroy Lord Chesterfield.[3] In 1758 the wealthier Catholics formed the Catholic Committee in Waterford to present their respectable and loyal request for a repeal of the laws. Before long, most counties had their own committees. On 14 January 1766 the Papacy finally ended its support for the Jacobite royal line and from then on recognized George III as the lawful ruler of Ireland. In 1767 the Jesuits were expelled from most of the Catholic kingdoms back to Rome. These facts removed any real sense of threat from the Roman Church to the Irish establishment and led on to overdue reforms of many restrictions on land ownership by Catholics and Dissenters between 1771 and 1779 by the Irish and British parliaments. For a property owner such as Arthur it would have been obvious that when those who were disadvantaged were allowed to buy longer leases and freeholds the new demand would cause the overall value of property to rise, and this was seen in the 1780s. It was a time of changes.

The membership of the Kildare Knot was formed from the gentry, merchants and professionals, those in charge of the local cash-flows, many of whom had surnames of English or Scottish origin and would have been third- or fourth-generation British settlers. But they understood Ireland and its ways, and their settler-ancestors in the 1600s had usually paid for their land and then had to pay more to make it productive. In England these Anglo-Irish were considered to be Irish, and their use of Irish emblems, green ribbons and the order's toast to 'Ireland', all under the patronage of St Patrick, indicates that they identified themselves in their group as Irish. Given all the difficulties in Ireland, they could move to England or America at any time but chose not to. All the Gaelic-surnamed members in the Knot were Protestants, and all the Catholic members had Old English or Norman surnames, the latter including members of the Kildare Catholic Committee. It was an inclusive group, clearly trying to forge a new identity at that social level by moving to improve or eliminate the religious divisions apparent since 1691.

A similar group to the Knots emerged among Irish-Americans. In 1781 George Washington was made a member of the Philadelphia-based Friendly Sons of St Patrick. Founded in 1771, this was a charitable, non-sectarian, largely Presbyterian Irish-immigrant group with its own badge; later, in the 1840s the society raised large sums for Irish famine relief.[4] Also, by 1780 a new Order of St Patrick had just been formed in Dublin, with a middle-class patriot bias. In 1783 the first royal Irish order was created for the nobility, called the Knights of St Patrick. Arthur's order was just the first of many, all dedicated to Ireland's patron saint.

By St Patrick's Day 1777 the Kildare Knot had grown to some seventy members, with Arthur Guinness elected annually as its secretary. He was now its longest-standing brother, and so perhaps it was a case of Buggins's turn, but he would not have been elected to the post unless he was competent. His handling of that pickaxe and his use of 'much improper language' in 1775 did not disqualify him. It gives us a sense of his standing in the Knot, whose members must have heard about that amusing and ongoing little fuss concerning his water supply in Dublin. In any case, a smart new membership book was ordered by him, bound in red Morocco leather and covered in ornate gilt designs, flourishes and letters reading 'Principal Knot of the County of Kildare 1777' and with a lozenge in the centre stating 'His Grace the Duke of Leinster President' (Plate 11). As well as its social import, it is the only highly decorated object that we can say was commissioned and approved by Arthur. Possibly the gilder was introduced by Samuel, as he was making 'gold of a peculiar sort for book-binders' back in 1753. The book starts with a list of the members in 1777, and Arthur took the opportunity to place his name directly under the Duke's (Plate 12).

William FitzGerald, the 2nd Duke of Leinster and 21st Earl of Kildare (1748–1804; hereafter 'the Duke') (Plate 34) had inherited his father's august titles in 1773, aged just twenty-five, and in 1774–5 he was elected Grand Benevolence or head of the entire Friendly Brothers Order. He was the premier peer in the Irish House of Lords, having been an MP in 1769–73, and he controlled a group of Kildare MPs in Parliament. He had inherited Carton, Leinster House and his family's 60,000 acres in County Kildare.[5] His aunt Louisa was married to Friendly Brother Tom Conolly of Castletown. Given the Duke's interest in the order, it must have seemed inevitable to Arthur by 1774 that the grandest man in Kildare would be elected president of the Kildare Knot whenever he wanted. This kind of involvement was entirely unforeseeable nearly two decades past when Arthur had joined the new group as its third member in 1758.

The young Duke was generally quiet and dutiful, and he had faced the possibility of a duel in 1774. In the background, his widowed mother, the dowager Duchess, had set up home with Mr Ogilvie, the family's tutor, causing scandalous rumours to fly around Dublin. That year his sister, Lady Emily, was betrothed to marry Lord Bellamont, but on his arrival for the wedding at Carton on 20 August Bellamont lost his temper and called his mother-in-law-to-be 'a whore', whereupon 'a general fracas followed', and not surprisingly there was 'talk of a duel'.[6] William would have issued the challenge as head of his family but could not, being a Friendly Brother. Bellamont was eventually 'harried and cajoled towards the minister' and the marriage proceeded. Bellamont was known to have duelled in London in 1772 with the retired Lord Lieutenant of Ireland, Lord Townshend but lost and recovered from a wound in the groin. The cause? He had sought a sinecure post from Townshend in 1771 but had been turned away by 'a mere minor official'.[7] His fantasy-portrait in feathers and pink silks is one of the eye-stoppers in the National Gallery of Ireland.

Given his position at the top of the Ascendancy, the Duke was also a liberal in his views and was opposed to the Penal Laws and any unnecessarily irksome links with Britain. On his Grand Tour of Europe in 1766–8 he visited Rome where he found the Pope to be a 'very agreeable man', and when he kissed the Papal toe he found that it 'was very sweet'.[8] Clearly he was not a Protestant bigot. He went on to help found the Order of St Patrick in 1783 (and was styled KP, a Knight of St Patrick), became Grand Master of the Irish Freemasons, took memberships of the Dublin Society and the Royal Irish Academy, joined the Kildare Grand Jury and acted as a director of various charities and canal companies. His life was laden with titles and duties, and he had many siblings to support.

The Duke's younger brothers, Lords Charles, Henry and Edward Fitz-Gerald, were subsequently elected as Kildare Friendly Brothers between 1779 and 1783, no doubt at his suggestion, so the Duke must have found the Knot a pleasant and useful local group. Lord Henry's proposed membership was even 'seconded by all the Members present' in 1779 – how obsequious – but it seems that he never actually swore the required oath. That did not stop him attending dinners and helping to run the Knot's dances. Others of the Duke's relatives, in-laws and employees were Friendly Brothers, such as Frederick Faulkner, the Chevalier d'Estours, Captain George Napier, James Spencer – his agent in Athy and Rathangan – and Peter Bere, who supervised Carton.

For such a grandee, dining with the Kildare Knot was also a useful means of keeping in touch with what was happening locally around his vast estates and was an opportunity to drop any class or social barriers, which worked in both directions. The Duke chaired forty-two of the fifty-six meetings listed in the book, styled 'His Grace the Duke of Leinster President in the Chair'. The ethos of the Knot was one of a settled certainty that did not want its members' family and property arrangements to be overturned suddenly by a stupid insult and an unlucky shot. They were already gentlemen and felt no need to duel to impress society.

However, duelling was then becoming increasingly popular and visible. Professor James Kelly's statistics suggest that before 1770 there were about three duels a year in Ireland, but thereafter the annual average increased to fifteen.[9] In 1780 Arthur Young blamed Irish duels on 'excessive drinking': 'Who is it that can reckon the most numerous rencontres [duels]? Who but the bucks, bloods, land-jobbers and little drunken country gentlemen. Your fellows with round hats edged with gold who hunt in the day, get drunk in the evening and fight the next morning.' These were the 'half-mounted' rural squireens, the lesser gentry.[10]

But many duels were also fought between politicians, and so the Duke ensured that his nominated MPs in the Irish House of Commons were safe by enrolling them all as Kildare Friendly Brothers. With his MPs, family and agents all members, and given his wealth and exalted social position, the Knot became a local political support group with Arthur at its centre, just as Ireland's patriot politics reached boiling point. Never mind that the order's rules of 1763 forbade 'all religious, political, national or Party Debates'.

In March 1778 His Grace was – naturally? – re-elected as Knot president and Arthur was again 'Electd Secretary'; however, 'the honr. of wch. office he is forced to decline for want of time to attend it'. Whatever his want of time, most likely perfecting the brewing of porter beer, he continued writing up the Knot meeting book in 1779 and dined with the Knot until 1785 when he was aged sixty. From Dublin to Maynooth took several hours on horseback, and he was getting on. It was a part of his social life for twenty-seven years, his longest affiliation outside family and business, and as we shall see that it linked into many of his other activities.

In the background, between 1778 and 1783 the Irish Volunteer movement had created a national Protestant patriot militia of over 50,000 men to protect the island from invasion by the French. There was a veiled threat to the administration, as the Volunteers could not be challenged on the ground by the British garrison, and reforms ensued. The Crown, under pressure in America, was persuaded by the patriot supporters of Henry Flood and Henry Grattan to improve Ireland's terms of trade.[11, 12] Also the power to vote money bills – taxation – was devolved from Westminster to the Irish Houses of Parliament directly under the Crown. The American War of Independence was winding down after the British defeat at Yorktown in 1781. An element of political devolution was created when Ireland's legal independence was confirmed by the British executive and Parliament between 1780 and 1783, helped in London by the Duke's first cousin Charles James Fox.[13]

The lawyer and memoirist Jonah Barrington, just down from university, recalled:

> The general enthusiasm caught me . . . I found myself a military martinet and a red-hot patriot. The national point was gained . . . The Irish Parliament had refused to grant supplies to the Crown for more than six months. The people had entered into resolutions to prevent the importation of any English merchandise or manufactures. The entire kingdom had disavowed all English authority or jurisdiction, external or internal; the judges and magistrates . . . declined to act under English statutes . . . we completely set up for ourselves, except that Ireland was bound . . . never to have any king but the King of Great Britain.[14]

How closely the Friendly Brothers and the Volunteers overlapped in Kildare can be seen by the insignia of the Castletown Union Volunteers in Celbridge, set up by Tom Conolly. They also wore a Maltese cross, also described as a St Patrick's cross, also hanging from a green ribbon, with the inscriptions 'Quis Separabit' and 'Castletown Union 1779', and were launched at a grand dinner at Castletown on St Patrick's Day 1779.[15] Conolly had simply absorbed most of his order's Irish emblems and elements for his Volunteers' insignia. Beyond such accoutrements, the Clane Rangers Volunteer song of 1779 included ten Friendly Brothers out of the sixteen men named, and out of the fourteen commanders of Kildare Volunteer units forming up in 1779–80 we find another ten Friendly Brothers. These overlaps are significant in terms of numbers and also of timing, as about a third of the final total of 220 Friendly Brothers joined the Kildare Knot in 1776–80, which was the Volunteers' hey-day.[16] The Duke encouraged the movement at national and local levels and commanded the Dublin Volunteer regiments.

Another famous patriot in the Kildare Knot was Walter Hussey Burgh who had joined in June 1767. A landlord with 2,785 acres at Caragh near Naas, an over-achieving barrister who became Prime Serjeant of Ireland in 1777, he was also a member of the Clane Volunteers in 1779. Elected MP for Athy in 1769–76 and then for Dublin University, he became Chief Baron of the Irish Exchequer in 1782 before his untimely death in 1783 aged just forty-one. He had earlier disagreed with Grattan, as had Flood – as in all groups there were divisions, but they shared a common ethos.

On 30 October 1779 the Duke signed himself as Leinster at the top of a list of ninety-eight Kildaremen meeting at Naas, the county town, including many of his fellow Volunteers and twenty-four Friendly Brothers. The list was described as a Non-Importation Agreement, and their aim was to liberalize Irish trade terms with England and to repeal the Navigation Acts that had restricted Irish trade since the 1650s. If ignored, they would boycott English imports into Ireland.[17] Arthur was not present in Naas, but as a Dublin merchant knowing all about such disabilities he would have entirely agreed with their aims. Freer trade or a boycott of English porter would certainly do him no harm. Then on 4 November the Duke inspected a parade of the Dublin Volunteers that filled College Green, famously painted by Francis Wheatley. Guns sounded, flags waved and the Dublin crowd cheered. A cannon held a placard reading 'Free trade or this'. By December the Crown had quickly amended the relevant laws as England needed to export its goods somewhere – anywhere – finding itself again at war with most of Europe.

As these leading Volunteer–Friendly Brother patriots in Kildare were repeatedly electing Arthur as their secretary, and as he went on attending their dinners, he clearly shared their political views. Everything we know about him fits the bill: the annoyance at English imports, the unfair excise duties between Britain and Ireland, his continuing dislike of the useless but divisive Penal Laws, his longstanding membership of a non-sectarian club, his evident sense of Irish ancestry and, as a man of the world, knowing that the Dublin Parliament could and should control more of Ireland's affairs.

Unlike the former American colonies the Irish patriots did not want universal suffrage, and anyway suffrage was limited in that new republic to white males. The colonists' Congress had had an anti-Catholic paroxysm in 1774–5, slavery continued, the Continental Army forbade the enlistment of 'lunaticks, ideots and negroes' and the Amerindians came under pressure when the British left in 1783. The norm in Europe at that time was that the franchise – in those few countries where one could vote – came on the acquisition of some wealth and thereby having a stake in society, having something to lose. The progressive patriots felt that in removing the Catholics' and Dissenters' legal disabilities they would slowly acquire wealth as farmers, and merchants would benefit from the improved terms of trade. Increasing numbers of them were allowed to vote as 'forty-shilling freeholders' from 1793; by then most Irish Protestants were still not rich enough to vote. Such a system was found in European republics such as Switzerland, Genoa and Venice for the franchise or for public office.

Joep Leerssen (1996) has separated the Irish patriots of the 1700s from the nationalists of the 1800s in his examination of Irish literature. Similar to the anti-monarchical movement in his native Holland, the Irish patriot ethos sought a localized rule, free trade, philanthropy and personal freedom of worship. The link with the British monarchy and that strong navy would remain in a confederal sense, so long as it was useful. The aim was heteronomy, not autonomy. While the Crown was seen as important for continuity in international affairs and as a part of the checks and balances of the parliamentary system, it was also hoped that royal pensions foisted on the Irish taxpayer would be reduced. Laws would forbid absentee landlords from taking too much money out of the Irish economy. Self-confidence went with self-rule, their Catholic neighbours would eventually be fully included, increased wealth would gradually increase the franchise and no resentments would persist after a generation or two. All could be accommodated and led by the most virtuous men, such as the Duke. There would be a reasoned and beneficial purpose in all they did. That was the plan.

But, as Leerssen then indicates, this patriot ideal ended with the union with Britain in 1801, following on the failed United Irish revolt of 1798: 'it pulled the parliamentary rug from under the ideological feet of Irish Patriotism . . . what elsewhere in Europe was to become a left-right polarity turned, in Ireland, into a unionist–nationalist one.'[18] Each of these two later models often proved to be exclusive, divisive and introspective, largely based on sect and even on notions of race. Also, long before 1801, the patriots had divided over whether social progress and the reform of religious disabilities should be fast or slow. We shall find that Arthur supported the fast group. There was a large grey area of divisive transition in the patriots' opinions between 1783 and 1800.

By now even many of the landed oligarchy felt that the Penal Laws were outdated. The English economist Arthur Young discussed them with a landlord and senior judge, Chief Baron Forster, in 1777:

> In conversation upon the popery laws, I expressed my surprise at their severity; he said they were severe in the letter, but were never executed . . . There are severe penalties on carrying arms or reading mass; but the first is never executed, for poaching (which I had heard), and as to the other, mass-houses [Catholic churches] are to be seen every where; there is one in his own town. His Lordship did justice to the merits of the roman catholics, by observing that they were in general a very sober, honest and industrious people. This . . . brought to my mind an admirable expression of Mr. Burke's . . . 'Connivance is the relaxation of slavery, not the definition of Liberty'.[19]

For men such as Forster, a pillar of the Ascendancy establishment, any faith or value system that promoted good behaviour in his neighbours was better than none. The unspoken logic was that the laws were an anomaly, an embarrassment, irrational in the Age of Reason and only of intangible benefit in the minds of the insecure poorer Protestants but still obstructive to clever, ambitious and useful Catholics. Why hold back or deny the vote to anyone who was 'very sober, honest and industrious'? Once the latter were unbound, the economy would thrive. Anyone with Arthur's background would know that there was no racial or inherently different capacity between the Irish and the English, and a fairer system of commerce would provide the best proof of that. Young's *Tour in Ireland*, stuffed with good advice and statistics, was published in 1780 and sold well to improving landlords and patriots.

Arthur's views in regard to social change have not really been studied and understood. Dunne says that '[Arthur] was publicly opposed to any political or social change that might threaten the rights of his property'.[20] This echoes Lynch and Vaizey, who say that he was 'opposed to political or social revolution, as it threatened the rights of property'. 'Publicly opposed' is certainly wrong, and there was no full revolution in his lifetime, but many things changed. When laws were passed in 1771–9 allowing Catholics and Dissenters to buy land normally, he and many patriots supported the reform, not only from a sense of overdue justice but also because the ensuing new demand would increase property values. Wealthy Catholics could now buy land or lend money and take land as security. Here was one example of a large and long-awaited political or social change that might in theory 'threaten the rights of his property' as a Protestant, but surely the opposite was the case. We should not forget the enormous changes that had arisen in his parents' families; Lynch, Vaizey and Dunne were looking at Arthur alone and have decided to ignore the bigger picture over the previous century.

Arthur was in favour of sensible political and social change to the end of his life, but, naturally, as a businessman he also wanted to increase his wealth. Having worked all his life, having reached a position of some wealth after his ancestors' generations of toil and hardship, and, given the times he lived in, it is hard to think what would motivate him to want to let all his property go, having a wife and ten children to provide for. That would be unnatural, a denial of his life and a betrayal of his forebears' efforts. Of course, from a modern socialist point of view, all personal wealth and capital is unacceptable and should be limited, but such a view did not exist in his day and has never held majority support in Ireland. One can be wealthy and want everyone else to become wealthier, too.

Lynch and Vaizey were economists and did not examine Arthur's patriot views, and Dunne, a sociologist, seems to have paraphrased them without further analysis. None of them seems to have considered life as it was lived. The patriots had secured a limited independence by 1783. The Irish economic boom of the 1780s had enriched many. The terms of trade had changed for the better. The Penal Laws were crumbling. The American colonies were free. Rome recognized the Hanoverians. All these changes would have been unimaginable developments as recently as 1760 and would have seemed much more dramatic by 1785 than they do to us today. The Kildare Knot's overlap with the patriot Volunteers reveals Arthur's politics at this stage: many of these reforms were planned and led by the people he knew. The patriot plan for Irish conciliation was to provide security for the rich and opportunity for the hard-working poor, and many modern states work on that broad principle. But it was impossible to provide for all the poor, as the Irish population had more than doubled in the eighteenth century – no law reform could prevent that.

In that most Irish people lived on the land, and as Arthur owned no farm-land, the removal of any legal disabilities from the 1770s and any enrichment of the peasantry could do him no harm, only good. Dublin had also grown, and, given that beer drinkers were generally poorer people, any change or increase in their wealth would allow them to buy more of his beer. Why would a brewer oppose that? Far from Arthur being opposed to change, we should instead consider how well he thrived during a time of great changes.

Arthur's position can also be understood in the light of the very different lives of the playwright and politician Richard Brinsley Sheridan (1751–1816) and the orator Edmund Burke (1729–97), who became an MP in 1766. The three shared a descent from the underprivileged parts of the Irish population, being well aware of the awful 1600s, and yet were now improving their lot by using their wits within the ruling oligarchies. Then each tried, in his own way, to help others up the ladder and to break down barriers.

Burke detested the arbitrary and unlawful misuse of power and violence, 'It', whether applied by the Crown, by the Tipperary gentry in the 1760s, by the anti-Catholic London mob in 1780, by Anglo-Indian officials or by self-selected French and Irish revolutionaries in the 1790s. Sheridan, when an MP, was allied with the liberal Whig Charles James Fox, who also happened to be a politically supportive cousin of the Duke of Leinster. Both also opposed the African slave trade in the 1790s. In the process, they found some good people within the British system who they believed should be encouraged. The aim was for civilized, inclusive, gradual improvement, as bloodshed in their day would only cause bitterness in the future as it had in the past. Sheridan the realist once wrote: 'Justice is a lame, hobbling Beldame, who can never keep pace with generosity.' This can be paraphrased as: Work for justice, but you will achieve

# CHAPTER TWELVE

# Social Aspects of the Knot

*B*EYOND THE POLITICAL aspects and, given their sense of Irishness, there were inevitably some interesting social angles to the Friendly Brothers, all of which emphasize the Knot's focus on the Duke. We can imagine what Arthur saw. The 1777 book was made to list those who attended each meeting, but there are also occasional notes that cast more light on this group.

The Knot met and dined at three public houses in north-east Kildare: Toole's in Kilcock, Vousden's (which became Maxwell's) in Maynooth and Read's (also called the King's Arms) in Leixlip, all on the main Dublin–Galway road (today's N4 and R148). In 1777 it met once in the splendour of Carton. Typically, an upstairs room was taken for the night for some privacy, and the twenty or so diners crowded around the dining-tables once they had discussed their membership and persuaded new members to swear their oath. The dinner would have included, one hopes, the usual Georgian plethora of courses served together, washed down with copious amounts of claret or ale, followed by toasts to brotherly love, Ireland and to each other over the port. The Friendly Brothers had their own song, so there was some musical element. Then they would swing on to their horses and ride home or take a room near by for the night.

Being central in the north-east of the county, so convenient for the Duke, most meetings were in Maynooth. Out of the fifty-six meetings listed in the book, forty-three were there – or forty-four if we include that meeting at nearby Carton. The average number of diners each night was twenty-five in 1777–9, fourteen in 1780–4 and nineteen in 1785–91. The highest ever attendance was fifty and the lowest was six. Meeting dates were listed in the newspapers, reminding us that this was not a secret society. The meeting book includes a loose receipt dated 1 October 1791 from the *Dublin Evening Post* for seven insertions that cost £1. 19s., presumably for their meeting in August 1791.

The only misfortune in the Knot was the thorny problem that arose in 1778 concerning the membership of a Turk, Doctor Achmet Borummadal. He ran a Turkish bath ('Hot and Cold Sea-water Baths') on Batchelor's Walk in Dublin, most convenient for any brine-encrusted sailors landing at the port after a long voyage – and perhaps diversions other than bathing were available upstairs. Dr Achmet's baths were set up with a grant from the Irish Parliament in 1771. He was also described by Sir Jonah Barrington as 'Borumborad', a tall Turk with an 'immense black beard', and there was 'something cheerful and cordial in the man's address . . . he cut a very imposing figure'. He secured further annual grants by inviting up to thirty MPs to lavish dinners.[1]

On 30 September 1777 this Levantine paragon was proposed for Knot membership by the Duke and seconded by Samuel Forster and the secretary, Arthur – strong support. Then on 11 October the Knot met at Carton, the only night it did so, and doubtless the grandeur and beauty of the mansion helped secure a big turn-out of forty-seven members that night, one of whom was Arthur. Eight invitees were 'ballotted for and admitted', including Dr Achmet. His new interest in Kildare turned on a plan to open a second Turkish bath at the Curragh racecourse.[2] On 17 March 1778 Achmet put on his green ribbon, swore his oath never to duel and dined as a 'novice' with his new friends on the Knot's annual big day at the King's Arms, Mr Read's tavern in Leixlip. Unusually the Duke was absent that night, but Arthur and his Leixlip-resident brother Richard Guinness were among the twenty-three that dined. Achmet also took the opportunity to propose two new members, Doherty Gorman and Oliver O'Hara, who were seconded by Captain Brady of Gazebo Park above the town.

This was highly unusual in Kildare at the time. Achmet was surrounded by an exotic aura, accentuated by his proposal for membership by the Duke himself. The Ottoman Empire was another world away. By way of example, in 1788 the Irishman Thomas 'Buck' Whaley made a successful bet at Leinster House that he could travel from Dublin to Jerusalem and back inside two years. He later noted that: 'The Bedouins as well as the Turks are not allowed to wear green in any part of their apparel.'[3] However, at the next dinner, the secretary minuted some awkward correspondence from Dublin:

A Letter was read which had been received from the Principal Secy. of the General Grand Knott complaining that it appeared from our return to their

Knott that a person known by the name of Dr Achmet Borummadal had been received into the Noviciate State in our Knott . . . & signifying their desire not to admit the sd. Dr Achmet to any further Degree in the order without their Approbation.

The Knot agreed briefly in writing to this request, Arthur signing off thus:

I am your faithful brother & Obedt. hble. Servt. Arth: Guinness Secy. P.S. . . . some friends of Dr Achmet's have told me that he can produce sufficient Proofs that his admission is not contrary to our Statutes. If this can be made appear it shall be laid before you in due time.

The issue was not Dr Achmet's Turkish origin, nor his unusual business, but whether or not he was a Christian or a Muslim. Designed to be non-sectarian in Ireland, Rule 17 stated simply and clearly that 'No Person whatsoever shall be admitted into this Order, who does not profess himself a Christian.' The reply was read out at the following meeting on 28 June 1778 at Toole's public house in Kilcock, and the word from Dublin was that the good doctor 'does not appear to be a proper person to be made a Member of this Order'. He never dined with the Kildare Knot again, and it was the only expulsion.

The young Duke controlled several MPs, and Achmet would have wanted to curry favour with him to prolong his grants. One night all his distinguished but drunken parliamentary guests somehow managed to fall fully clothed into his enormous bath. The grants ended years later when he fell in love with a Miss Hartigan and agreed to shave off his immense black beard and to convert to Christianity. Thus the truth emerged: he was not a Turk but a conman, one Patrick Joyce from Kilkenny. Whether Achmet was also running a brothel or *bagnio* upstairs is unclear, but it would have been typical of such bath houses. His proposal by the Duke could tie in with Margaret Leeson's memoirs of her life as a Dublin madame. If she was truthful, her list of clients included the Duke.[4] Where does that leave Arthur – dutifully seconding this unusual man only because the Duke wanted him to join, the Duke perhaps being one of the wealthier clients of Achmet's brothel? Arthur must have quietly resented the Irish Parliament's continuing generous support for Achmet compared with its treatment of the brewers in 1773.

In any case, Patrick Joyce had run rings around them all. Not a Turk, not a doctor, he thrived with a ton of charm and a neck thick enough to reinvent himself for a decade. He was simply giving them what they wanted. He was gone before anyone could think about prosecuting or suing him – the case might be too embarrassing to go to court – disappearing with Miss Hartigan into the sunset.

An entry from October 1778 in the Knot's membership book in Arthur's hand states: 'A Motion was made & agreed to that a Ball shou'd be given by the Friendly Brothers for the Entertainment of the Friendly Sisters at Vousden's in Maynooth the day & Terms to be agreed upon at the next meeting.' Vousden's inn is now the Leinster Arms and was the Friendly Brothers' favourite venue, chosen for its nearness to Carton and the Duke. The dance was fixed for 6 May 1779, and a ten-man committee of 'Stewards' was chosen to run it and to 'to Regulate the Terms', comprising 'his Grace the Duke; Capt. Friend; Capt. Brady; Dr Percy; Capt. Moore; Revd. Kane; Capt. Burgh; Francis McManus; Capt. Shepherd; Arth: Guinness'.

It must have been a success for the members and their Friendly Sisters, as another dance was arranged for 15 January 1781, with much the same commit-tee excepting Arthur. The cost per member seems high at £5. 2s. 9d., but this covered three people: 'a Tickett for himself and two for admittance of Ladies'. Clearly they were not misogynists. There were also some minor social niceties to sort out after the first dance; the entry was written by George Tyrrell, who was by now the secretary, having joined days after Arthur in 1758. 'It is Recom-mended to the Stewards to see that no Gentleman sitte Down to supper till the Ladies are all seated. It is further resolved that the Reverend shall bring to the Ball any Number of Gentlemen he pleases!'

On 10 July 1781 another ball was planned for 4 October, 'no member in arrears to be admitted'. Others were held in September 1782, January 1783, October 1784, October 1785, September 1787 and September 1788. Now aged about sixty, Arthur volunteered again to be a committee member and steward for the dances in 1784 and 1785, joined by Lord Henry FitzGerald, Lord Edward FitzGerald, Major Brady, John Tyrrell, the Reverend Cradock, Michael Aylmer and Henry Hamilton. While the handsome Lord Edward loved flirting and dancing, his black servant Tony Small ('faithful Tony') was very likely in the bar next door, acclimatizing himself to Ireland and revealing his unusual life story as a freed American slave to the other patrons.

The Friendly Brothers decided to build a ballroom beside Vousden's tavern

in Maynooth for their meetings and dances. It is a detail that links the Duke
further to 'his' Knot.[5] This room (in Tyrrell's hand again):

> for reasons of Oeconomy and Convenience shall be annex'd to the tavern and
> to obtain said room it is proposed that each member shall subscribe 3 guineas,
> one to be immediately paid and the two Others on Roofing of the Room . . .
> the Duke of Leinster shall be apply'd to to Give the Ground adjoyning the
> tavern in Maynooth . . . to which his Grace was pleased to assent and Conde-
> scended to be Treasurer. Mr Henry Conway is to be Architect all amounts to
> be certified by the Architect and Counter Signed by the Treasr. & then laid
> before a Meeting of the Brethern of Whome a Majority are to Admitt
> [approve] the Accts. & Order Paymt.

His Grace could not have refused his patch of ground to his Brothers, and
we note his prearranged agreement. Entrusting their guineas to the Duke was
not a trust in the usual sense, he was above that, he was a rock, certain. 'Conde-
scended' had the sense that he was glad to work with them as an equal in this
project, indeed as their friendly brother – condescension carries a different
nuance today. Maynooth had been the Duke's august family's base since the
Middle Ages, it belonged to him, it held his ancestors' long-shattered castle, and
by encouraging any business and development there he was increasing the local
cash-flows that ultimately went towards the slowly increasing rents paid to him
– enlightened self-interest. Besides, his Brothers were paying to build a room
that would be a long-term asset on his property, and it extended the main street
another 120 feet further westwards on to a vacant site. The ballroom is seen on
Thomas Sherrard's 1781 map of Maynooth, by which time Vousden's had
become Maxwell's. Today it is the bulk of the Leinster Arms building.

Arthur Young had visited 'Cartown' in 1776 and mentioned 'Manooth,
which the duke has built; it is regularly laid out, and consists of good houses. His
Grace gives encouragement for settling in it, consequently it increases, and he
meditates several improvements.'[6] As well as developing his town whenever he
could, the Duke was an investor in the Royal Canal in the 1790s. The extra
expense of diverting it towards Maynooth to boost the town's commerce and
to deliver coal more cheaply to him at Carton by building the enormous,
costly, hand-dug earthen aqueduct over the Rye river at Leixlip led to the
canal company's financial difficulties. That aqueduct was also wide enough to

take the railway line that carries today's commuters from Maynooth to Dublin, a long-term benefit of over-engineering unforeseeable at the time. His major achievement for the town, which really put it on the map, was in helping establish the Royal College of St Patrick for training Catholic seminarians in 1795, now a college in the National University of Ireland.

The Friendly Brothers may have opined that building their room in Maynooth would guarantee the Duke's continued prestigious support for their Knot, as Carton is just two miles away. By 1780 137 members had joined the Knot, so the room's budget was around £430. Any 'oeconomy' was notional – what mattered was the 'convenience' of being near the Duke. The building costs in stone and slate in Kildare were mentioned by Arthur Young in 1777: 'a house 50 foot long, 16 wide, 2 stories high . . . [with another 2,000 square feet of outbuildings] . . . would cost about £300 [if built] of stone, the house slated'.[7] The ballroom was 120 feet long on two storeys, and so the budget suggests that the internal decoration was not elaborate. After the expense and effort of building the room, which focused the Knot on Maynooth from 1780, there were just four meetings at Read's in Leixlip. The last of the staged payments were soon cleared. In August 1781 Arthur and his Brothers resolved to meet on 19 September 1781, 'on which Day the Accts. and Mattrs. of the new Room will be Regulated', in good time for the ball to be held the following month.

It would be reasonable to suppose that Arthur would look forward to the occasional convivial dinner and dance with his Knot out in the country, taking in any gossip from the gentry who owned and ran his native county. Drinking in mixed company has always been a great social leveller. A record by Barrington of a week's carousal by the rural gentry between Christmas and New Year included an unsophisticated but plentiful menu. 'chickens, bacon and bread were the only . . . viands', to be washed down by 'Claret, cold, mulled or buttered . . . Wallace and Hosey, my father's and brother's pipers, and Doyle, a blind but a famous fiddler, were employed to enliven the banquet'.[8]

The Knot's dinners included much the same ingredients and others prepared to a higher standard. A Dublin Corporation feast in the 1780s would have been even more elaborate. But, on one occasion, Arthur felt that a grand dinner given by a new alderman was too extravagant, considering the needs of the city, and was setting Dubliners a bad example of how the rich should behave. Lynch and Vaizey (1960) cite an example, undated, where he wanted the money to go to the Blue Coat School charity instead of on food and drink.[9]

For this stance he was 'universally scouted' by his fellow councilmen, who said that 'good eating and above all good drinking, were strong bonds of good fellowship and unity'. Although a single case, this has given the impression that Arthur could be rather a self-righteous prig, unusually for a brewer, and apparently contradicts the social activities of his Knot.

The settings explain the apparent contradictions. In the Kildare Knot Arthur was doing as others did in the countryside, and any extravagance at table was understood as an ordinary part of the gentry's or, indeed, the Duke's, lifestyle. Clearly, the Friendly Brothers drank, sang, ate and danced in promoting 'good fellowship', and Arthur had helped to arrange their dances. Maynooth was a prosperous, well-fed and well-farmed parish, and a villager gazing in a ballroom window was not likely to grumble. Too modest a table for what must have seemed to be the Duke's private club might even cause a loss of face. But in Dublin an alderman's dinner would be widely known about and would be held, as it were, under the noses of the many poor, or of the poorer voters, who would then have grounds for complaint, envy and jealousy, even if the new alderman was footing the bill himself. The city's corporation was supposed to be rather more meritocratic than the landed gentry, and one should set a good example in public to inspire further merit in the city.[10] All considered, it seems that he was not a prig but was merely concerned with the public image of the Corporation in its city.

In reference to the gentry, Arthur Young had pronounced on their 'excessive drinking' leading to duels, but heavy drinking was very much expected in Arthur's Knot. Just because they were anti-duelling did not make them Puritans; on the contrary, it allowed them to unwind more than most, as any drunkenly offensive mistaken comment would never be followed by a duel the next day. Some examples were recalled in 1866:

It did not need the example of the Duke of Rutland to make hard drinking the fashion in Ireland. The anecdote, 'Had you any assistance in drinking this dozen [bottles] of wine?' 'Yes, I had the assistance of a bottle of brandy,' gives an idea of the extent to which the practice reached. Few songs were sung save those in praise of wine and women. Curran sang:[11]

> My boys, be chaste till you're tempted;
> While sober be wise and discreet;

And humble your bodies with fasting,
Whene'er you've got nothing to eat.

'It was an almost invariable habit at convivial meetings,' observes an infor-
mant, 'to lock the door lest any friend should depart. The window was then
opened, and the key flung into the lawn, where it could not be found again
without much difficulty. An Irish piper was stationed behind the door, where
he jerked forth planxty after planxty as the toasts progressed. A certain baronet
used to knock the shanks [stems] off each guest's glass, to necessitate draining
it to the bottom before he could lay it down again. Gallons of buttered claret
were drunk, and morning found the convivialists lying under the table in heaps
of bodily and mental imbecility.'

Sir William Johnson and his friend Dawson were invited out to dine. Some
time after dinner Sir William came to him and said: 'Dawson, am I very
drunk?' 'No,' said the other; 'why so?' 'Because,' said the Baronet, 'I can't find
the door.' It would have been hard for him, for the host had a mock bookcase
which moved on a spring, and when required closed up the entrance. After
making another trial, Sir William gave it up, and quietly resumed his seat.
Dawson escaped out of a window, got upstairs to a sleeping apartment, and
knowing that all the party would remain for the night, bolted the door and
barricaded it with all the furniture he could move. Next morning he found two
of the gentlemen in bed with him, who had effected an entrance through a
panel of the door.

We shall never know if these were extreme examples that passed easily into
anecdote. Such drinking bouts by the gentry were entirely acceptable to Arthur in
the countryside and were normal across Europe. But how could any member of
Dublin Corporation command public respect by spending a fortune on delicacies
and follow it by reeling around like a 'dram-drinker' on the city streets?

We must consider and speculate on the Knot's importance to Arthur and
the Duke from the 1770s to 1785. Between Dr Achmet, the dances, the ballroom, his entourage and his regular attendance, we can sense Leinster's
pervasive influence over the Knot. He needed it as part of his local political life
but never wrote about it. He headed the entire order at national level for a year
at each end of his mature life, in 1774 and 1795, but he was involved in many
other groups as well. It is hard to place exactly where he saw it in his life. Kildare

itself, the local gentry, benevolence, the Enlightenment, anti-duelling, deference to his family, civility, patriotism, non-sectarianism, the Volunteers, a decent meal with some rousing toasts – many aspects must have appealed to him. The order's homage to St Patrick was reflected in his later involvements in the Knights' Order of St Patrick and the seminary in Maynooth. The three groups accommodated the different ranks that mattered to him: his gentry and merchant neighbours, his fellow Irish peers and the Catholic hierarchy. The FitzGerald badge since the Middle Ages had also been the diagonal red cross of St Patrick. If anything, its inclusiveness of men a few ranks down from his position may have appealed most.

The Duke is seen today as rather a political 'wet' compared with his brother Lord Edward, but, given his background, his centuries-old inheritance – which had to be passed on intact – and the Ireland he lived in, it is hard to think what more he could have done in a practical way for his neighbours and his country. He was unsuccessful in many of his political wranglings with Dublin Castle after 1783 and knew that he was not a natural politician, but if we take him off his ducal pedestal he was a decent liberal man trying to do his best. The story of the Knot confirms the analysis by Dr Liam Chambers, the author of the masterpiece on Kildare in the 1790s: 'Kildare at the end of the eighteenth century was one of the most liberal counties in Ireland. This was largely due to the powerful influence, politically and geographically, of the Duke of Leinster.'[12]

Although the Knot and Arthur's membership of it must be seen as a small part of the Duke's life, the underlying inclusive ethos remained a part of Arthur's political credo. It encouraged those 'generous Sentiments of Candor, Benevolence and Friendship for all Mankind'. Naturally, people who went out of their way to trouble him, such as the Excise men and the city's water-pipe committee could not qualify for his generous sentiments. Had Arthur not been invited to join the Knot at its start in 1758, it seems less likely that he would have been invited in the 1760s, being based in Dublin, and was perhaps even more unlikely in the 1770s when it had become very grand – but who can say? In the Duke's absence in October 1784 Arthur sat as chairman for one evening, being well respected enough to take His Grace's seat, so he had made his mark. Critics will say that the group's inclusiveness was limited to wealthier people, but one had to start somewhere. In his book on Irish duelling Professor Kelly (1995) adds: 'The membership of the County Kildare Knot . . . reads like a

*Who's Who* of local life in the late eighteenth century.'[13] These were the men who thought highly enough of Arthur to elect him as their secretary, which speaks for itself.

Throughout, one senses that Arthur steered an interesting social middle course between the rural poverty of his ancestors and the commercial and social heights of his day. He would meet and talk with both the poor and the rich and needed them both for different reasons. The poor included his essential workers, consumers and suppliers; the rich conferred respectability. There was, of course, no social limit to his ability to do business. Ultimately, he had to avoid slipping back into poverty, while on the other hand he could never become an aristocrat. He had to understand the nuances of each but always belonged in Dr Johnson's 'middling station of life'. Politically, his aims were those of all such men in the centre – that the 'lower orders' would become more civilized and that the gentry above him would grow more tolerant. This becomes clearer in the 1790s.

If there was an element of snobbery about such a man being in the Knot, he had been a member from its outset in 1758, and it involved the more pro-gressive – by the standards of his day – gentry and merchants in Kildare. He stepped down as secretary when he had to and left it when he chose to. No family anecdotes survived about Arthur's smart acquaintances – it was thought until recently that he had no such friends – so snobbery and name-dropping was not an important element. Within the small circle that was running Dublin his link to the Duke would have been known about in a general sense, adding to his respectability in the city, but many others were also members of groups that the Duke joined. He must have been excited by the Duke's progressive patriot stance: here was a man whose family had made history in Kildare for nearly five centuries, so anything was possible. However, it is telling that in all the voluminous correspondence and books about the Duke's grand and well-connected family, the Knot is barely mentioned and Arthur never.

In 1783 Lord Edward FitzGerald, a future leader of the republican United Irishmen and a younger brother of the Duke, had just returned from serving in the British Army against American gentlemen-patriots and found himself back at home surrounded by these Irish gentlemen-patriots. His uncle Tom Conolly had even placed a marble bust of the gentleman-republican George Washing-ton in his beautiful Palladian entrance hall at Castletown, where it still stands today. From 1783 the Duke nominated Lord Edward as 'his' MP for Athy, gave him an income and ensured that he was elected to the Friendly Brothers on 8 October that year.

But this was not enough. He was restless and bored after his time of risk and danger and wrote to his mother from Carton on 3 August:

> Really a man must be a clever fellow who, after being a week at Carton and see-ing nobody but Mr and Mrs B. can write a letter. If you insist on letters I must write you an account of my American campaigns over again, as that is the only thing I remember.[14]

Today this sounds like a case of post-traumatic stress disorder. 'Mr B.' was Peter Bere, the Duke's agent at Carton, who was also a Friendly Brother. Lord Edward remained a charming, handsome, wandering, *bien-pensant*, restless, romantic soul. The patriot Brothers could not imagine that he would help destroy their gradualist dreams of progress in a decade or so and help divide the Irish for another two centuries. That was not their wish nor his intention.

# CHAPTER THIRTEEN

# Networks

URING THE 1780s the fruits of Arthur's production can be seen. The decision to brew porter was working. Most importantly, the Irish economy was booming and Dublin was developing rapidly, which assisted his sales. As with the expansion of the Kildare Knot after 1758, this boom was unforeseeable when he moved to the city. By 1783 the patriot-inspired Irish Parliament was almost independent of Westminster, but on the political front the Crown was now disentangled from America and was deploying patronage to hinder progress by the patriots.

As well as being a patriarch and businessman, Arthur was also a great joiner of groups. Considering his contacts through the City Council, his wider family, his staff, his business, his guild, his Church and the Knot we see a network stretching across Dublin, Kildare and beyond. We also know of his wider family and its circumstances and origin. By now he knew how the world revolved, even if he could not always make things happen.

Arthur's religious life was also consistent, and he had no reason to change it. Within the Protestant ethos he performed 'good works' and attended Methodist lectures as well as his regular church. One of his in-laws, Edward Smythe, was a Wesleyan minister at Bethesda Chapel on Dorset Street; Arthur may have agreed with the Methodists that all men were equal in God's sight, but he did not join them. Wesley had criticized the Irish Penal Laws back in 1748: 'Nor is it any wonder that those who are born Papists generally live and die as such, when the Protestants can find no better ways to convert them than by Penal Laws and Acts of Parliament.' At one level, religion is the history of ideas. At the time of the European Reformation in the 1500s the new Lutheran and Calvinist sects were inspired by a frighteningly zealous millenarian faith, while their brothers who stayed with the mainstream

Roman Church were exhorted to do good works. By the late eighteenth century the situation was largely reversed. Catholics would still do good works, but their devotional faith was now much more remarkable, particularly in Ireland, as Catholic doctrine did not accept the Copernican model of the solar system until 1835. For literate and commercial Protestants, ever-enquiring in the manner of Locke and Newton, embracing progress and living in the Age of Reason, faith was not so important, but good works were now the best practical everyday means of demonstrating a desire to help humanity. Being seen to assist in the community was also an important part of the Irish-patriot ethos.

As well as educating his eldest son Hosea for the Church, which would have been seen as a good social deed in his day, Arthur assisted in the education of those on his doorstep. First, he made a loan of 250 guineas to the choir school at St Patrick's Cathedral and refused repayment, and then he helped establish Ireland's first Sunday School in 1786.[1] The children came from all backgrounds and were being helped up the ladder as he had been: education was everything. The first family link to the medieval cathedral was made, a building that a grandson would restore in the 1860s for what would be an unimaginable expense in Arthur's time – the repairs cost several times Arthur's wealth at his death some sixty years earlier.

There was another hidden network connection in the background here, as William Cradock, Dean of St Patrick's, had joined the Kildare Knot in July 1780 and was elected as its chaplain. He had also been appointed Registrar (secretary) to the new Order of the Knights of St Patrick in 1783, being a friend of the Duke of Leinster, and had helped with Arthur in arranging the Knot's dances in 1784 and 1785. His link to Kildare was his family home at Craddockstown, just east of Naas. He was also a governor of the Meath Hospital. All considered, Arthur's support for the schools was well intentioned and practical but not entirely surprising, given his contacts. He may have hoped that Cradock would let the right sort of people know about his generosity, people such as the Duke perhaps. This support for Dublin's main cathedral has to be understood in the light of being seen to do good works for the community. However, the advanced *philosophes* of the Enlightenment had by now moved on from such conventional moderation. Frederick the Great (1740–86), the philosopher-king of Prussia, reflected in his political testament that Christianity was 'an old metaphysical fiction, stuffed with miracles, contradictions and absurdities . . .

some fanatics espoused it, some intriguers pretended to be convinced by it and some imbeciles actually believed it'.

In the field of health care, the work was *pro bono publico*. Dublin had nine hospitals for the poor, regardless of their backgrounds, and treatment and payment were entirely different from today, as hospitals were sponsored by the charitable rich. One example was Simpson's Hospital, set up in 1781 for 'the reception of poor decayed, blind and gouty Men'. The Dublin College of Physicians was refounded and expanded as the Royal College of Surgeons. As Georgian medicine was ignorant of the causes of infection, many cases might have been better off out of hospital, but bone settings and amputations were usually successful. Richer cases were usually treated at home. There were other clinics, and Parliament paid for a Pharmacopoeia Pauperum 'for dispensing Medicines to the Poor of this Kingdom'.

Arthur supported the Meath Hospital, which had been founded in 1756, so called as it was for the 'Relief of the poor Manufacturers in the Earl of Meath's Liberties'.[2] The committee that ran the hospital and paid for food and bedding also arranged for doctors to inspect the cases without charging a fee. It was often not enough in terms of resources, but Georgian Dublin was doing its best, again in a similar way to that found in the rest of Europe. Some were callous towards the labouring poor, who had a hard time across Europe and needed help.

In 1773 the Meath was in trouble as the 'Finances have been considerably lessened by the failure [bankruptcy] of a late Treasurer'. Mulcted once, the subscribers found a more reliable pair of hands in Arthur. Besides, there might be some demand for a nourishing beer at the hospital. If unpaid, merely being entrusted as treasurer with such a responsibility added to his social respectability. The subscribers were generous and had also recently invested in a new building:

> anxious to render this Charity as extensively useful to the Public as possible, have erected a plain commodious Building on the *Comob* [Coombe], originally constructed for an Hospital, capable of containing eighty Beds, on which they have expended their whole Fund, amounting to near two thousand Pounds.[3]

Parliament then assisted with an annual grant of £100 to cover running costs, and the new building became the County Infirmary for County Dublin in 1774.

By 1778 it claimed to treat 250 to 300 interns and 'at least 3,000 Externs Yearly'. Eight doctors and one apothecary handled the patients. One of them was surgeon Israel Read, who joined the Kildare Knot on 28 October that year. Perhaps he was another distant Kildare Read cousin, as he lived in Leixlip. A worsening socio-medical problem was apparent by 1787: 'In the last Year, six additional Beds have been fitted up, appropriated for Venereal Patients, which are constantly kept full.' It was a poor, crowded part of the city, and for decades the soldiers from the barracks across the Liffey had met up with the girls in Twatling Street just below Arthur's brewery. Its name at least had been sanitized, as it were, to Watling Street from about 1760.[4] His children were protected from such sad and ungodly sights, being safe in the nest at Beaumont.

The historian J.C. Beckett (1966) was critical of the overall provision: 'Ireland had no provision for the sick poor, except for a small number of privately endowed hospitals, most of them in Dublin.' By 1775 all but two counties had county infirmaries but 'even at their best . . . the infirmaries benefited no more than a tiny fraction of the population [and] made no provision for the treatment of infectious fevers . . . it was impractical to convey patients over long distances'.[5] All true, and so the Meath Hospital's £2,000 in donations must be seen as an unusual charitable collection for the time, although not the largest. Dublin was different in a modern and beneficial way from the rest of the island, and Arthur was involving himself in that difference. The results across the rest of Ireland were inadequate for Beckett, writing in the modern era of public-health provision, and he gave a reason: 'lack of cooperation by the country gentry, who were undoubtedly more selfish, more negligent and more ignorant than their contemporaries in England, or even in Scotland'. Here is a further reminder why Arthur and his forebears had urbanized: to get away from such men, so that one's chances in life might not depend on an incompetent or unlucky landlord.

A subscriber to the Meath Hospital paid three guineas yearly, or £20 for life. Each then had 'a Power at all Times when there is a Vacancy, or upon any sudden Emergency, of sending a Patient into the House'. In the event that a brewer became injured or feverish, Arthur could send or convey him several hundred yards southwards for treatment. This was the precursor of the brewery's own health clinics set up in the 1870s; free care for the poor but in the hands of the limited medical knowledge of the time. In turn they were the models used when the Irish Free State organized its clinics from 1922. It made practical sense for

Arthur to be a subscriber, as he would gain the goodwill of his workforce – enlightened self-interest again – but in acting as unpaid treasurer for decades he had gone the extra mile. His only reward was that it added intangibly to his respectability within his networks of contacts, being seen as 'a safe pair of hands'. In 1787 he was voted 'the Thanks of the Governors for his diligent and faithful discharge of the Office of Treasurer and for his unwearied Exertions for the Benefit and Welfare of the Charity'.

By 1778 Arthur was on the committee of men who owned the Hibernian Fire Insurance Company, which had a capital of £40,000 subscribed in varying amounts by its ninety-two members, an average of £430 each. They charged a higher percentage for higher amounts of risk, unlike today. A sample premium on hazardous insurances was 5s. per cent (0.25 per cent) for £1,000–1,500 of cover. Whatever amount he invested, it was another diversification of investment and risk, and, of course, he had to insure the brewery, Beaumont and all those buildings in Leixlip against fire. The brewery backhouse fire in 1765 may have prompted him; as well as paying his premiums to his company, his membership of the Hibernian could produce an extra profit. His brother Samuel was also a subscriber. The word Hibernian – the Roman name for Ireland was Hibernia – was often used by patriots, as it denoted classical civility as well as Irishness.

Another member becomes of interest later. Valentine, Hugh and 'Malacky' Connor, merchants, were trading at 16 Bachelor's Walk and so, as it happens, were near to Dr Achmet's Turkish baths.[6] They were Catholics, and in 1793 we shall see Arthur's response when Valentine was not allowed to become a Freeman of the City. Given the name Hibernian, it is not a surprise to find some subscriber-brothers of his Friendly Brothers. The company's secretary was Christopher Deey, whose lawyer brother Robert was in the Kildare Knot. Robert married Mary-Ann Tyrrell, whose brothers were in the Knot. The Deeys and their brother William were on the boards of many other companies and institutions in Dublin, a commercial network in themselves. Subscriber Ebenezer Geale's brother Daniel was also in the Knot, and their brother Benjamin was repeatedly elected as the Dublin Corporation's Treasurer in the 1770s. Hibernian Insurance still trades today.

This Christopher Deey was also a turnpike-road commissioner in the trust that maintained the main road west between Lucan and Kinnegad.[7] Tolls were levied at various points to pay for repairs, but, unlike today's toll roads, all the profits had to be reinvested in repairs. As such each turnpike was run as a charitable trust, occasionally supported by Parliament. The other trustees in the 1780s included the now-famous Henry Grattan MP, Tom Conolly MP of Castletown, Captain Brady of Leixlip (soon to be a colonel), Thomas Wogan Browne of Clongowes and, unsurprisingly, Arthur Guinness. Four of these were also Kildare Knot members, familiar faces in a familiar world.

At least Arthur had an interest here, as the main road passed his brother Richard's Salmon Leap Inn and his brewery and then on between his own investment properties in Leixlip. Further west the road passed by the walls of Carton and the ballroom in Maynooth where the Friendly Brothers met and then on near to Carbury where his Grattan in-laws lived. He had travelled every inch of it, and while, mending it was beneficial to him and his family, his public involvement alongside Grattan was part of the patriots' ethos. In 1795 the Dublin–Mullingar Turnpike Act extended the trustees' responsibilities in both directions, almost to the St James's Gate brewery itself. In March 1803 the trustees declared a vacancy on Arthur's death that had to be filled; he had served with them for the benefit of his corner of Kildare until the end.[8]

Being an urban man, Arthur did not need join the grandly titled Dublin Society for Improving Husbandry and Other Useful Arts, founded in 1731 and incorporated by charter in 1750, which is today the Royal Dublin Society. It promoted agricultural improvements and the study of arts, even including Gaelic literature, but had nothing innovative to offer an urban brewer. However, dozens in his Knot were members, and his son, Arthur II, joined. But historians such as Wilson (1998) have seen his son's name and have wrongly assumed that it was he.[9] Likewise, he was not a member of the Ouzel Galley Society, Dublin's main commercial arbitration body, although his son was.

The ongoing water dispute was finally resolved with his fellow city fathers on 16 July 1784. Following his unseemly outburst in 1775 he had obtained that injunction to put the Corporation on the wrong foot if it did interfere, and he had bricked over the culvert alongside the brewery to ensure that it was not easily dug up or blocked in his absence or at night. The matter went to arbitration, not the courts, as his brewery lease had obviously ignored the separate lease on the adjacent culvert. This was a civilized solution, as he had effectively been misled in 1759. In sum, the city's case was not so watertight for it to be certain of winning in court, and by now he had taken a free water supply for twenty-four years. In the background the water-pipe officials knew that his social networks were wider than ever. The eventual favourable agreement allowed him the flow from a two-inch pipe 'to his concerns adjoining' for a modest £10 per annum. As with Giles Mee's water lease of 1670, a long lease of 8,975 years was granted on the small area around where the pipe entered the brewery, to end tidily when his brewery lease ended. In the interim he could readjust his brickwork and repair or replace the pipe, if he ever needed to, without technically trespassing on the city's property.

The increasing canal-water supply and his continuing interests and his membership of the city's Common Council have generally been ignored in the context of the arbitration and settlement date. The focus has been on his out-burst in 1775 – interesting, of course, and a human reaction, showing him clearly at fault but missing the big picture. Paying £10 for a year's water was nothing to him, but it seems he was right to drag his heels for so long. Closing the deal earlier when the supply was limited to a part of the small Poddle flow could have been much more costly. He had started to plan his arguments only after that ruckus in 1775, and going to arbitration reduced his legal costs. His Friendly Brothers in the city corporation may have been loath to treat him too harshly, but, as we have seen, there were other good reasons for patience.

On the political front, mid-1780s Dublin was generally quiet and prosper-ous. As gratifying was Grattan's Parliament's imposition of higher duties on English beer and sugar imports in 1782. Even the Castle administration, nomi-nated by the government in London, agreed that these new duties were reasonable.

The British Prime Minister William Pitt then tried to introduce equality in the form of a trading common market between the islands in 1784–5, but this foundered. This must have interested Arthur, as his products could have been put on a level playing-field with those from Britain. As his labour and material costs were lower than in England it could allow him to undercut the English brewers, and with any export sales obligingly protected by the Royal Navy. On the other hand, the large-scale English brewers might also have dumped their surplus production on Dublin, which could have destroyed him. The patriots successfully opposed the plan as the common tariffs would have been fixed in London.

The strength of British trading power was emphasized in 1786 when the short-lived Eden treaty was signed with France. The French had insisted on this at the end of the American war, but, as the economic historian Fernand

Braudel said, France was then flooded with 'an avalanche of British goods: cloth, cottons, ironmongery and even quantities of china – causing an outcry in France'.[10] William Pitt described the treaty as Britain's 'true revenge' for its losses in America. For Arthur and the patriots, some continuing link to Britain's ever-growing financial and productive strength was clearly a good thing, so long as British beers did not flood into Ireland. Braudel concluded that from 1780 English merchants had taken over the British market and had control of the world market. Despite Ireland's new, albeit rather theoretical, political independence, the reality of the fast-growing British economy on its doorstep could never be legislated nor wished away.

The economic boom of the 1780s in Ireland was still an exciting time in Dublin. The Bank of Ireland was set up in 1783, the Four Courts and the Circular Road were built, the Post Office and a new Customs House was started and the main goods-carrying canal reached from Dublin towards the Shannon. Construction on a second canal, the Royal, was begun. The Grand Canal was of double benefit to Arthur. It carried a huge amount of water to the City Bason reservoir and enabled a new way of distributing his beers to the hinterland of Dublin, although this was a slow process, as many rural areas often did not use cash. Its branches reached Robertstown in west Kildare in 1784, Athy in 1791, Tullamore in 1798, and the River Shannon by 1804, nearly five decades after the first sod was cut. The canal raised land values where it ran, but as he was not a rural landlord he had no reason to invest in the project; this proved lucky as it collapsed when railways were laid in the 1840s.

On his brewery doorstep the weavers in the Liberties also prospered, an important local market for Arthur. By 1784 they were running 1,400 silk looms and some 11,000 people were employed in the area. The Liberties Corps of Volunteers advertised for recruits and allowed Catholics and 200 of the 'lowest class of citizens' to join their ranks, which was considered inclusive at the time. However, this new prosperity did not stop the 'Liberty Boys' from indulging in their rare but traditional street fights with the butchers in Ormonde Market across the river. 'On some occasions more than a thousand combatants were engaged . . . all business in the district was suspended; the shops were closed, and peaceable citizens were confined to their houses.'[11]

It would have been much less restrictive to be confined within a four-acre brewery, but this savagery could come as close as Thomas Street, just yards east of St James's Gate. 'At one time, the Ormonde Boys [northsiders] drove those of the Liberty [southsiders] up to Thomas-street, where, rallying, they repulsed their assailants and drove them back as far as the Broadstone, while the bridges and quays were strewn with the maimed and wounded.' The butchers used their cleavers to stab or hamstring their enemies, but on one occasion the weavers hung some butchers up by the jaws on their own meat-hooks. 'On May 11, 1790 one of those frightful riots raged for an entire Saturday on Ormond-quay, the contending parties struggling for mastery of the bridge; and nightfall having separated them before the victory was decided, the battle was renewed on the Monday following'. One wonders how truly penitent they all were in church on the Sunday. 'A friend . . . stood quietly the whole day looking at a combat, in which above 1,000 men were engaged.' These riots could erupt within minutes and must have been something to watch out for whenever Arthur rode home to Beaumont.

Occasionally the students from Trinity College would weigh in on the Liberty Boys' side, a reflection of Dublin's northside–southside polarity. It was said that:

The gownsmen were then a formidable body, and, from a strong *esprit de corps*, were ready, on short notice, to issue forth in a mass to avenge any insult offered to an individual of their party who complained of it. They converted the keys of their rooms into formidable weapons. They procured them as large and heavy as possible, and slinging them in the sleeves or tails of their gowns, or pocket-handkerchiefs, gave with them mortal blows. Even the Fellows participated in this *esprit de corps*. The interior of the college was considered a sanctuary for debtors; and woe to the unfortunate bailiff who violated its precincts. There stood, at that time, a wooden pump in the centre of the front court to which delinquents in this way were dragged the moment they were detected, and all but smothered.[12]

On one such occasion:

a passing Fellow of the college called out: 'Gentlemen, gentlemen, for the love of God, don't be so cruel as to nail his ears to the pump.' The hint was immediately taken; a hammer and nail were sent for, and an ear was fastened with a ten-penny nail; the lads dispersed, and the wretched man remained for a considerable time bleeding, and shrieking with pain, before he was released.

It is likely that any beer sales by Arthur into the college would have to have been paid for in advance.

As well as mob violence the higher social ranks included duellers, whom we know Arthur disapproved of, and the bucks or dandies who would 'pink' strangers with their swords. We met the 'Slackers' of 1760. The 'Chalkers' were 'in the habit of mangling others . . . with the wicked intent to disable and disfigure them'. 'Houghers' preferred to hamstring their victims. Sometimes the Army was called in, as the police force, the City Watch, 'thought themselves well acquitted of their duty if they escaped from stick and stone'. All considered, Arthur seizing and waving that pickaxe back in 1775 was unremarkable in the Dublin of his day – even if it was hasty and foolish – but it was unusual for a merchant.

Politically, matters started to fray after the revolution in France in 1789. Based initially on French economic grievances and taxation, by the end of 1790 the outcome was still uncertain. In 1788–9 England also saw George III go mad, and in the ensuing regency crisis the Duke of Leinster wanted the Prince of Wales appointed as Regent of Ireland, just as his cousin Fox wanted him made Regent in England. On the king's recovery the Duke lost much official support for his stance, and his main sinecure worth £20,000 a year was removed.

Although Arthur's last visit to dine with the Kildare Knot was in 1785, and the group was subsequently dissolved in 1791, his general view seems to have remained similar to the Duke's liberal progressives: social changes were badly needed in Ireland, but a link to Britain should remain. The Knot meetings ended when John Tyrrell, a conservative secretary, split with the Duke politically in 1791 and held on to the membership book. At its end the Knot included Kildaremen who would support the republican United Irish in the 1790s, and such a broad spectrum of membership probably hastened its demise. Arthur must have heard of this and must have thought back to the Knot's beginnings in 1758 and the men he had met as it grew. Its division and end became a tiny metaphor for Ireland's politics in the 1790s – even the Duke and his brothers were divided between revolution, steady progress and conservative stasis.[13]

# CHAPTER FOURTEEN

# Family Matters in the 1780s

*I*F A BOOM was on and politics were in exciting turmoil, at least Arthur's family could be planned for, as his father had planned for his in his day. Education, civility and his sons' involvement in business were the main concerns. Arthur also launched into and expanded an entirely new business with his customary caution and sense of timing.

His eldest son was born in 1765 and was christened Hosea, meaning, in Hebrew, Jehovah has saved. Perhaps it was a difficult birth. Recalling Olivia's grandmother's English ancestry, which reached back twelve generations through a nondescript series of names to Archimer, a male relation of William of Wykeham, Hosea was packed off in about 1777 to Winchester College, Hampshire, where there can have been few if any Dublin boys. Following that, Hosea proceeded to Oxford University in the 1780s, where he studied divinity at New College. Wykeham, an Archbishop and the Chancellor of England, had founded both institutions in the 1380s.

As Hosea was considered Founder's Kin at both places, enrolling may have been easier, and the fees would have been substantially reduced. At each place the young student would have found himself almost back in the Middle Ages. The school at Winchester could have been confiscated and sold off by Henry VIII in the 1530s, but it had survived untouched. In the chantry Hosea would have noticed that its beautifully coloured medieval altar decorations and the statue of the Blessed Virgin had been preserved from the iconoclasts of the 1550s Reformation and from the Puritans of the 1600s. In the cathedral near by, in which the republican Oliver Cromwell had deliberately and offensively stabled his cavalry, Wykeham's tomb had survived, the man whose benevolence had made Hosea's education possible. Every summer and at Christmas he would have been able to make the long trek back to Beaumont to see his family. As with his Uncle Samuel in 1750, he came back to Ireland after Oxford, taking his doctorate in divinity at Trinity College before joining the clergy. With an eye on the costs, and via an unusual route, an exposure to the wider world had been gained. Hosea had received the very best education within reach, and any ensuing social benefits would be given back to Dublin and Ireland. People might criticize an uneducated brewer's son joining the Church, but nobody could complain when Hosea had two degrees behind him.

Arthur II, who came next, was born in 1768 and lived until 1855. He was educated locally in Dublin at Whyte's Academy in Grafton Street and worked in the brewery instead of attending university. The contrast between Hosea and his younger brothers is marked. Edward, the third son (1772–1833), became a solicitor. Benjamin (1777–1826; named after his grocer-uncle) and William (1779–1842; named after William Read) were also brewers. John (1783–1850) was christened John Grattan Guinness in homage to Henry Grattan and ended up in the Indian Army in 1804. The dates over more than two decades indicate that Arthur and Olivia were still sexually active – or were at least doing their Biblically ordained duty to multiply. Six hands, eyes and nostrils could now ease their father's brewing chores in old age. They would take on the endless checking of stores, of the quality of grains and hops, and sniffing and tasting the continuous brewing process itself to ensure consistency. From twenty-one births, of which ten children survived into adulthood, these three sons were a distillation but quite enough for continuity if all went well.

Hosea was not the only English-educated boy in the wider family, as Samuel's son Richard followed his father's footsteps to London. Having studied law in Dublin and by now aged twenty-three, he enrolled on 14 April 1779 at the Inner Temple to train as a barrister. On his way he visited the aged Dr Johnson at Lichfield – possibly as a kind of homage – and then saw the Sheridans in London. He spoke at a debating club when Edmund Burke was present, and the orator commended him.[1] Back in Dublin he was called to the Irish Bar on 28 November 1782. Samuel doubtless sponsored his son, just as his father had sponsored him in the 1740s. As with Hosea, Richard had studied abroad and acquired a further layer of polish, wit and some anecdotes, but he would live and work in Ireland. After all, he was Irish. England might be less in control of Ireland now, thanks to Henry Grattan, but it still had its uses.

In September 1783 Richard married Mary, daughter of George Darley, builder and stonecutter, of Mercer Street. We have seen that his aunt Frances married John Darley back in 1763; although childless, it was evidently a successful union. The Darleys provided a neighbouring house at 9 Mercer Street that they had built for her dowry. They could thus keep an eye on the young couple and any children and had acquired a resident lawyer if they ever needed one. Richard's house was several hundred yards south of his parents in Crow Street, and he could call in on them on his way to the courts. (Ninety years later one of their granddaughters would marry Arthur's brewing descendant and in time become the first Lady Iveagh.) In their portraits Mary is a handsome girl, but Richard looks rather shady and secretive (Plates 33, 32).

Richard was very fond of the nine surviving children of the twelve born, but they were costly. He was asked to subscribe towards a book about to be published, but he replied:

> What can I do, I have my own works to subscribe to, nine volumes, three of them folios and six in duodecimo. I have found the binding very expensive, I am labouring to gild and letter them in the back, the paper is tolerably good, the character, I hope, clear and neat, but I assure you I have found the press very expensive. In a word, I cannot protect anyone's productions but my own.[2]

His pun on 'the press', a euphemism for sex, was deftly made. Wanting to invite a friend to dinner who was unpopular with his daughters, Richard promised each of them a new dress, and they consented to the invitation. At the end of the evening the guest thanked the family for his enjoyment of its hospitality and good food and remarked how much he looked forward to his next visit. Richard said: 'Alas, to entertain you has cost me so much that I am afraid I can never again ask you to dinner.' The guest retorted that 'a cut out of your leg of mutton cannot ruin you', whereupon Richard teasingly revealed his bargain in front of his daughters, to their horror and embarrassment. A memorable lesson in hospitality had been made.

Unlike his Uncle Arthur, Richard was not opposed to duelling, once fighting with his fellow barrister Peter Burrowes; both survived and they later became great friends. Clearly social and voluble, Jonah Barrington later described him as 'Mr Dicky Guinness, a little dapper, popular, lisping, jesting pleader', which adds to his portrait. On another occasion Pierce Butler insulted him in open court to provoke a duel, but:

> an uproar ensued, and the Honourable Pierce hid himself under a table. However the sheriff lugged him out and prevented that encounter . . . Pierce with great difficulty escaping from incarceration on giving his honour [to the judge] not to meddle with Dicky.[3]

What a difference between the first and third Richard Guinnesses. 'Dicky' is also dutiful to his family, but his sparky self-confidence contrasts with the quiet application of his grandfather. In the 1790s we shall find him involved on several occasions with his radical republican friends.

His handsome brother Samuel could not have looked more different (Plate 31). In 1789 he was called to the Irish Bar and married Mary Eccles, but they had no children. They lived in Ely Place, moving to Mercer Street in 1810, two doors from his brother. An erudite barrister until his death in 1826, he was elected treasurer of the Royal Irish Academy in 1806.

With these Guinness–Darley marriages in 1763 and 1783, it is no surprise that Arthur's eldest child Elizabeth, named after his mother, married Frederick Darley, stonemason, in April 1785 when she was twenty-two.[4] They had children and lived and worked in Abbey Street, with Frederick becoming in time a lay magistrate and Lord Mayor of Dublin in 1809.

Sales were good in the Dublin boom in the 1780s, and it was time for Arthur to diversify and invest elsewhere. In 1782 he bought flour mills in Kilmainham, a mile west of the brewery, on the south bank of the Camac River between Golden and Bow bridges. Knowing the grain markets, he was now processing dry wheat instead of wet malted barley. Naturally, being a patriot, he named them the Hibernian Mills.

The bakers of the city needed more and more flour to feed the ever-growing population, but there was also a new element of competition for the Dublin millers, as a successful bounty scheme for carting flour milled in the countryside to Dublin was launched in 1784. Although this bounty must have been a challenge, it quickly sponsored large new areas under tillage, providing Arthur in the long run with a greater availability and choice of wheat and barley; a mixed blessing perhaps. In the event, the quantities of flour carted or ferried into the capital by his new rural competitors were unpredictable and highly volatile, and were, in tons:[5]

1782 – 0
1783 – 106
1784 – 2,386
1785 – 4,493
1786 – 10
1787 – 0
1788 – 0

This was clearly a difficult market to plan around, and so he did nothing for several years. The year 1785 must have been a challenge – as with the brewers' troubles in 1773 it must have seemed that he had bought into the wrong business. But in 1788 he rebuilt his mill, taking advantage of the apparent lull in competition from the rural millers, who were now bypassing Dublin and exporting flour directly to the richer markets in England. By now Dublin itself consumed about 300 tons of flour every week.[6] The French consul in Dublin noted this new export market:

> this . . . is proceeding with inconceivable rapidity. Ireland . . . which was for-merly dependent on England for the grain consumed in the capital . . . has been in a position for several years to export considerable quantities of it . . . Thus a people which is poor, but used to privation, is feeding a nation [England] that has far more natural wealth than itself.[7]

Whether exported to England or sold in competition with Arthur and the Dublin millers, the rural poor were not going to benefit greatly wherever this flour was sold.

These changes were dealt with head on. From a letter Arthur sent to a creditor in 1790 (below) we learn that he reinvested over £7,000 of his profits to rebuild the flour mills and within a decade was taking annual profits of £2,000 from them, a very good return.[8] By 1793 the supply pendulum had swung back, and the rural millers sold increasing quantities of flour into Dublin, much of which was shipped quickly and cheaply along the new Grand Canal. The investment was sensible and successful but was not in any way hasty.

> No doubt you were surprised at my not remitting to you sooner; the reason was that I was disappointed in receiving a sum of upward of £1,200 which

was due to me, and was to have been punctually paid to me, above a year ago, of which I have received but £200 which much embarrassed me, as I have within these last two years expended between four and five thousand pounds in erecting flour mills near Dublin, which when I had completed required a capital of three thousand pounds to carry on the business in them. All of which weighty matters, I thank God, I have now completed, and have my Mills in full work.

The great increase of my Family required every exertion of mine to make this great extension of my Business, in addition to my Brewery which is still extending. One of my sons is grown up to be able to assist me in this Business, or I wd not have attempted it, tho' prompted by a demand of providing for Ten Children now living out of one & twenty born to us, & more likely yet to come.

Thankfully for Olivia, perhaps, her twenty-one births had ended in 1787. By 1790 he was sixty-five, she was forty-eight, and so 'more likely yet to come' was somewhat boastful.

'One of my sons' – Arthur II – was aged twenty-two in 1790, and had by this time worked for several years alongside his father. In such a multifaceted, hands-on, quality-dependant and people-orientated business, it was the only way to ensure his son's future success. This was more useful and practical than taking a university degree for social reasons. Arthur must have cast his mind back to the very different world of Celbridge in the 1730s and 1740s when his father had in his turn taught him whatever he could. The letter reminds us that £1,000 in 1790 was still a lot of money to Arthur, as Olivia's dowry had been a generation earlier. He was prospering gradually, he could mention thousands in the letter, but £1,000 owing and unpaid to him was not something he could raise to pay his creditor. The underlying message is clear: he is rich enough to pay and the creditor will be paid, but he must wait until the mills are rebuilt. A planned investment is much more important than an unplanned debt.

The expansion and importance of these flour mills led to his firm's redescription in the Dublin almanac of 1793 as 'Guinness, Arthur & Co., brewers and flour factors' and later 'Guinness, Arthur & Son, brewer and flour merchant' up to 1807. As these mills were sold in 1838, most Dubliners have forgotten about this decades-long involvement in Kilmainham. According to

Lynch and Vaizey (1960), when the brewery's profits fell after 1815 the flour mills' cash-flow kept the family afloat during a few lean years, perhaps saving the brewery itself. By 1838 the Guinnesses were moving from rich to very rich and wanted to expand and focus entirely on their main business. Just a few years later Charles Dickens sarcastically contrasted the social status of those in the bread and beer industries in *Great Expectations*: 'I don't know why it is such a crack thing to be a brewer; but while one may not possibly be grand and bake, one can be as grand as never was, and brew.'[9]

# CHAPTER FIFTEEN

# Turning the Corner – the Tax on Beer

AGED SIXTY-FIVE in 1790, Arthur might have considered it time to think about retirement and handing things over, but his last decade became his busiest in all areas – business, politics and his family. Taking into consideration the investments in the busy 1780s in milling, his adoption of porter as well as ale, his participation in the Hibernian Fire Insurance Company and ownership of the properties in Leixlip, we can see the standard diversification of assets that is essential for preserving wealth. In these boom years he had reinvested his profits in the mills and was to rebuild his brewery from profits in 1797–9. But beer imports from England and the Irish whiskey business were still growing, and so the continuing political focus was to reform the duties on beer. This was achieved by 1795 and provided a vital foundation for the brewery's success over the following century. It had taken time and patience, and Arthur must have seen it as a great opportunity for his family, allowing him to expand the brewery in the late 1790s. His industry was out of the woods at last. The 'steady drip' method of reform had eventually worked for him over several decades within the existing system.

Although Henry Grattan was more interested in constitutional matters and found that debates on finance cramped his oratorical style, he was supportive of the Irish brewers in 1791, again as part of an anti-spirits crusade – to improve themselves socially, those at the bottom of the ladder had, at least, to be weaned off spirits. Spirits were, he said, 'the destructive poison of the people', and higher duties were essential 'to put them out of the reach of the mechanic and the labourer'. He hoped that country landlords would restrict the issue of drink licences across the island and thereby reduce public drunkenness. By contrast, beer was 'the natural nurse of the people entitled to every encouragement'.[1] Hogarth's Beer Street and Gin Lane were still in the public mind. The 1791 measures were, however, not stringent enough for reasons of trade and taxation. Grattan went back on the attack: 'whatever is done to promote sobriety in this country must be done by Parliament . . . Revenue and not reform was the evident object of Administration.'

To be fair, the administration felt that restricting liquor licences would push many to drink homemade poteen, which was untaxable and often lethally badly distilled. Elizabeth Malcolm (1999) has found that spirit consumption rose from the 1750s, with homemade poteen becoming more prevalent (or more visible?) from the 1780s. While some 8,000 licences for inns and taverns to sell spirit drinks were sold in 1790, spirits were also available in some 90,000 other premises around Ireland.[2] In 1791 Parliament increased the cost of licences and required each licensed premises to have at least two hearths to eliminate the smaller and poorer publicans.

Clearly, Arthur had a vital financial interest here, but most spirit drinkers lived in the countryside and were not his potential customers anyway, so to that extent any desire to reform the rural poor was disinterested on his part. Essentially, he would have wished that they would follow the sensible methods of his ancestors and move up the ladder. The main worry for him was still the ever-increasing amount of beer imported from England. On 14 February 1792 Arthur appeared again before a parliamentary committee as the 'House had resolved itself . . . to further examine whether the late [1782–1791] Regulations for encouraging the Brewery [trade] and preventing the excessive Use of spirituous Liquors have had the desired effect'. A series of statistics had been laid before the committee that showed a recent but definite improvement. Also, an account was made on the three types of brewer in Ireland at the end of 1790, in and outside Dublin:

|  | Dublin | Rest of Ireland |
| --- | --- | --- |
| Strong brewers | 29 | 207 |
| Small brewers | 18 | 37 |
| Retailing brewers | 0 | 646 |

Small brewers were brewing a weak beer for the table, something like root beer, and the retailing brewers would have included his brother Richard in Leixlip, brewing and retailing for a local market.[3]

This political campaign also had a much wider and more inclusive aspect. The earlier narrower focus had been on the Dublin brewers and their large excise tax contribution, and they were headed by George Thwaites through their guild, whose members in 1773 had to be Protestants. In contrast, by 1792 the aim was to show Parliament that hundreds of tax-paying brewers, both large and small, of every religion and background, were in competition with the local distillers and poteen-makers across the whole island and needed help.

Regarding competition, imports and production over two years, in the nine months up to Michaelmas, the trends seemed favourable, except for the continuing avalanche of English beers:

|  | 1790 | 1791 |
| --- | --- | --- |
| Irish-made spirits (gallons) | 2,297,986 | 2,202,082 |
| Imported spirits | 888,063 | 661,464 |
| Imported beers (barrels) | 70,601 | 88,456 |
| Irish-brewed beers (barrels) | 346,838 | 386,517 |

Assessing the excise tax paid in the previous year, in the six months to Lady Day, the brewers were paying much less than in the 1770s. Some items showed a tax paid of:

| | |
| --- | --- |
| Imported beers | £8,234 |
| Tobacco | £37,500 |
| Wine | £52,163 |

As against:

| | |
| --- | --- |
| Irish beers | £1,252 |
| Import duty on hops | £3,026 |

These amounts show the relative importance to the Irish tax collectors of these desirable but non-essential items. While the tax on beer itself had been lowered, other taxes, such as that on hops, were effectively an extra tax on beer. A reasonable person might have thought that all was going well, but the brewers continued to complain that the distilleries were under-taxed in terms of the relative alcohol content of each drink and that the English brewers would drive them to the wall. On 27 February the proceedings were disturbed when the Parliament building suddenly caught fire. Along with all his colleagues and the politicians, Arthur, now aged about sixty-seven, had to seize his papers and make an undignified scramble for the doors. Within hours the building had burnt to the ground.

At a subsequent meeting near by on 5 March the Irish MPs resolved to reduce but not repeal all taxes on beer. The 1792 Act even reduced the cost of licenses where publicans in the bigger cities sold over seventy-five barrels of beer. Fines for infringements were increased, and workmen's wages could no longer be paid in a pub nor be paid in liquor. Parish vestries could appoint over-seers to check that pubs and inns were being run in an orderly manner. Both sides in the parliamentary debate were agreed that the poor had to be protected from themselves – this seems paternalistic today but indicates that the improve-ment of the lot of the poor was being addressed. The campaign was succeeding and was continued.[4]

Henry Grattan was the brewers' supporter, and his political rival was the Right Honourable Mr John Beresford, who was in charge of the Irish Revenue. Indeed, it was so much his personal fiefdom that he had just built a beautiful new Customs House on the north bank of the Liffey, and the street at its rear is still called Beresford Place. Beresford was also a senior member of the con-servative 'junta' that ran Ireland between 1783 and 1801 and which frequently stonewalled Grattan's other proposals for social reform. Debating the tax on beer was just another arena in which these two parliamentary rivals engaged. The *Freeman's Journal*, once a patriot mouthpiece, was on Beresford's side from 1784, edited by Francis Higgins.[5] It argued that the recent tax reductions on beer enabled the brewers to afford to use more malt and hops when brewing each barrel of beer and thereby sell a richer and more delicious product to help wean the poor off spirits. The brewers' longstanding argument about the social evil of the idle whiskey drinkers was being subtly turned against them. This extra material would cost something; naturally the brewers had hoped to keep the tax savings all for themselves, in order to allow them to undercut the English brewers, and had not intended to spend it on extra malt in each brew. Adding malt would be to admit that their product was not already of the best possible quality. Ground down between the Irish distillers and the English brewers, and cornered by the *Journal*, the Irish brewers were being asked to spend money to help the distillers' consumers when they needed that same money to counter the threat from England.

Yet Arthur and his guild members must still have raised an eyebrow at the harsh editorial comment in the *Journal* of 2 November 1793. The brewers had been given 'every possible encouragement, with a view to procure for the laborious part of the people, a substantial and wholesome beverage, to induce them to refrain from an excessive use of ardent spirits, which is a bane to the lower orders of the people" It deplored:

> the avaricious conduct of the brewers. That now sold by many brewers for *porter*, is not near so good as the *common ale* drank in this country a few years ago . . . there is no good well-bodied malt liquor of Irish manufacture . . . that offered in general to the public is a poor, sour trash, unwholesome and disgusting.

What could the poor drink except spirits, having no 'good malt beverage'? But after their initial shock, the Dublin brewers, being realists, would have known that behind this sweeping criticism lay the *Journal's* underlying support for Beresford against Henry Grattan.

Parliament finally repealed all taxes on beer in 1795, and Grattan hailed this victory in a famous letter to the Dublin brewers. 'It is at your source that Parliament will find in its own country the means of health with all her flourishing consequences, and the cure of intoxication with all her misery.'[6] This must have seemed like a logical consequence for Arthur – what was good for Grattan was good for Ireland and good for him, too. Imports of beers from Britain now dwindled away from a sizeable 125,000 barrels in 1793 to some 60,000 in 1803 and to just a trickle by 1813. By 1795 Pitt also eliminated duties on beer imported into England to foster the Irish export trade. This made the difference and gave Arthur a favourable tax climate that modern Irish exporters would understand, despite differing systems and duties. Further, the higher taxes on malt barley in England worked to the advantage of the exporting Irish brewers up to the 1830s. The way was now clear for Arthur to plan to rebuild his brewery so as to expand production, and this overhaul started in 1797, as we shall see. For Arthur, at the age of seventy, and having been a brewer for four decades, a certain degree of useful advantage and business potential had finally passed from Britain to Ireland.

In 1794 we find the first public representation of Arthur's porter beer, in the English *Gentleman's Magazine* (Plate 21). The drinker is not, however, a gentleman, as he wears an apron, a rough belt and a tousled neckerchief and has no wig. Yet he wears breeches and buckled shoes, so he is not a penniless *sans-culotte*. He raises his tankard in one hand and holds a tobacco pipe in the other. He is enjoying his reward after the working day, and his ruddy cheek and solid build suggest that he is a skilled craft worker, a man of some experience and judgement, the salt of the earth. The table holds a loaf of bread, a round of cheese and perhaps chops on his plate, which are about to be washed down by his lifted pint with its foaming head. Behind him stands a hogshead of ' Guinneſs Porter' above floor level. London, the birthplace of porter beer, has taken note, and with a caption suggesting a toast: 'Health, Peace and Prosperity'. Who could argue with that? Despite this visible success with his porter, Arthur would still brew ale as well until 1799. He must have been very proud that his hand-crafted product, copied just sixteen years earlier, and even his surname, would be noticed for the first time by gentlemen subscribers across the Isles and around the empire. If, a year previously, the *Freeman's Journal* had stated that 'there is no good well-bodied malt liquor of Irish manufacture' and that Irish porter was 'a poor, sour trash', in respect of this particular Irish brewer they could now swallow their words.

# CHAPTER SIXTEEN

# Marriages

*T*HE TIME HAD come for Arthur's three eldest sons to think about getting married, Elizabeth, his eldest child, having done so in 1785.[1] The three wives' families tell us something about his wishes for the next generation. There had to be a dowry and some sort of record of family success and achievement. But can it be chance alone that in two generations only two out of seven Guinness wives had living fathers when they married? It seems that their widowed mothers were perhaps too anxious to get their girls off the shelf and settled down quickly. They would have preferred for their daughters to marry into the landed gentry, with a secure rental income, and marriage into a merchant family with a riskier income may have seemed second best. In turn, such a fatherless girl might allow a brewer to marry above his rank, in a sense that we cannot fully understand today. In such circumstances, those in the 'middling station of life' understood the advantages of such unions.

Arthur II, his second son, married Ann, aged nineteen, daughter of Benjamin Lee of Merrion, County Dublin, at St Mary's Church, Mary Street, on 8 May 1793. In rough terms of natal origin, if Arthur was rural-Irish and Arthur II was Dublin-Hiberno-English, the Lees had been in the heart of the Dublin business world for over a century.

Despite a somewhat colourful past, the Lees were a respectable family – so respectable that for the next generation or so the brewing branch was known as the Lee Guinnesses. Ann, like Olivia and Sarah on their marriages, was a fatherless teenager, and she brought with her a dowry of £2,000. Arthur II pledged the brewery lease in their marriage settlement, and this is the first proof that he, the second son but the eldest brewing son, would at least inherit the ground on which the brewery stood as distinct from the business itself.[2] Ann's rich father Benjamin Lee (1745–86) had married Sarah, daughter of the

Revd John Smyth of Drogheda, County Louth. The Smyths claimed a distant royal descent that now seems unlikely.[3] A diversion into the Lees' experiences in the 1700s is instructive.

Benjamin Lee had been fatherless in his turn but from birth. His mother, Dorcas Cullen, was mentioned in his father Benjamin's will, which was drafted shortly before he died in 1745. As it said 'Dorcas Cullen' and not 'my wife Dorcas', they were not married. Being rich, this must not have mattered to the elder Benjamin, son of Henry Lee (d. 1713), but when he died leaving his sister Anne Norton to administer his estate, his lover Miss Cullen had a battle on her hands and the writs flew. The will included:

I have a Daughter living by the said Dorcas Cullen and she is now with Child. I bequeath to the Child she is now ensient of [pregnant with], if a Son, all my Estate . . . same begotten by me on the body of said Dorcas Cullen.[4]

Despite the impersonal legalese, he was making provision for them, and luckily for Dorcas the baby was a son. Perhaps because of this, Benjamin's aunt went into court in August 1745 to secure guardianship of the four-day-old baby. In September, with all of the estate coming her son's way and wasting no time, Dorcas started collecting her late lover's debts and hoped to rent out vacant premises in Stafford Street. In a pertly worded advertisement in the newspapers, she said: 'Proposals will be received by Mrs Dorcas Lee, widow and administratrix . . . and Notice [is] given to Persons indebted not to pay Debts to James Deiring, formerly a Clerk to said Benjamin Lee.'

But her not-quite-sister-in-law Mrs Norton, the real administratrix, who was now employing Mr Deiring, counterattacked in the press on 14 September:

Whereas Dorcas Cullen by the name of Dorcas Lee published . . . last Tuesday wherein she stiled herself the Widow of Benjamin Lee . . . Now I Anne Norton . . . aunt and administratrix shall not pay to Dorcas Cullen any sums without my joining in a Receipt . . . by which name she accepted the administration.

Dorcas was also obtaining credit before her payment from the estate under her newly assumed name of Dorcas Lee and was passing herself off as the widow, which she was in a sense but not in law. Clearly he had loved her.

While that case was being settled, another Benjamin Lee, alias Furniss, appeared out of nowhere in 1747. He was a nineteen-year-old who had gone off for years on a merchant ship to Holland and who claimed to be an elder half-brother of Dorcas's children. A son by a former lover, two by his last, all those writs and press notices – even by the standards of Georgian Dublin this was bordering on the disreputable, and, much worse than the sexual shenanigans, it was all being played out in public. Furniss had not received a penny and sued Dorcas, Anne Norton and his toddler half-siblings for a share, but by now Miss Cullen was in the driving seat: 'and particularly Dorcas Cullen has possessed herself of all or most of the Assetts'. Benjamin was clearly a popular name in the family, but, sadly for Furniss, the will was very clear about 'all my Estate'.

The main Lee property was at Merrion, then just south-east of Dublin, where they made stock bricks to build the growing city. To complicate matters further, their landlord, Viscount Fitzwilliam, next sued them all in March 1749. Trees had been felled, pits and holes had been dug in the ground and the Lees 'are proceeding to dig and raise large Quantities of Clay thereout for the making of Bricks'. What did he expect, renting out his land to brickmakers? No reply was made to the writ, and the brickmaking continued. Then in January 1752 a writ was issued by the fiery Dorcas on behalf of her young son against a Mr McMullan for mismanaging lands and losing silverware, a case that dragged on into the 1760s. In 1770–71 a first indirect link to the Guinnesses' city-based cousinage appears when young Benjamin rented out properties for £40 per annum in Love Lane and Glovers Alley to George Darley of Mercer Street, still described as a stonecutter. We recall that Frances Guinness had married George's brother in 1763.

The remaining wealth, after the lawyers had taken their fees, was clarified in the marriage settlement of 1772, when Benjamin junior married Sarah Smyth. As well as the Merrion brickworks, now busier than ever as Dublin expanded towards it, and the properties rented to the Darleys, there were two large houses in Dawson Street. These had been built decades earlier at the edge of the city as his grandfather, 'Henry Lee, bricklayer', had cleverly bought a vacant site there in 1712, 'a portion of the west side of a new Street, called Dawson's Street, leading from Patrick's Well Lane [Nassau Street] to Stephen's Green in the Suburbs'.

Henry had paid Joshua Dawson a ten-shilling premium and a rent of £10 per annum for the site. Benjamin senior had built on it just before the area started to become fashionable with the building of Leinster House in 1745.

From bricklayers and brickmakers to property developers, the Lees had done very well.[5]

In Henry Lee's will of 1713 we see that even a bricklayer could be rich. He had three sons, and the third son, Benjamin, was left £1,500 as well as his share of the properties including that land at 'Meryoung'. Henry was, in turn, the son of Thomas Lee of Milltown, County Dublin, who married Sarah, daughter of Henry Paris, a Dublin iron-master. His grandfather was another Thomas Lee of Milltown, a humble tenant-farmer, whose will was proved in 1680.[6] As with the Read and Guinneas families, farming and living so close to Dublin had given them an edge. All of this impressed Arthur in 1793, as these new in-laws represented old Dublin merchant wealth and had helped to build the city itself over the last century, even before his father had first moved to Celbridge.

What we know of the Lees comes from legal paperwork, from their problems, but Arthur must also have heard many other stories about them and their properties in Dublin between 1760 and 1793. Miss Cullen's steely nature was a very good thing in the background, balanced by some sort of distantly nebulous link to royalty through the Smyths. And yet, what a warning to keep one's affairs in order. Arthur II and Ann presented Arthur with a grandson in 1795, but it was their third son, Benjamin Lee Guinness (1798–1868), who managed and expanded the brewery from 1839 and then repaired Narcissus Marsh's Library before famously restoring St Patrick's Cathedral in the 1860s. Given his Lee ancestry, it was in the blood.

A few years later, in 1804, Benjamin Guinness, the younger brewing brother, married Ann Lee's younger sister Rebecca, proof that the Lees and Guinnesses still held each other in high esteem. By then Arthur was dead, but who could doubt that he would have approved? They lived in comfort at Brookville in the leafy suburbs and at 26 Eccles Street. They had just one child, Susan, and so his share of the brewing partnership merged back in 1826 into his brothers' shares. As with Richard junior selling his Leixlip pub and brewery in 1803, having had four daughters, it was then considered impossible for a lady to be a brewing partner, today an illogical and impractical view. Benjamin had made a huge contribution to the family business over his working life, and his share of the family partnership ended on his death only because of the vagaries of biology.

In contrast with the Lees, Hosea's marriage to Jane, daughter of Colonel Simon Hart, on 19 June 1794, was into a more quietly respectable suburban-gentry family, with the family's first links into the wider British Empire. Colonel Hart had retired from the East India Company, doubtless on a good pension, and lived at Goose Green, Drumcondra, not far south of Beaumont. Hosea and Jane had thirteen children, of whom one went to India and then settled in New Zealand in 1852.

As well as being rector at St Werbergh's Church in central Dublin for thirty years, by 1801 Hosea was also taking direct action as a clergyman in helping the poor and unlucky of the city to rebuild their lives. It would have been easier to turn a blind eye to the poor, as many clergymen did, but, like his father, he realized that the opportunity for them to progress was essential for the city and the country, and so it was part of his role in the community as another patriot. He was chaplain at the Magdalen Asylum in Leeson Street and acted as secretary of the Association for Discountenancing Vice, both of which were working to reform prostitutes – an unfashionable cause – and with the latter publishing religious material and establishing multi-faith schools.[7]

Hosea was also on the committee for the Society for the Encouragement of Servants, which aimed to ensure that they would be well trained and motivated. He knew what a perfect servant should be from his days at Winchester College, as the school's leitmotiv is a large surreal painting of the 'Trusty Servant'; a man with stag's legs (speed), a padlock on his lips (discretion), a donkey's head (patience), a pig's nose (tolerance of bad food), an open hand (trustworthy) and so on (Plate 19). Here was an interesting lesson, not one of English colonial trade nor of militant empire building but how best to serve and be useful. Hosea also had the simple example of his servant-grandfather Richard: work hard, be reliable, save money and set your children up in business. This may all sound patronizing today, but in the days before social welfare such 'encouragement' could save lives and, at its best, lay the foundations for prosperous future lives.

In 1803, on Arthur's death, Hosea inherited Beaumont House and all the investment properties in Leixlip to guarantee him an income. He was apparently the most Englished of Arthur's sons, if we consider his years at school and university there, his marriage to a daughter of the empire, his social position as a senior Dublin clergyman in the Church of Ireland and as a wealthy pillar of society, whose children would marry into the Church, the Army and the gentry. Yet it was he, being the eldest son, who approached the Herald in Dublin Castle in 1814, so conveniently close to St Werbergh's, and sought a formal grant of the arms of the Gaelic-Jacobite-Catholic Magennis clan as used by his father.

By then, had his sons wanted, they could forget Arthur's silverware and seal and claim any identity or none. The Herald, Sir William Betham, could not find a written link back to the Magennis viscounts for this eminent man of God – today's genetic results explain why – and so he granted a recoloured version of the arms. About a hundred Magennises with a lineage were alive back in 1700, including some Richards and some Protestants, all descended ultimately from Murtogh (d. 1348), and all their legitimate offspring were listed. Given this lack of lineage, now the unspoken assumption was an illegitimate descent from the chiefs, but even this was preferable to Hosea and his brothers than no link at all. The new motto *Spes Mea in Deo* (My Hope Is in God) was copied from the Dublin brewers' guild, so the new arms reflected the past and the present: the claimed Milesian origin mixed with the new urban commercial reality. Hosea could easily have buried the continuing County Down ancestry legend with its newly apparent tinge of illegitimacy if that origin embarrassed him in any way as a Protestant prelate, but he could not and would not bury it because it was his identity also, having come down from his father.[8] It was an inherited article of faith.

One question remains: why did Hosea not include Richard's father Eoin/Owen Guinneas in the lineage in 1814? The Guinneas/Guinis farm had ended on George's death long ago in 1731. George and William the gunsmith were ignored. County Dublin had only been a stepping-stone on the way from County Down, so the small dairy farm was edited out. The likeliest answer is that Richard had ended up described as a 'gent' on his remarriage in 1752, so it was socially desirable to start the lineage with him. As Richard was born (*c.* 1690) when the last Magennis viscount left Ireland (1691), at a time of war and upheavals, some judicious pruning of the family tree by the Heralds made the claimed descent from the viscounts seem more credible. This may also explain why so little paperwork and anecdote remains of Richard.[9]

Uncle William's family were still very much alive, however. Arthur's gunsmith cousin Richard Guinness's mixed marriage to Anne Bourke in 1764 produced four children who were also married by 1793. Largely and wrongly ignored, being overshadowed perhaps by the story of the brewery near by, their trades were also busy and skilled-urban, and there were other interfaith marriages.[10] Like his father, Richard was a Freeman of the City, but, unusually, on 9 November 1776 he 'begged leave to resign the . . . Freedom thereof' with another five men, which was granted by the corporation.[11] It could be that he was not thriving financially or that he was contemplating conversion or had converted to his wife's religion, and no Catholic could be a freeman until after 1793. Whatever the case, he changed his mind, as on 17 October 1777 he and some others were 'praying to be restored to their respective freedoms of this city; granted'.[12] Keeping one's fingers in as many pies as possible is usually a good thing.

This Richard's eldest son, William (1765–c. 1840), was a merchant tailor on Ormond Quay, Dublin, being first admitted to the Guild of Smiths in 1789 'by right of birth'. In 1791 he married Rebecca Harpur, daughter of Thomas Harpur, a cloth merchant of Leixlip and Islandbridge, whom Arthur would certainly have known and perhaps introduced.[13] Harpur's products included a popular chintz of the Volunteers on parade in the Phoenix Park in 1782.[14] The next son, Richard, was a calico printer of Dublin, Leixlip and then at Green-hills near Tallaght, who converted to Catholicism on marrying Bridget Blake, a sister of Michael Blake, Bishop of Dromore, County Down. Benjamin was a tailor at 1 Upper Ormond Quay, called the Emerald House, who married an unknown girl. Mary Anne, the youngest, married 'Joseph Kavanagh of James's Street Dublin, Roman Catholic', and they lived in Aungier Street. None of the sons produced a male descent that survives today surnamed Guinness, but it would be interesting to know if they have living descendants.

Edward, Arthur's third son, a solicitor, was, in March 1796, the next to marry. His spouse was Margaret, daughter of the late James Blair of Lucan, County Dublin. Described by the family's historians only as a 'coach spring maker', Mr Blair was also a rich landowner and a self-made man with a past. His ancestors came from Perthshire – being described in a Chancery Bill of 1772 as a 'native of Scotland' – and he had a brother Daniel living there at 'Hornhill'. Hornhill is not identifiable today, so perhaps it was a very small place or James was hiding his true origins.

James had married the widowed Jane Richardson, alias Stoker, of St Peter's parish, Dublin, in 1765, and they had six children. But seven years into the marriage, the Bill of 1772 issued by one Anne Watson must have come as something of a blow.[15] Miss Watson averred that *she* had married James on 17 August 1754 and that her father had paid Blair a dowry of £200 and so was bringing her case for 'jactitation of marriage'. She had been married, deserted and robbed, as it were, of the money; he had remarried bigamously, and she wanted the money back if she couldn't have him. Informal marriages were sometimes legal into the 1750s.

Blair's defence suggests a louche start to his life in Dublin. Anne and he had lived together, on and off, for six years when she was a servant living in William Street, but there was no proof of a marriage nor of the £200. And why had she taken eighteen long years from the alleged marriage and seven years after his marriage to Jane to bring her case to court? He admitted having been on 'familiar terms' with her, but her 'irregular manner of living' and her 'frequent and excessive drinking of strong liquors' had caused them to part. 'This suit is merely an attempt to extort money from this defendant without any just ground.' The case was dismissed for lack of evidence – yet one wonders how a penniless Scotsman could have done so well had he not had a helping hand such as £200 from his fiancée, but this is countered by questioning how Anne Watson's father could have had so much as £200 put by and yet had tolerated his daughter working as a servant. Whatever the truth, James returned to his lawful wife.

Blair had amassed a great amount of property by his death in 1794 and had clearly benefited from the boom of the 1780s. He bequeathed leases on houses in St Stephen's Green, King Street, Bridgefoot Street and numbers 21 and 22 Aston Quay. Around Lucan he had long leases on 180 acres at Huntstown, bought from the Lutterells of 'Hanover Square, Co. Middx.', and nearby Lutterellstown Castle, as well as 154 acres at Westmanstown and Coldblow. He also owned an ironworks in Lucan, as he was, indeed, a busy coach-spring maker. The latter bare description has told us very little – there was something to hide. Not surprisingly, Blair left enough in his will for a dowry of £2,000 for Margaret, the same as Ann Lee. But Edward's and Margaret's lives were unlucky. He moved from the law into iron-mastering but hit financial troubles in 1811 because of unreliable debtors, and they went to live on the Isle of Man. One of their daughters, Elizabeth, was married in 1837 to Arthur II's son Benjamin, and so they, too, are ancestral to the brewing Guinnesses. Whatever he knew of the late James Blair's past, Arthur must have felt in 1796 that the newlyweds were well set up for life.[16]

Two deaths had also occurred. Arthur's sister-in-law Sarah died in 1794, and Samuel followed her on 24 January 1795, aged about sixty-seven. Here, for Arthur, was a break with the past that went all the way back to their childhood at Celbridge – and much had changed since then both in the family and in Ireland. Samuel was more urbane and more international in his outlook than all his siblings. The first in the family to launch out and engage in the business world, he shared fewer interests with Arthur than their brother Richard, and Arthur has unfairly overshadowed him in the intervening two centuries. Two of their descendants married in 1873, and so the brewing branch of the family descended from the first Lord Iveagh shares Samuel's ancestry. Yet nobody can say where this interesting couple were buried, most likely at St Werbergh's, and the only record of Samuel's death was in the *Dublin Evening Post* of 3 February 1795, saying that this 'eminent trader' had died after a lingering illness. Was it brought on by the gold refinery fumes or from a broken heart?

# CHAPTER SEVENTEEN

# Politics and Identity

W E ARE NOW on the edge of the slipway that will launch us into a darker period in Irish history, one that was filled with mistrust and which ended with the deaths of tens of thousands in 1798. Most Irishmen, including Arthur, did not seek trouble in their lives, but we learn most about people from how they react under pressure. Despite some reforms, the irritant for many was still based on religion, no longer on land ownership but on the vote and involvement in politics. Arthur's stance of allowing Catholics to take a full part in Irish politics emerged. He had been doing business and socializing with Catholics all his life, some of his cousins in Dublin were Catholics, and he was lucky to have none of the inherited defensive fears of many of the Protestant gentry. But for many of his neighbours it remained a contentious matter, especially given that another war had just started with France, the fourth in Arthur's lifetime.

In the background, Arthur's views were practical but too rose-tinted, and at the national political level the patriots had now divided into liberals and conservatives. The Duke of Leinster had supported a regency during George III's first fit of insanity in 1788–9 and set up the Irish Whig Club in 1789. Although his Kildare Knot had folded in 1791, he headed the entire Friendly Brothers Order again in 1795, just as he had in 1774. The Catholic Committee revived itself in 1790 with a wider support base and repeated its demands for an end to the remaining Penal Laws. An inadequate initial reform was made by the Irish Parliament in 1792. The patriot aim of inclusiveness was being slowed markedly by the more reactionary section of the Ascendancy led by the junta. In Parliament, Grattan patiently sought reforms, with occasional success.

Out in Celbridge the elderly Tom Conolly pledged his considerable support for 'Catholic Relief' – the vote for Catholics – at Castletown in September 1792. His persuaders must have seen his bust of George Washington. One was

Kildareman Theobald Wolfe Tone, by now the secretary of the Catholic Committee, and another was Thomas Wogan Browne of Clongowes, like Conolly a
former member of the now-defunct Kildare Knot.[1] As a fellow landowner and a
former Friendly Brother, Wogan Browne could ease his radical political associate
into the august presence of Squire Tom. Also in 1791 the first Republican
United Irish groups formed, soon to be led in Leinster by the same Wolfe Tone
and Lord Edward FitzGerald, and the organization became oath-bound in 1794,
with some 280,000 sworn adherents by 1798, a very sizeable body but still less
than 10 per cent of the population. They sought a male franchise, as in France
and the United States of America, based on three hundred constituencies, a
republic and the end of the link with Britain if the people so desired.

Politics within Ireland and Europe were in turmoil following the endless and
chaotic changes in France from 1789. There, the nobility and clergy quickly
gave up their tax privileges but were then faced with confiscation and execution.
Louis XVI remained a figurehead monarch until 1792 when extremists came to
power. He was sentenced to death in January 1793 by a narrow margin and
was publicly executed within days. His Most Catholic Majesty's remains were
unceremoniously lowered into a quicklime grave. Declaring war on Austria in
1792 and on Britain in February 1793, at home the French republicans carried
out the frightful September Massacres and the Terror. The war caused an economic slump in the Irish countryside, and the hardships of the peasantry led to
agrarian unrest.

Even before the war had started, peasant groups of 'Defenders', followers of
the Whiteboys, were forming and were attacking and looting farmhouses for
weapons. Some acts of cruelty seem gratuitous. One night in January 1791, near
Dundalk, 'the house of the parish schoolmaster was surrounded by a banditti,
who, having broken in, took the man, his wife, and their son, a boy fourteen years
old, and cut their tongues out of their heads; after which they took the father and
mother and chopt off their fingers.' The underlying cause was that the landlord
who had appointed this teacher had refused to renew some farm leases, and so
a soft target linked to the landlord had been attacked.[2] In the same area, by
January 1793 it was said that the activities of 'a banditti, calling themselves
Defenders, grow daily more alarming; near forty houses have been attacked
belonging to Protestants, for the purpose of plundering them of their arms. This
banditti are linked together by an oath of secrecy and they have their regular
leaders.' A new organization was emerging.[3]

The capacity for such group violence was latent in a country with no police force except the Army. Perhaps we should be surprised that life was so quiet. Many Defenders merged into the United Irish in the later 1790s. When the French war started in February 1793, Ireland was considered a soft target by the French leadership, and as the republican United Irish were France's natural ally on the ground a liaison was established. In contrast with the Defenders, the more visible loyalist Orange Order was formed in Ulster in 1795. Members of both groups carried out indefensible atrocities on defenceless people. In Arthur's native Kildare, which was largely free of petty sectarianism, just one Orange 'lodge' had been founded by 1798, and that was at Monasterevin, at the opposite and more rural end of the county from Maynooth, the focus of the non-sectarian Kildare Knot.

In such changing times Arthur's political views were made public. In early 1793 Catholics of some means petitioned to George III, and the parliaments allowed them to vote for the first time since 1728 if they were at least 'forty-shilling freeholders'. On 27 February 1793 Grattan had argued in his Parliament that a recent fall in the value of the Irish funds (the government debt) was not caused by 'the prospect of catholic emancipation; on the contrary [by] the despair of it . . . the catholic body in Ireland are now too important, and too wealthy to be excluded from the franchise'.[4] On 15 October that year the Dublin Guild of Merchants welcomed eleven Catholics who had applied to join, including one Valentine O'Connor of Dominick Street, just before the corporation's next admissions to the franchise.[5] On 18 October the corporation's Board of Aldermen considered these eleven merchants and another nineteen Catholic applicants, of whom they rejected twenty-nine, but they put Valentine's name forward for approval; Dublin might have a single Catholic voter for the first time in decades. Later that day the Common Council had to decide whether to admit him on to their electoral list, but he was rejected by a vote of sixty-six to twenty-nine. A Mr Stevens argued on Valentine's behalf without success. Mr Howison spoke for those against, saying that there was nothing objectionable about Mr O'Connor himself, but 'he was opposed against opening a door to so dangerous an innovation as that of admitting Catholics into the corporation'.[6]

On 19 October the *Dublin Evening Post* was the only newspaper to give proper coverage to this exclusion, as it and the other Irish papers were avidly reporting the staged trial of Marie-Antoinette, Queen of France, which had resulted in her judicial murder by the republican government. One of the charges brought against her was for committing incest with her eight-year-old son; Paris, considered to be a fount of European civilization, had apparently gone completely mad. It was too remarkable. Regarding Valentine, the *Post* was sarcastically on his side: 'on the question of admitting Mr O'Connor to his freedom, that *wise* assembly have set themselves in *direct opposition* to the WILL of the Monarch and the legislature . . . Probably some remedy may be found for this EVIL in a short time.' Worse, the aldermen had turned down the other twenty-nine applicants out of hand.

A rumour went around that Arthur had cast one of the votes against O'Connor. Unable to get about the city and meet people as in his youth, he denied this and made his views crystal clear in the press for all to see.[7] Speaking in the third party, which might seem pompous today, the tone is that of an old man who has something important to say, one who wants a very different Ireland for his children:

> It was absurd to suppose otherwise, from a general view of Mr Guinness's conduct during life, having on all occasions showed the most anxious desire to have every civil and constitutional privilege which he enjoyed extended to his Catholic Brethren; having ever esteemed it the best means of healing divisions and establishing confidence and affection between his fellow citizens of every persuasion.

This has been quoted before but never in context. Arthur's fellow subscribers in the Hibernian Fire Insurance Company in the 1770s had included Valentine Connor of Batchelor's Walk. Just as Daniel O'Connell's father had reattached his ancestral Gaelic O', so also Mr O'Connor had 're-Hibernified' his surname by 1786.[8] By the late 1790s we find him and Malachy (formerly Malacky) trading as wholesalers in Dominick Street. Arthur had done business beside him for two decades, and he may well have known him for longer, but the length and nature of their relationship has been ignored. As such he must have respected O'Connor's judgement of insurance risk and business sense, and their capital had been commingled and invested together over many years in a common purpose. O'Connor had even appeared before a parliamentary committee in 1792 as an expert witness on Dublin's coal trade.[9] Why refuse the franchise to such a practical man who had helped in the city's business for decades simply because of his religion?

'Catholic Brethren', 'every civil . . . privilege', 'healing divisions': the progressive patriot aims could not have been put more clearly. I have said that Arthur's and the patriots' view on property law reform in the 1770s might have been motivated in some part from self-interest, but by 1793 Catholics had property rights and the vote, if not quite in Dublin. Here he was declaring that much more should be done. It was a matter of opportunity for all his countrymen – 'every civil and constitutional privilege' meant that he supported further law reforms to allow Catholic MPs and lords in the Irish Parliament, along with judges and state officials, as did Henry Grattan, which were all forbidden until the Act of Emancipation in 1829.

Arthur was publicly in favour of full emancipation before the emotive word was widely used.[10] The philosophy behind this stance was that there was no inherent difference or superiority between or in any religion, nor indeed between people of Irish or English origin – they were all living on the same small island and they had to get on together. Fostering trust and wealth creation would be the means. Regardless of their religion or their past, a country of self-governing 'fellow citizens' was exactly what the progressive patriots aimed to encourage in Ireland, under a distant Crown. But the republican United Irishmen had a more radical and violent formula.

The *Post* reconfirmed Arthur's public position on 2 November, naming and shaming all those who had turned down O'Connor's application. 'We hear the following gentlemen voted for and against the admission of Roman Catholics to the Freedom of the city' was accompanied by a list of the city guilds and the votes cast within each. Arthur was out on a limb even among his fellow brewers on the Common Council, as the paper listed James Magee, George Thwaites and Samuel Madden against and only one vote in favour, that of Arthur Guinness.[11]

This was followed by a typically patriot analysis of the result in the *Post* of 7 November: 'every attempt to exclude them as Catholics . . . can have no effect other than that of exasperating the minds of both parties . . . and of tearing open those wounds which are now so nearly healed, and rendering Ireland again a divided country'. Undoubtedly Arthur was of the same opinion, and the *Post* had even paraphrased his 'healing divisions'. He would have been saddened if he could have known that over a century later Ireland would be divided violently into two states because of sectarian mistrust. The continuing exclusion from power of the numerous Catholic middle class further divided the patriots and was a factor in their decline.

By now the Ascendancy hardliners were also moving against moderate patriots on the heels of the royal executions in France. The *Freeman's Journal* of 5 December 1793 ridiculed an imaginary 'Pseudo-Patriot's Creed', which included 'the infallibility of Mr Fox' (Charles James Fox MP, the Duke's liberal English cousin) and 'Tom Paine is the Apostle of Truth', grouping two very different men together. All reformers were being tarred with the same brush. Arthur sympathized broadly with Fox's opinions but probably not with Paine's new book, *The Age of Reason*, which criticized all monarchies and organized religions out of hand.[12]

Regrettably this support for O'Connor has either been ignored or quoted without analysis, and so Arthur's views on the sectarian aspect of Irish politics in the 1790s and his long personal association with Mr O'Connor have not been recognized. The continuity of his opinion at least back to the 1760s and the early days of the Kildare Knot – can we say, from his youth? – must be apparent, through the Volunteers' heyday and on with the reformist Henry Grattan in the 1780s and 1790s. Arthur was not wealthy enough to be a politician in Parliament, but he publicized his views because at his level he understood the need for a steady drip of opinion on this issue, reminding the city merchants of the immediate and practical need for serious reform. It was his only weapon, casting into the balance all the status and respectability that he had gathered over decades in the city, and casting it on the side of decency.

Arguably Arthur's apparent sense of good timing in business was being applied to his political views. It seems that the patriots' largest division over reforms hinged on the years around 1793 and the outbreak of war, and the O'Connor saga gave him a chance to declare his views when they mattered most. Any political risk from Catholics abroad had ended by 1766; power should be shared. The cause for equality for Catholics was just in the Age of Reason, and a level playing-field would be good for Ireland and its economy. This was a further sign of his self-confidence: as a Protestant, he trusted a Catholic majority in Parliament to help run Ireland at least as well as the Ascendancy was doing. He could have kept his views to himself as many others did. Notably he did not move towards safe conservatism, given his age at the time (sixty-eight) and the majority view of his fellow councillors. The latter felt that change in a time of war was dangerous, or that enough had been changed – all could see that the initial modest reforms in France had led to mayhem in just four years. In a sense they were pessimistic and fearful about the outcome of further reform, while men like Arthur and Grattan were trusting optimists.[13]

According to Liam Chambers and others, this support for O'Connor in Dublin is mirrored by the views of his former Knot president in Kildare, the Duke. Leinster had established the Association of the Friends of the Constitution, Liberty and Peace in December 1792. Their view was 'That the permanent peace and welfare of Ireland can only be established by the abolition of all civil and religious distinctions arising from difference in religious opinion, and by a radical and effectual reform in the Commons House of Parliament'.[14] This group wound down almost at once on the French declaration of war in February 1793, but we shall see its credo echoed also by Arthur's son in 1797. Chambers adds that at this point 'the duke even made approaches to the liberal wing of the United Irishmen through Thomas Addis Emmet'.

Arthur's and the Duke's views were still in line, years after their 'brother-hood' in the Kildare Knot. Note that the Duke wanted to reform just the Irish House of Commons but not yet the Lords; some things were sacrosanct to a duke, and a system of checks and balances had to be maintained. But they both supported the idea of an Irish Parliament where Catholics would probably be in the majority in the Commons before long, most likely the trustworthy and busier middle-class Catholics – practical men like James Farrell and Mr O'Connor – who already had so much to lose if the system was overthrown. Such a majority would take part in public life and adjust the unpopular tithe laws. The Papacy recognized the Hanoverians, so a sensible link to the Crown would remain. The Papacy had lost all its French property during the French Revolution, including its centuries-old estates around Avignon, and the French republicans and the Gallican Church loathed each other. The Irish Brigade in the French Army had disbanded, not wanting to serve a godless republic. Of course, this solution by emancipation never matured, but the Duke's support in 1795 for the Catholic seminary in his town of Maynooth, funded by the administration, was a logical and practical part of this vision.

The question arises – given this position as an 'extreme liberal' by the definition of Professor R.B. McDowell, concerning Catholic inclusion in Irish politics[15] – what Arthur thought would happen to his son Hosea, who had by now entered the establishment's Church? The answer must be that he would thrive best in Dublin, where he was a clergyman and where he was not supported by the unpopular tithes on agricultural produce. Hosea should hold his own, given his education and the higher percentage of Protestants in the city. The matter of national justice was the most important consideration, even if it might slightly hinder his son's career. In any case there was a spiritual parity between the good men in all the main churches.

All these complex tangents were ignored by historians such as Lynch and Vaizey and Dunne. Their too-bald opinion was that Arthur 'was opposed to political or social revolution, as it threatened the rights of property'. It appears that, being economists, Lynch and Vaizey missed Arthur's liberalism and that Dunne then followed them without further enquiry. There were many grey areas of opinion in Dublin, with some very rich liberals, well examined in some recent books on Grattan.[16] Property was considered then to be the foundation of prosperity, yet Arthur's friends in politics were still trying to find a national accommodation and were even sailing close to the radical wind. In that wealthy people can be progressive and have driven much real progress in the last few centuries, Arthur was progressive for his day. Only those who lacked self-confidence were opposed to social change. But could change be managed sensibly, or would they all be swept away by a violent revolution?

Arthur's quest for reforms did not mean excluding himself from the system, indeed his involvement within it might be a practical help, and in the previous month the *Freeman's Journal* listed Arthur being sworn in, on 7 November, as one of the twenty-two grand jurors for the City of Dublin.[17] Being a grand juror was a sign of one's respectability and good sense, being seen – again – as a safe pair of hands. Grand juries set the 'cess', the annual rate on property levied for public works such as repairing streets and bridges, in his much simpler times the part-equivalent of today's town and county councils. A balance had to be struck between the infrastructural needs of the city and the amounts his fellow businessmen could pay.

Reconfirming his sense of origin, Arthur had a metal seal made for completing documents and sealing his letters with a small blob of wax. It was over thirty years since his wedding cup displayed the Magennis crest (Plate 16), and he could have dropped or played down that identity by now if he wanted to. He was aged about seventy and had no need to impress. The seal was used on leases dated 23 March 1795 and was passed on to his solicitor son Edward.[18] The detail on the instrument was much too fine to be made out at a glance. Few could have been so expert as to squint at a formed seal and recognize the Magennis viscounts' arms, not shown publicly in Dublin since James II's 1689 patriot Parliament, and certainly not since 1693 when their lands had been confiscated.

The seal was further proof of Arthur's continuing feeling about his ancestry and an affection in his heart for the former culture in another part of Ireland. Earlier in the same year a new viceroy, the Earl of Fitzwilliam, was sent over from London and proposed a solution with Grattan to remove the disabilities of Dissenters and Catholics, by now some 85 per cent of the population. London replaced him within days; it was an example of British stupidity and must have been a bitter blow for Arthur's hopes for the future. At that time, perhaps, the seal was some consolation, a confirmation that his family had struggled through all the difficulties of the past and would somehow survive the increasingly ominous 1790s. The Milesian insignia, with its rampant lion beneath the red hand of Ulster, is still seen today carved in stone in the pediment near the top of Iveagh House at 80 St Stephens Green, which was the brewing family's Dublin townhouse from 1856 to 1939.

This decades-long Magennis clan affiliation and Arthur's support for the patriots, Mr O'Connor and Catholic empowerment all tend to argue against Sean Dunne's view in 2003 that:

> The one aspect of Arthur's life which makes the most compelling case against the claim of his Irish identity would be Arthur's political allegiance. Arthur, like many members of the elite minority, was closely aligned with the forces of English colonialism. Arthur was directly opposed to any movement towards Irish independence, and wanted Ireland to remain under English control.[19]

Nobody has ever made a 'claim of his Irish identity', it being beyond dispute. This interpretation either misunderstands or deliberately ignores the aims of the progressive patriots, as all historians are agreed that they were not 'opposed to any movement towards Irish independence'. The Magennis affiliation is brushed aside.

The patriots wanted a beneficial link with Britain with the largest amount of self-government for Ireland, and to misunderstand the reasons for this is to exclude from Irishness all those who can live with a useful shared sovereignty. Grattan had put it neatly: 'The Channel forbids union; the Ocean forbids separation.' The nationalists of later generations sought much the same arrangement in 1886 and 1893 and saw it decided, but not effected, in 1914. An island needs overseas links. Most of Ireland is now independent but in a qualified way. The patriot view is still worth considering in our very different times, as the island is part of a useful confederacy in the European Union that some are inexplicably trying to make ever more federal. Not so much post-colonial, Ireland may now be in an inter-colonial era. As in the British era, the ongoing debate revolves around the trade-off between controls and rewards. In Arthur's time there was some good and some bad in the British connection, and the bad could be slowly reformed, but clearly for him the vital reforms and solutions in 1793 had to be effected between Irishmen.

At war, and with Ireland as the weak link in the chain, it was the British Tory cabinet that had pushed for better trade terms in 1795 and improved the various relief Acts in 1793 that allowed Catholics to vote again and to sit on grand juries. The Hearth Tax that hit the poor hardest was abolished, but sporadic rural disturbances continued at a low level. As a liberal, Arthur would have applauded these improvements but wanted much more. Under pressure, Pitt had, surprisingly, achieved more for social progress in Ireland than all the liberal Irish groups put together. If the well-meaning Viceroy Fitzwilliam had been allowed to effect his reforms in 1795 there would have been more hope for the future, but the republican United Irish would still have continued their activities.

Limited social reform was introduced elsewhere in the 1790s. The movement to abolish slavery had started in London, and freed slaves were shipped to Freetown, which had just been established in West Africa. In British India, Hindu widows could no longer be burnt alive on their husbands' corpses. In the background, although not in power, men of goodwill in London, such as Sheridan, Fox and Burke, had consistently promoted the necessity for these and other sensible changes, in Parliament and at social events, and their steady-drip approach had also played its part. But in May 1797 Grattan and his Irish Whig patriots withdrew from the Irish Parliament, frustrated at being endlessly stonewalled by the local junta and most of the oligarchy. It must have been a point of low morale for his supporters, including Arthur. His reactionary or untrusting opponents felt that changes introduced at a time of war and tension would only lead to more trouble and more demands for reform: the argument of the slippery slope.

# CHAPTER EIGHTEEN

# Rebellion

*I*T IS IMPOSSIBLE to try to imagine someone's feelings at a distance of more than two centuries after their death. From the known facts and Arthur's record so far we have to deduce what he thought. It seems that he believed that a revolt would not happen. The United Irish movement offered nothing worth risking his life and property over. In the context of the brief 1798 rebellion much has been speculated in the last century about the republican mentality, their views on freedom, national independence and brotherly love that does not always stand up to close examination. Arthur was more a practical patriot than an emotional nationalist. So let us attempt to consider what was in his mind, a liberal networker with a Dublin perspective, who sought non-violent change, given the general situation and what might follow. By contrast, his nephew Richard, the barrister, had interesting and unmentioned links to some United Irish leaders that have been ignored to date. Both ends of the stick must be examined.

The year 1798 was the culmination of a struggle that had been under way in Ireland for nearly a decade. None could predict its outcome. The French might arrive in great force to support the United Irish or not at all. In the event, having established mastery in much of Europe in between 1795 and 1797, in 1798 they sent their forces off to Egypt. Ireland was a sideshow for them. They had attempted a naval landing in the far south of Ireland in 1796 under General Hoche, which failed. Wolfe Tone, the United Irish leader, was in France coordinating the effort, as help and war materials were needed from the new republic. But what was the French Republic's method in such cases? What might they do if they and the United Irish took control of Ireland? In Holland in 1795 the French had, at the invitation of its rulers, entered to protect the new Batavian Republic: 25,000 troops manned the eastern border forts and Paris demanded a vast subsidy of 100 million golden guilders. The Dutch republicans, being romantic idealists, protested and offered a lower amount. What about their mutual brotherly ideals? But Sieyès, a French leader, reminded his colleagues that 'it is not for them to cede but for us to take', and the gold was moved to France.[1] The French imposed a paper currency from 1796, which caused inflation, evasions, fines and heavy punishments for the liberated but ungrateful Dutch.

Then, in 1796–8 a new star, Napoléon Bonaparte, entered northern Italy and took it from its rulers, setting up the new Cisalpine and Ligurian Republics. He stripped them of wealth and works of art to pay for their protection. From the former Venetian Republic Paris received even the four bronze horses from high up on the façade of St Mark's Basilica, which had stood there for six centuries. In Switzerland the new Helvetic Republic made its forced contributions, and at Aachen in Germany the French generals boasted of 'leaving the inhabitants only their eyes, so they could weep'. The Papal States were next to be occupied, causing revolts that were crushed with severity. Monasteries were plundered and confiscated, and Pope Pius VI was driven into exile.

Duff Cooper commented in 1932 that 'The Directory, which ruled France for four years . . . to November 1799, had only one principle – to protect in their existing situation the large number of people who had made substantial profits out of the Revolution.'[2] Should such men arrive in Dublin, what would they not take? They would not protect the new Irish Republic for free. Not only would lives and businesses be lost but also any gold and silver, anything of value that they could remove. What remained would be an impoverished satellite protectorate. Looking at all the evidence from elsewhere in Europe by the start of 1798, these French republicans were state larcenists.

Arthur II, now aged twenty-nine, set out his own political views in late 1797. Naturally they were those of his father, who had already entrusted him with so much and with more to come. By now, many rural areas had suffered from rough weapons searches, and hardship had been compounded by some cruelty. He spoke at a public meeting and regretted 'the strong measures at present adopted for the suppression and prevention of tumult and disorder'. Next, he suggested a way towards peace and justice: 'The things most likely to produce this most desirable end are the total removal of the remaining barriers between us and our Roman Catholic Brethren and a constitutional reform in the representation of the people in Parliament'.[3]

The younger Arthur intended this within Ireland but also foresaw what would become the Reform Acts, as did his father and the Duke. A wider franchise with a lower wealth qualification – a broader involvement – might give enough people enough say and enough hope for the future. The nobility's control of Parliament would have to be reduced. It was a progressive comment, allowing justice without bloodshed, and Arthur II would support Daniel O'Connell's campaigns for emancipation and electoral reform in the decades to come. It was the progressive patriots' argument again, with more voters included sooner. Near radical in 1797, he was calling publicly for laws that would not be enacted until 1829 and 1832.

The Irish Whigs and Grattan had published a report on Irish social and economic conditions in July 1796, which called *inter alia* for an increase in labourers' wages and for full equalization of tariffs between Ireland and Britain. Both of these were necessary and would also have been good for Arthur's sales at home, as labourers were his principal customers and a stronger economy should help the whole of Ireland. Bills introduced by Grattan and the Irish Whigs in Parliament to allow the election of Irish Dissenter and Catholic MPs and to reform the franchise were rejected in 1796 (by 143 to 19) and 1797 (170 to 30). Significantly, Arthur II had made his progressive points after their rejection by Parliament and was not concerned about any ridicule from the supporters of its majority.

In contrast with Arthur's and his son's opinion, the Dublin aldermen and Common Council, often Whig supporters in the 1780s, had taken a stand against further emancipation in the 1790s. In January 1792 they had called on their MPs, including Grattan, to oppose any changes that might 'subvert the Protestant Ascendancy in our happy Constitution'. As we have seen, they denied the wealthier Catholics the city franchise by a wide margin in 1793, even though the right to vote had just been granted by their own Parliament. It would have made for a quieter life for the family to follow the majority line in Dublin's establishment. Both Arthurs would meet the city fathers socially or on business on almost a daily basis. By now they were somewhere in the city's merchant élite, but clearly they did not share its politics. As with Arthur's adoption of the Magennis arms back in 1761, this suggests a basic self-confidence along with a sense of justice. Considering Arthur's support for Valentine O'Connor back in 1793 and Arthur II's solution in 1797, both publicized in their home city, holding on to their progressive liberal and non-violent views must increasingly have felt like walking a tightrope.

There had to be pressure from the other side as well, and a radical gave his opinion in print in late 1797, undated, in what was described as an 'assassination journal'. The newspaper was *Union Star*, edited anonymously by Walter 'Watty' Cox, and it started with a threatening preamble: 'The Star offers to Public Justice, the following detestable Traitors, as Spies and Perjured Informers', and a list of dozens of names followed. The sixth read: 'Guinness – a brewer at James's gate, an active spy. United Irishmen will be cautious of dealing with any publican who sells his drink.'[4]

How could Arthur be a traitor when, like most of the population, he had not sworn allegiance to the United Irish? An 'active spy' at the age of seventy-two? His position with his clients, the city's publicans, was to seek favours and orders from them, not to ask for information that might result in their deaths. In early 1798 the United Irish leadership advised: 'Avoid as much as possible meetings in public houses, either of societies or committees, because they might be attended with much danger . . .'; it was a continuing concern for them. The *Star's* position became ambivalent:

> We are constantly witnessing the impudent affectation of cowardly moderation, acting in partnership with tyranny, against the Union Star, which they accuse of inculcating principles of assassination. We certainly do not advise, although we do not descry assassination, as we conceive it is the only mode at present, within the reach of Irishmen to bring to justice the royal agents, who are constantly exercising rapes, murders and burnings, through our devoted country.[5]

Arthur had been a man of moderation for decades but would not have considered himself to be 'cowardly' by, for example, sticking his neck out in calling for Catholic civil rights. Impressionable hotheads might see him listed and equate him with those 'exercising rapes, murders and burnings', which was clearly not the case – and by 1797 the United Irish had indulged in unprovoked murders, thefts and arson for some years.

The outcome at the end of the 1798 rebellion was telling. Cox sang like a bird to the Castle authorities, happily betraying *his* sworn comrades, having helped to wind them up into a civil war.[6] With hindsight, being called a traitor by such a turncoat must have seemed like a backhanded compliment. Having saved his own neck, and in receipt of a British pension for some years, Cox went

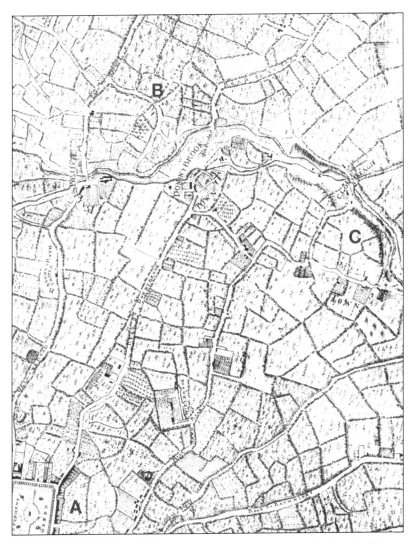

**36.** Map of Symonds Court and Milltown around 1760. The fields and villages would have been the same when Arthur's father Richard lived here during his childhood. Arthur's uncle moved to Milltown in 1726.

A = edge of Dublin, B = Symonds Court (now Simmonscourt), C = Milltown

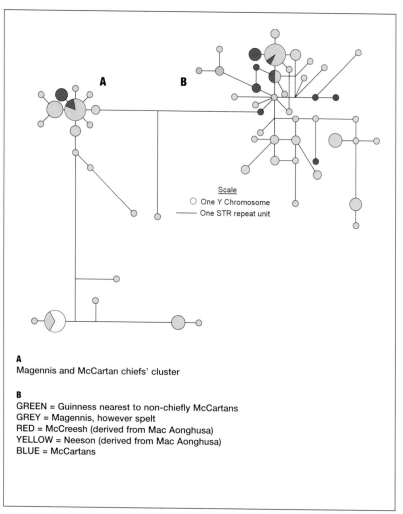

**A**

**B**

Scale
○ One Y Chromosome
— One STR repeat unit

**A**
Magennis and McCartan chiefs' cluster

**B**
GREEN = Guinness nearest to non-chiefly McCartans
GREY = Magennis, however spelt
RED = McCreesh (derived from Mac Aonghusa)
YELLOW = Neeson (derived from Mac Aonghusa)
BLUE = McCartans

**37.** Dr Brian McEvoy's genetic map (2004) of 100 Magennis and McCartan
men, showing that most were not descended from the Magennis chiefs and
that today's Guinnesses are nearest to a group of McCartans. This provides
conclusive proof that the Guinness family's theory of descent from the
Magennis chiefs was wrong but confirms that they came from County Down.

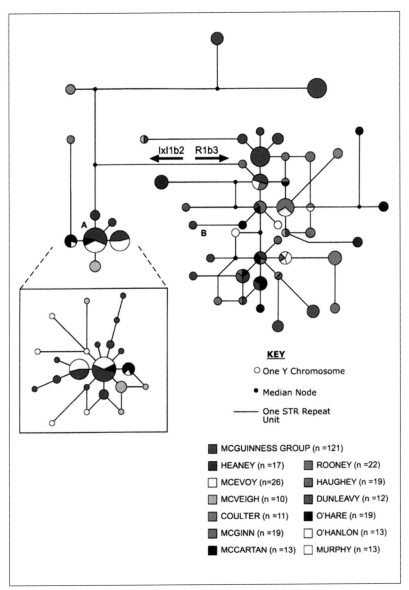

**KEY**

○ One Y Chromosome

• Median Node

—— One STR Repeat Unit

▮ MCGUINNESS GROUP (n =121)

▮ HEANEY (n =17)  ▮ ROONEY (n =22)

☐ MCEVOY (n=26)  ▮ HAUGHEY (n =19)

▮ MCVEIGH (n =10)  ▮ DUNLEAVY (n =12)

▮ COULTER (n =11)  ▮ O'HARE (n =19)

▮ MCGINN (n =19)  ☐ O'HANLON (n =13)

▮ MCCARTAN (n =13)  ☐ MURPHY (n =13)

**38.** The East Ulster genetic landscape, showing the relatedness of 315 men with surnames linked to the region before 1600. As in the genetic map in Plate 37, the Guinness results were closest to some McCartans.

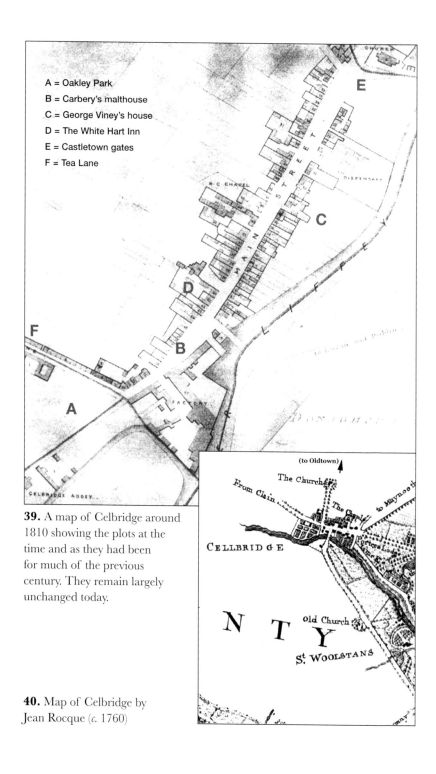

A = Oakley Park
B = Carbery's malthouse
C = George Viney's house
D = The White Hart Inn
E = Castletown gates
F = Tea Lane

**39.** A map of Celbridge around 1810 showing the plots at the time and as they had been for much of the previous century. They remain largely unchanged today.

**40.** Map of Celbridge by Jean Rocque (*c.* 1760)

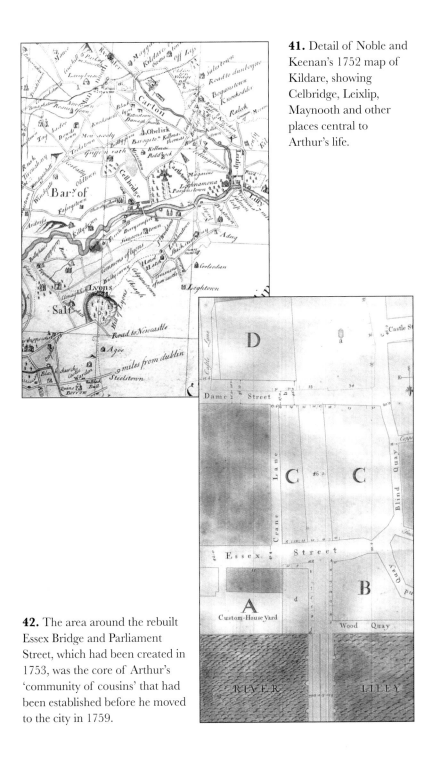

**41.** Detail of Noble and Keenan's 1752 map of Kildare, showing Celbridge, Leixlip, Maynooth and other places central to Arthur's life.

**42.** The area around the rebuilt Essex Bridge and Parliament Street, which had been created in 1753, was the core of Arthur's 'community of cousins' that had been established before he moved to the city in 1759.

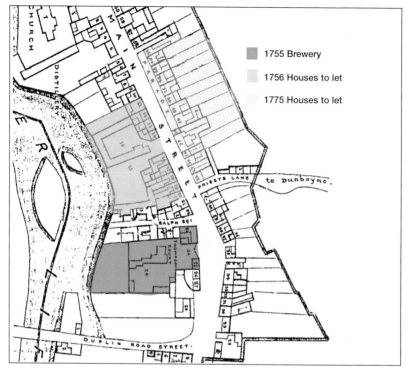

Legend:

1755 Brewery
1756 Houses to let
1775 Houses to let

**43.** Properties leased 'for three lives' by Arthur in Leixlip.

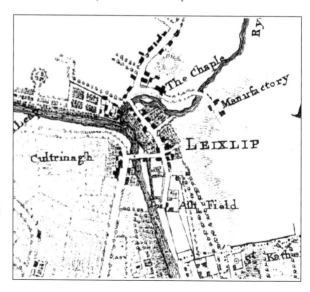

**44.** Detail of Jean Rocque's map of Leixlip (*c.* 1760), showing individual houses but not the continuous range of properties built by Arthur.

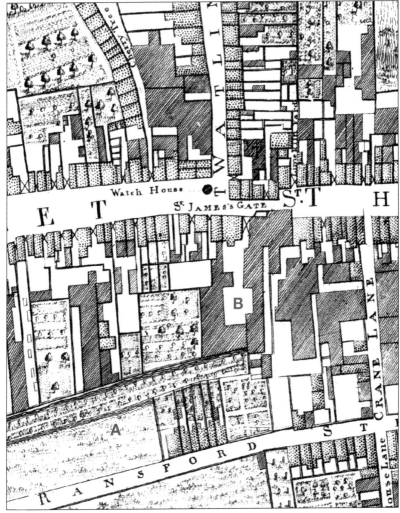

**45.** Detail of Jean Rocque's 1760 map of the St James's Gate area in Dublin, showing the city watercourse (A) running behind the brewery (B).

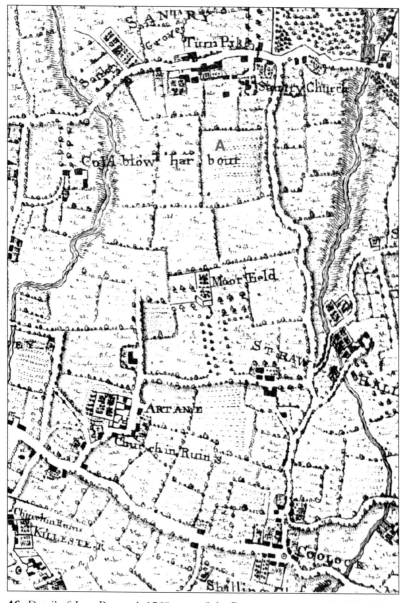

**46.** Detail of Jean Rocque's 1760 map of the Beaumont area north of Dublin, where Arthur moved into Beaumont House, his 'gentleman's box', in 1764. The house itself does not appear here, but its location is marked A.

on to edit the *Irish Magazine* from 1808. He commented in 1815: 'It is very probable that the said Guinnesses would be soon reduced to the humble condition of their grandsire [Richard], that of driving other people's coaches instead of their own.' He had quite a chip on his shoulder; nothing is so hateful to a radical as a wealthy liberal.

While in France, Theobald Wolfe Tone, the United Irish leader, wrote in his personable memoirs, which were eventually published by his son in 1826:

> as for merchants . . . they are no great hands at revolutions . . . Our independence must be had at all hazards. If the men of property will not support us, they must fall; we can support ourselves by the aid of that numerous and respectable class, the men of no property.

The question is begged: did he not wonder why had he had failed to convince more of them to support him, at least those merchants of practical ability and goodwill? What would tempt a progressive and wealthy man such as Arthur, whose forebears had slowly triumphed in adversity, to join the United Irish? A handbill that was short on specifics but long on emotion was printed for 'the more wealthy classes of United Irishmen'.[7] Such men would 'make up by pecuniary contributions for the deficiency or neglect of other exertions'. It condemned 'the polluted spy, the blood-thirsty magistrate, the merciless bravo, the venal and sanguinary senator' and looked forward to freedom with 'a general shout of *Ireland as it should be*'. Arthur had his own clear views on that.

Further, the Army's violent excesses in the late 1790s were brought down on the heads of the innocent because of the activities of the United Irish; they were part of the problem and not the solution. The French ideology had moved on since 1789 from personal freedoms and security of property to the doctrine that all property belonged to 'the nation' – anything could be confiscated at any time by a government that often consisted of a dozen overworked men around a table. Unlike the new American system, a French merchant could never be sure that his property would be his tomorrow. The republican ideology in Europe was vehemently opposed to the Catholic Church, yet the United Irish were playing on Catholic disabilities to gain support, which must have seemed dishonest. Such aspects are often overlooked today. The *Dictionary of Irish Biography* refers to Arthur's 'opposition to the United Irishmen', but he never publicly opposed them.[8] It is fairer to say that they were ideologists exploiting and worsening Ireland's difficulties and had nothing to offer him. The nub of it was that an American-style revolution supported by familiar and experienced faces might have gained his support, but the French system imposed by untried and unknown men could not.[9]

However, Santerre in Paris and Sweetman in Dublin were rare examples of brewers who were radicals.[10] Their view of Arthur's opinions would have been that, despite his good intentions, he had not convinced enough of his fellow patriots to reform the existing system quickly enough, so he should either move aside or join them and let them finish what he had started. There was some logic in this. The American, Dutch, Italian, Swiss and French republics were established by now; for good or ill, Ireland would be next, and soon most, if not all, of Europe would consist of republics. Best to work for a speedy overthrow, work on the teething problems and start to build 'Ireland as it should be'.

But Tone's support in Leinster consisted of many disaffected people in the countryside and a small number of modern thinkers, few of them achievers. His 'at all hazards' only made sense if you had nothing to lose. The radicals' impatience must have rankled with Arthur, given that he knew how long it really took to get on – several generations in his case. As for independence, why risk everything to swap a known degree of authority from London for an unknown degree of control by Paris? And why risk it for this man, whom many in his native Kildare said was the natural son of a neighbouring landlord, Theobald Wolfe – another of Arthur's Friendly Brothers – and who may have been motivated ultimately by mixed feelings over his paternity?[11] If a rebellion was started the Orange alternative was equally unpleasant: a willingness to kill any number of Irishmen, including suspects and prisoners, in defence of their modest privileges.[12] As we know, Arthur had wanted those privileges to be reduced by persuasion, which the French war had made much harder to achieve. Neither extreme would foster long-term trust on the island, and, in Edmund Burke's terminology, both could and did qualify as 'It', the haphazard and illegal violence of the mob or by soldiers.

The activities of the United Irish movement had led on to martial law and much casual brutality by the British forces. In April 1798 Terence Sheel, a clerk to Mr McAuley, a Dublin merchant, was stabbed to death from behind at night as an Army patrol passed by in South Great George's Street in the centre of Dublin. A surgeon pronounced him dead, and shortly afterwards the coroner found a verdict of murder by persons unknown, as witnesses could not be sure of the regiment or officers involved. The parishioners of St Andrews immediately formed a committee to find out, assisted by Alderman Exshaw. That Sheel was a Catholic and the parishioners were Protestants was quite irrelevant; they were all Dubliners. The Army revealed that an officer of the Fermanagh Militia was the suspect. Facing execution, he was arrested but escaped, and £400 was subscribed 'in less than five minutes' by citizens as a reward for his recapture. On 12 April the Army's 'garrison-orders' for Dublin made it clear that 'no step will be left untried . . . to bring him to justice, and to the punishment such unsoldier-like behaviour deserves . . . we lament the loss of a fellow creature, and feel ourselves ashamed of the conduct of a brother officer'.[13]

Dublin was again different from most of the rest of Ireland, as its citizens could combine to create this type of extralegal ad-hoc pressure on the Army to curb its psychotic element. Newspapers ran the story. In few other places would a surgeon and a coroner be on the spot to do the paperwork, nor would most rural parishioners have been able to protest so coherently for a local politician to deal directly with the general in charge. Most villages did not have £400 to raise. Without this urban social network victims in the countryside had few means of redress against haphazard Army brutality and not enough contacts or literacy to make their case. It was naturally simpler to blame all redcoats, and by extension the entire system, and seek redress in a different way, meeting violence with violence.

Despite the unsettled politics in the air, the trade depression and the war, Arthur reinvested over £6,000 of his profits back into rebuilding his brewery between 1797 and 1799. As we have seen, the tax situation had improved in 1795, allowing a year for planning. It was also a good time to have ready cash to offer in his negotiations with the builders, as on 2 March 1797 the Bank of Ireland had had to suspend payments in gold and silver coin and briefly resorted to paper. The unhurried commercial sense of his timing is obvious once again, but this is also the vital sign that he thought in 1797 that nobody would be so rash as to launch a rebellion. Anyone with £6,000 who was nervous about an imminent revolution would have bought portable wealth such as jewels or gold.

His son Benjamin wrote in early 1798:

Our father was very unwell last week, but is now quite well. He generally comes to James's gate every day and stays here for an hour or two and sometimes rides out to the Mills; this gives him good exercise which is quite necessary. The business goes on very well considering the situation we are in here with building. The sales of the Brewery last year up to the 31 October were nearly 12,000 barrels, the profit £6,000 including barms and grains. The flour mill also did very well; we sold about 7,500 barrels, the profit about £2,000. We have already laid out above £4,000 on the new Brewery and £2,000 more will not finish it.[14]

Through his profession Arthur's barrister nephew Richard – 'Dicky' – saw radical politics from a very different angle. In late 1793 he had acted for a Wexfordman whose case had been referred to the King's Bench court in Dublin by the local court. Mr 'Kairin', a phonetic spelling, was charged with administering an illegal oath and was bailed on security of £100, a small fortune.[15] Other such men had fled abroad before trial, and the court was taking no chances. Richard's assistant counsel, who followed his client to Dublin, was the Wexfordman Beauchamp Bagenal Harvey, who, like him, had studied at the Temple in London and was soon to be a famous republican leader.

In April 1795 Richard assisted the famous John Philpot Curran as junior counsel in the defence of the Reverend William Jackson, a United Irishman. Jackson was a French agent who was sent to Ireland in 1794 to meet Wolfe Tone who told him that the Irish would revolt whenever a French Army landed. He was arrested through an informer and was charged with high treason. As France had declared war in 1793 the verdict must have seemed inevitable, and so it was notable for Richard to take on the brief. Jackson's case was unusually difficult to defend, as he took poison and died in the dock. Richard promised to attend Jackson's funeral at the request of his widow, but on arrival he found that it was arranged as a demonstration against the government. This was a step too far for a lawyer, and he returned to his wife Mary in Mercer Street saying, 'I'm a ruined man.' To be on the safe side, he was persuaded to visit Lord Chancellor Clare, the head of the Irish legal world, explaining suavely that he could not refuse a request from a beautiful widow in deep distress.[16] Clare, another member of the junta, said that he had been unwise, and a vacant position that Richard coveted as a Recorder, a salaried minor judge, was given to another.

The barrister Sir Jonah Barrington recalled the Jackson trial and its sudden collapse:

It was discovered that previous to his coming into court he had taken a large quantity of arsenic and aquafortis mixed in tea . . . He had a splendid funeral; and to the astonishment of Dublin it was attended by several Members of Parliament and barristers! – A Mr Tighe and Counsellor Richard Guinness were amongst them.

If 'Dublin' knew of this, and Barrington recalled his surprise at the news, then Richard's quick explanation to Lord Clare was a sensible precaution.[17]

Henry Guinness (1922) mentioned an 'account preserved by his family' revealing Richard's 'sympathy with the advanced party', a delicate way of describing the United Irishmen. Richard had dined in April 1798 with some interesting men at Bargey Castle in County Wexford, including his host Beauchamp Bagenal Harvey, Captain Keogh, Henry and John Sheares, Mr Colclough and Mr Hatton, who were the leaders of the Cork and Wexford United Irishmen, and Jonah Barrington. The diners around the table numbered thirteen, a very bad omen, and all except Hatton, Barrington and Richard were to die within a few months.[18] No more was said, but could the conversation between such men have avoided politics?

By chance, Jonah Barrington wrote about a previous dinner with some of these United Irishmen in Wexford town that month, in a party of seventeen. He was invited by Harvey to dine at Bargey Castle the following evening, 'to meet some old Temple friends'. There the company included 'Captain Keogh [who was Barrington's cousin], the two unfortunate Counsellors Sheers . . . Mr Colclough . . . Mr Hay . . . Mr William Hatton' and 'a gentleman of the Bar whose name I shall not mention, as he still lives'.[19] Barrington's *Recollections* were published in 1827, and Richard died in 1829, so it seems certain that he was the 'gentleman of the Bar', as he had also enrolled at the Inner Temple as a trainee barrister back in 1779. Politics were indeed discussed:

Temple freaks were talked over, the bottle circulated; but at length Irish politics became the topic, and proceeded to an extent of disclosure which utterly surprised me . . . The chances of success, in the event of a rising, were openly debated . . . All this was being talked over without one word being uttered in favour of rebellion – a system of caution which I afterwards learned was much practised for the purpose of gradually making proselytes without alarming them. I saw through it clearly . . . I found myself in the midst of absolute though unavowed conspirators . . . the explosion was much nearer than the Government expected, and I was startled at the decided manner in which my host and his friends spoke.

Barrington concluded: 'Every member of that jovial dinner-party, with the exception of myself, the barrister before alluded to and Mr Hatton, were executed within three months.' If he was 'startled at the . . . manner in which my host and his friends spoke', it appears that Richard Guinness was one of those 'friends', and, as a fellow barrister, Barrington was covering up for him nearly thirty years later. If by 'friends' he had meant *just* the rebel leaders and not Richard, why did he maintain Richard's anonymity? He could mention Richard attending Jackson's funeral in 1795, but that dinner in Wexford in 1798 was too compromising. Richard became a minor judge within a decade, and his official reputation was untarnished by his revolutionary associations. Being a lawyer who was in a financial position to be able refuse to take on difficult, dangerous or unprofitable cases – and representing revolutionaries was certainly all of these – his visible involvement between 1793 and 1798 is notable.[20]

By the time of Richard Madden's partisan commentary in several volumes (1843–60) Richard's little secret had been forgotten, barring that 'account preserved by his family'. One wonders what other details Madden may have missed. In the close examinations in the following century of secret payments made by the British administration to many spies and 'felon setters' in the period 1795 to 1805, some of them United Irishmen, it emerged that none were made to Richard nor to his Uncle Arthur.[21] This indicates that Richard was a closet republican or sympathetic enough not to want to inform on his United Irish friends, as Barrington did, and also that Watty Cox had been wrong to list Arthur as an 'active spy' in late 1797. A real spy would know what was going on, would know what was planned; he would not be investing money in buildings and plant but would be squirreling it away. Instead, Arthur and his nephew were keeping their ears close to the ground around 1797–8 so that they could plan for the whole family's protection. Some pointed questions could have been misheard. Clearly Richard had covered his tracks.

Cox went on to attack everyone venomously in print, not just the administration but also the moderate Catholics Lord Fingall and Archbishop Troy of

Dublin. Like many gadflies and critics he had no real love for humanity. He finally reached the republican nirvana of New York in December 1819 during an epidemic but could remark only on 'this hideous climate and most detestable race of rascals . . . the wise men of Gotham . . . have perished in thousands and, in my opinion, the yellow fever would confer a blessing on the human race by continuing its capers.'[22]

Just before the outbreak of the 1798 rebellion Lord Edward FitzGerald was arrested after a struggle at 153 Thomas Street, quite close to the brewery. The United Irish ranks included numerous spies, and the government locked up many of the leaders, which reduced the possibility of a central command of any revolution. Dublin was peaceful, with heavier patrolling by the Army. The open rebellion started in May in Johnstown, then a hamlet on the Dublin–Cork road, by chance some three miles south of Oughterard Hill. Rebels mobilized in Kildare, around Belfast and in Wexford, but most of the country, including Dublin, remained quiet. In August a small French force arrived in County Mayo and swept through the west. Despite much personal bravery the rebel forces did not link up strategically from a lack of support, and the local militias and British forces mopped up each in its turn.

While the rebellion is often portrayed as a revolt against British rule and its aim being to set up an Irish republic, most of the fighting was between the rebels, who had strong Presbyterian support in Ulster, and the loyalist Irish forces of all religions. As such, it was more like a civil war, the worst type of war. The Catholic Church and its prelates remained loyal to the Crown. The Wexford leaders included Harvey and Colclough, with whom Richard Guinness had so recently dined. There, a republic was established for about a month, but it could not grow and was crushed.

Leaderless at the national level, the interesting and well-publicized United Irish ideals resulted in localized, resentful peasants' revolts with no thought of a person's worth or use. For example, James Spencer, the Duke's manager in Rathangan in west Kildare and a member of the Kildare Knot from 1776, was killed after surrendering to the rebels in a night-time assault on the town, although their leaders thought well of the Duke.[23] If the United Irish were ever to lead the country and make it more prosperous, they needed to persuade such men to assist, not to kill them at the first opportunity. If they had succeeded quickly with wider support it is likely that many such men would have assisted a new republican administration, whether from fear or from a desire to help. But to the rebels on the ground in Rathangan, the brotherly aims and future needs of their leaders were not important. What mattered to them was to sweep away all the visible elements of the system, all the local figureheads, and then see what would happen next.

Spencer had served on a Kildare turnpike-road trust from 1772 and had been Mayor of Athy in 1786. Managing Carton and then the Duke's estates around Rathangan, he knew the productive capacity, the people of all ranks, the transport realities by road and canal. In sum, he had learnt over decades what it took to run County Kildare. He was useful to any government, tying the local economy to the national – just the sort of man who would know how to feed a city or an army in a hurry. He had no dispute with Lord Edward Fitz-Gerald, and they had known each other personally for decades. By chance he had dined with the Knot on 8 October 1783, the night when Lord Edward swore his oath never to duel. It seems ironic that he was described as popular. Spencer also supported Grattan's Irish Whigs. If such a man and his helpless family could be killed reactively, and if such a rebellion had widened, then no man of practicality, usefulness and goodwill was safe.

In such a haphazard eruption, with no certain outcome, anything could happen to anyone. People such as Terence Sheel and James Spencer had hurt nobody. Many of the hazier or soft-focus histories of the revolt have ignored such examples. The French experience since 1789 had not been peaceful, steady or predictable, considering that the nobility had quickly agreed to abandon their privileges. By contrast, longstanding elected delegates of proven ability had led the American rebels from start to finish; they and their political formula of 1776 were still in place two decades later. Even so they had fought a hard struggle until 1781, and they had three European allies and the British were fighting 4,000 miles from home. How much harder would it be for the United Irish, with one ally and just sixty sea miles from Britain?

But let us suppose that the 1798 rebellion had been successful in a quick near-bloodless coup under a central leadership. We should consider that 90 per cent of Ireland's trade was with Britain, and that would end. Any trade with Europe or America by local shipping would have been intercepted by the Royal Navy. To protect its western sea approaches, a British re-invasion to take some of the Irish south-eastern ports was entirely likely. Therefore a French protective force and naval presence would be essential for the new Irish Republic. That, in turn, would lead to a French plunder to pay for its forces in Ireland, as had just occurred elsewhere in Europe.[24] In the many speculations on the rebellion, the illiberal reality in the event of its *success* is seldom considered.

Arthur had an urban perspective. After a Dublin trading career of nearly forty years he must have had a better overview of this larger European reality than a desperate cottier or tenant-farmer with a hungry family. Given the undoubted hardships endured by the peasantry in the 1790s, such a likely scenario between Ireland, Britain and France, even in the event of the rebels' initial success, would have led to further hardship. The peasants would pay a much lower rent or tax to the new republic and pay no church tithes, but as exports of agricultural produce would be impossible, the rural economy would have been reduced to a medieval self-sufficiency.[25] Certainly the great dairy and beef exports from Munster would have collapsed.

Considering that Ireland is an island, it is remarkable that the United Irishmen ignored the vital importance of the Irish export trade. Questioned after the revolt, Arthur O'Connor was clear that 'the old notion that a carrying trade is the most beneficial, is nonsense; the home trade should be the great national object . . . There is no convenience nor a comfort of life that we could not find in our island.'[26] Most businesspeople and consumers then and now would find such idealism impractical and incredible. It ignored the reality of life as it is lived, but a self-contained island economy free from the snares of foreign capital has long been the dream of inexperienced visionaries. When a policy of self-sufficiency was finally attempted from 1932 to 1960 in the Irish Free State and Republic, it led to a stagnant economy and emigration, causing a decline in population. Now it is better understood that capital and trade can be used wisely and need not be a trap.

With the likelihood of continued hardship post-revolt and a reinvasion with further bloodshed, it was also inevitable that harder men would come to power. As had happened in France in 1793, the initial revolutionary leaders, such as the *bien-pensant* idealists Samuel Neilsen, Wolfe Tone and Lord Edward FitzGerald, might well have lost their lives as had the French Feuillants and Girondins in a bout of auto-cannibalism. Further, most rebels were Presbyterians and Catholics, and it was doubtful whether their unity of opposition to the system would continue with quite the same degree of fraternal unity after the system collapsed. There were too many unpleasant possibilities.

Closer to home, a new republic would also have wanted to control Arthur's flour mills to feed the capital. If his brewery had been occupied and drunk dry in 1798, his notional brewer-successor would have had trouble arranging deliveries of barley, and hops would have been unobtainable. The skills of his workforce would be useless, and they would be unemployed or, at best, brewing a basic medieval-style hopless ale for the city. In a risk analysis of the 1790s it was at least *possible* that the United Irish movement might confiscate his hardwon assets if it took power. If opposed by British sea power, that possibility would become a probability. Given that element of doubt about their intentions it is hard to think what would motivate Arthur to support them against the certainty of protection under the existing legal system, imperfect though it was. For a considerable time life would have been hard for poor and rich alike, particularly in Dublin. The United Irishmen's plans were only viable on the establishment of a friendly British Republic, and that was never on the cards.

Arthur was neither opposed to Catholics coming into politics nor to loosening some links with Britain. Because of the war with France, the Irish export economy needed that powerful navy and market in 1798, and a new republic using state larceny to pay the French would set his family back to the level of his father in 1722. He had been assisted, yes, but he had maintained and built up a business in a cautiously entrepreneurial way. All that saving, those reinvestments, that hard work, that care for the poor, that endless sifting of grains and sniffing of brews, that patriotism, that self-control, that consistency, that acquisition of skills might, in the end, have proven to be an enormous waste of time. His ancestors had progressed from poverty through their own efforts to allow him a degree of wealth and security, but his entire life's work – and maybe his entire family – could disappear overnight. Was that just?

Arthur had known Lord Edward FitzGerald through the Kildare Knot, so he had at least made his acquaintance. He would have followed the establishment of the United Irish, and, as a patriot, he must have agreed with much of what they said about the hardship of many people's lives and the general lack of social justice. His hero Henry Grattan was in touch with them. His fellow turnpike-road trustee in Kildare, Thomas Wogan Browne, was an associate of Wolfe Tone. His voluble nephew Richard was perhaps a closet republican. This and much more must have been on Arthur's mind. He was a long-term social networker, and so it is certain that he made it his business to know or know about the people involved and the United Irishmen's arguments and methods. A clear dividing line was their espousal of violence, which in wartime meant that the government's forces were likely to be violent to civilians. But, at the last, like it or not, the odds were too long against the rebels' success. This analysis is confirmed by and explains his brewery redevelopment in 1797–9; nobody in his right mind was going to launch a revolt in 1798.

A similar analysis was made by Wolfe Tone's longest supporter, John Keogh, known as Gog. As a leader of the United Irish and a wealthy merchant, he had been involved at almost every step in the republican movement but tried in vain to stop the revolt at the last moment, realizing that it could not succeed. Most of the population also remained calm, in line with Keogh and Arthur. But, tragically, some 30,000 died, many of whom were killed as prisoners after the event, some indeed at the barracks just across the river from the brewery, and whose corpses were flung into the Liffey as a horrible public deterrent. It had been a disaster for Ireland, and the inevitable parliamentary union with Britain that followed made the progressive patriots' ideals impossible.

Perhaps as a result of being named in 1797 in the *Union Star*, Arthur's two younger sons Edward and William joined the Dublin Yeomanry when the rebellion started. It seems that the rebellion was over before their training ended. He would not allow Arthur II and Benjamin to sign up, suggestive of a less than wholehearted support for the administration and a prior concern for his business, his own little republic. Benjamin, aged twenty-one at the time, complained in a letter: 'I think myself unfortunate that I am so situated at this time that I cannot join the yeomanry, but really attendance required now in Dublin is such that if Arthur [II] and I went into the yeomanry the Business here must be entirely stopp'd.'[27] In 1798 this amateur militia marched to and fro giving the appearance of being omnipresent and succeeded in averting trouble in the city. A story goes that the youngest son, John, was wounded carrying dispatches near Santry aged just fifteen, but contemporary evidence is unavailable.

The rebellion prompted the union with Britain in 1801, but in the negotiations and bribery leading up to it, it was assumed that some Catholic MPs would sit in London, allowing a closer representation for those Irish Catholics who had the vote. This was delayed until 1829, which, inevitably, caused bad feeling. Entirely in line with all we know of Arthur's views, his son Arthur II supported this later emancipation of the Catholic middle class. The third Arthur (1797–1863) briefly supported the Young Ireland movement of *bien-pensant*, emotional nationalists in the 1840s, whose founders in turn admired Grattan.

New political ideas were not shunned by the family, but they had to be practical as well.

United or not, some economic link with Ireland's strong trading partner and its empire had to be kept. Simply put, it was the richest buyer of Irish produce and the richest country in Europe. Arthur II also saw the link as the best for the island's economy and therefore best for all the people. But in 1798, with a fast-growing population, competition for land, economic hardships and a new ideology for the common man, a sizeable minority felt that only an overthrow of the entire system could lead to better times. They put their lives on the line; no higher price could be paid. To the brewery's customers and suppliers in and near Dublin, with a wider world-view, an Irish Parliament with some links to Britain, with all its faults, was of much greater apparent benefit.

During the next century the story of 1798 was reinterpreted in many different ways, best examined by Professor Whelan.[28] In August 1898 the centenary of the revolt was marked in Dublin by nationalist processions witnessed by over 100,000 supportive bystanders. The veteran Fenian republican leader John O'Leary laid the foundation stone for a planned statue of Wolfe Tone. That evening, at a banquet hosted by the Lord Mayor, O'Leary revealed his more flexible hopes for the future in a speech, a vision that now appears quite close to Arthur's:

> he infinitely preferred that Ireland should be under her own laws, and not under English laws, and he did not mind whether it was a republic, an absolute monarchy or a limited monarchy; however, he was not an impractical man, and could conceive Ireland accepting something short of that.[29]

In the 1970s a French journalist asked Zhou Enlai, the longstanding Chinese communist leader, what he thought of the French Revolution of 1789. His answer was enigmatic: 'It's too soon to tell.'[30] The great amount of recent scholarship on Ireland in and around 1798 will give a wider view over time.

*CHAPTER NINETEEN*

# *Revolution*

*I*N ARTHUR'S TWILIGHT years the business was passed on
and expanded further in a very different and more successful type of Irish
revolution. Arthur had moved with Olivia to a house on Gardiner Street in
Dublin before his death on 23 January 1803. By then he had passed on his
father's torch, and the next generation had their turn. All that remained was to
look back over his life and his ancestors' gifts to him and to return to them, consistent to the last.

The earliest brewing workbook at the Guinness Archive at the Storehouse
in Dublin dates from January 1796. It is the key record of a transition, of a
change of gear in the business. Porter production figures are shown to 1815 and
ale up to its last brewing in April 1799, but already porter was the main product.
After more than forty-five years of brewing ale, Arthur's rebuilt brewery would
specialize only in varieties of porter. This was clearly the right decision, and the
family link of 109 years back to his grandfather's ale-selling licence of 1690 was
finally broken. It is apparent from the records that the quantity of each brew
could be tailored flexibly to meet any incoming orders.

It seems that he was continuing with ale for the local market. Reducing the
gallons, barrels and hogsheads in the statistics to barrels of thirty-two gallons,
we find that on 6 and 16 June 1796 he produced seventy-five barrels of ale
in two brews. His mix per brew was five barrels of brown malt to fifteen of pale
malt, with fifty pounds of hops added later. In rough terms these twenty barrels
of grains were added to about four times their volume of water, and the disposal
sale of the spent brewers' grains to farmers was an extra income for the
business.

In the same month Arthur and his sons started eleven brews of porter, pro-
ducing an average of seventy-three barrels per brew, although these were

actually sold in hogsheads of sixty-eight gallons each. Here the mix per brew was fifteen barrels of brown malt to thirty-five of pale malt with 273 pounds of hops added. The charred malt and hops were at a much higher percentage compared with ale, as one would expect. In 1796 he averaged 774 barrels of porter per month, some 198,000 pints, compared with about fifty-eight barrels of ale, or 14,848 pints. As we have seen from his son Benjamin's letter of 1798, the net profit was one pound on every two barrels, and so the family's wealth was increasing by nearly £100 every week. By contrast, a rural landowner would be paid his rent every quarter, or sometimes even annually; brewing allowed for a much faster turnover of cash.

By May 1798, while the United Irish rebellion broke out in parts of Ireland, Arthur's own quiet revolution of redevelopment was under way. We have seen that by 1790 he had planned, rebuilt and then was running his Hibernian Mills in Kilmainham to capacity. Continuing to brew while rebuilding the brewery must have been a much greater planning challenge, given the traffic of men and building materials as well as all the brewing inputs and outputs. Besides, his planning now had to cope with a widespread, if short-lived, revolt. Yet production did not drop that month: three brews of ale produced seventy-six barrels, and porter was brewed twelve times. In June 1798 Benjamin wrote that 'few in Dublin employ so many men as we do'.

In 1799 the statistics reveal the new reality. In March two brews of ale yielded sixty-three barrels, and beside the entries was written 'The last Brewing of Ale'. Emotional or not, this landmark statement was then crossed out and underwritten 'on other Side'. On the next page, on 22 April, we find the final ale run of forty barrels, using a slightly darker mixture of fourteen barrels of pale malt to six of brown malt and fifty-six pounds of hops. If it was already less profitable than porter back in 1773, Arthur had continued to brew it for another twenty-six years, so some local demand for his ale had persisted. (Is it ancestor-worship on my part to deduce that its quality must have been above the average?)

The porter output now jumped sharply, from seventy-six barrels on 11 April to 113 barrels in the brew started on 15 April, and in between them is written 'New Brewery'. By the brew started on 31 October 1799 the yield was already 142 barrels or eighty-eight hogsheads, nearly double what it had been at the start of the year. As well as a higher volume of porter per brew, more brews were started every month, with twenty-one by December 1799, and so the compound effect was almost to quadruple production.[1] This gave the business a greater economy of scale, allowing him to price his products more competitively. From the aforementioned 1796 production average of 198,000 pints per month, the output in December 1802, the month before he died, reached 724,000 pints, a fitting *grand finale* to his forty-seven years as a brewer. (With modern machinery, computerization and steel brewing vessels, today's much larger brewery, run by Diageo, can produce a daily average of three million pints.)

If he was expanding in the Dublin market, how did this compare with London? There, the largest porter brewery was Whitbread's, which sold 202,000 barrels in 1796 and 192,000 the following year.[2] This was many times Arthur's higher volume of production, so by 1800 he was still a minnow in terms of the entire British Isles market. The *Gentleman's Magazine* notice of his barrel back in 1794, when he was an even smaller minnow, seems all the more remarkable; again, the high quality of his product is the only explanation. The second largest porter brewery in London was still called Thrale's, by now selling some 140,000 barrels annually; the Barclays' enormous investment had paid off.

This was Arthur's own revolution at a time of upheaval – non-violent, progressive and beneficial to his family, his workforce and the Irish economy. Compared with the world outside the brewery gates it was a peaceful way of gaining at least a greater personal independence. As well as his three sons, from 8 September 1799 he employed John Purser Junior, who was always called 'Mister John', to oversee the accounts and tie them into the brewing process. This reminds us of his father, the original emigrant porter-brewer of 1776, and although the exact nature of the link between Purser and Arthur in the years 1776 to 1778 is still unclear, from now on the Pursers as much as the Guinnesses were overseeing the brews. Arthur and Mister John had a brief falling out over some long-forgotten matter, but he was quickly re-employed when Arthur II took control in 1803.[3] Everyone had long forgotten about the nutcase London Moravians. The interfamily relationship was such a success that it continued for another century.

Another early treasure in the Storehouse Archives is a 'Brewery Note Book' of October 1801 to February 1803, not written in Arthur's hand. It gives technical notes on each brew, with temperatures taken twice daily, sample dips into the kieves, the type of hops used and so on. A replication of a good brew would be impossible without proper records, and we see the adoption of scientific method. Doubtless there were earlier books that were burnt or thrown away during the rebuilding. Larger quantities are being produced in more brews, and the man himself, the aged expert Uncle Arthur with the big nostrils, the man who has held it all together for so long, is now too old to keep it all in his head. Besides, by now his sons understood all that he knew about brewing. A technical note such as 'Copper 1st Charge 34.0 dry Boiled 1 Hour Copper 2nd Charge 24.0 dry reduced to 36' is not the stuff of poetry, but the finished result might inspire it. Such was the growth of production volume in the New Brewery that from December 1801 the records of the many kieve dips were 'now kept in another book'.

On 14 December 1801 a brew was started 'for West India Porter', with 'Temp of atmosph: 22° [Fahrenheit] *very hard frost*'. Other brews were desig-nated 'For Keeping Beer'. The wider empire was now a potential customer, given porter's qualities. The British brewers had supplied this overseas demand over decades, and now the Irish brewers had a chance to compete on price. That was an achievable and realized patriotism: exporting to and profiting from England and its empire, while making use of its commercial system and its powerful navy. The tail was starting to wag the dog.

Increased production was the foundation for increased sales. By 1801 annual production was up to 9,805 hogsheads (15,884 barrels), and then a marked jump in Arthur's last full year of life to 15,602 hogsheads. There was no pause in output in the month of his death, January 1803, just as there was no pause during the rebellion nor during the brewery rebuilding. This suggests a close hands-on management by the three brothers, with John Purser and a con-tented and very professional workforce of which we know little. Static at 15,166 hogsheads in 1803 – when France and Britain were at war yet again – by 1810 it reached 38,448 and by 1813, a decade after Arthur's death, this had grown to 43,859 hogsheads, with a significant number exported.

The rebellion in the countryside had, by 1799, collapsed into a sporadic brigandage. Richard junior, still brewing at Leixlip and aged nearly seventy, claimed for his losses in the revolt at Sallins, near Naas. His horses, cows, hay and 'cloathes' were assessed at £40. 12s. 7d. Arthur lost some money and beer, but the difference between the rebels and yeomen was that the latter paid late for their beer while the rebels paid nothing. For example, the Forenaughts Cavalry, based near Oughterard, a yeomanry unit of seventy-seven men, final-ized its accounts from 1797 only in 1802, including £7. 10s. paid 'to Guinness, for porter', and £3. 10s. 5d. for cutlery to his cousins the Reads.[4] But the great loss in 1798, for which they could not claim, occurred when Catholic sectarians burnt the old church along Tea Lane in Celbridge, which probably held their parents' wedding record and definitely their own baptismal dates and records of any siblings who had died young. Some of the people whose prosperity and political future he had argued for had destroyed his own past, courageously burning the empty building at night.

The parliamentary union with Britain in January 1801 followed the blood-shed of 1798. Volumes have been written on it, recently and notably by Patrick Geoghegan and with a fine compendium edited by Daire Keogh and Kevin Whelan, but the political and social facts are perhaps examined more carefully than the economic aspects. Britain forced the union with bribery, paying the Irish MPs to dissolve their Parliament and for some to sit in London. Supporting the existing Ascendancy with the possibility of paying to suppress another rebellion during the ongoing French war would cost Britain too much for too small a return.

No record of Arthur's view survives, and he had no say in the matter. Most patriots were vehemently opposed, but some liberals saw it as better way to effect social changes. As with all political change there was bound to be some bad and some good, and one always has to make the best of circumstances. As a patriot there must also have been sadness that too many Irishmen – too many of the Ascendancy – had not seen the obvious need to work towards a better country for all. Peace was declared with France in 1801, being signed at Amiens after a lengthy delay. Although it lasted only about a year it was current at Arthur's death. That and the brewery's new capacity must have been a final comfort. French politics had changed yet again to a brief and progressive dictatorship under its First Consul. Bonaparte agreed matters with the Papacy, reintroduced a nobility with awards and medals and controlled the press. To the dismay of democrats everywhere he was pouring new wine into the same old bottles.

In 1802, in Arthur's last days, the wider world seemed to look forward to an exciting future for his children. Monsieur Garnerin demonstrated his hydrogen balloon in London, an improvement on the hot-air variety, and the launch was assisted by Mrs R.B. Sheridan.[5] Dr Jenner was awarded a prize for his life's work on vaccinations. On 24 March Messrs Trevithick and Vivian, Cornish engineers, lodged their seminal patent application to improve the steam engine 'and the application thereof for driving carriages' on rails. Out of hundreds of patent applications that year, just one was Irish, from William Speer of Dublin, to improve the hydrometers that were needed in all breweries. Modern brain-power and the best opportunities for technical progress at this stage were found overwhelmingly in England. Arthur II was to buy his first steam engine from there in 1809.

Beyond the aristocracy, politics and business, the links between Ireland and Britain already included social assistance, and the London Knot of a charity with a familiar-sounding name was helping the poor Irish there. The *Annual Register* recorded that on 17 March 1802:

> the benevolent society of St Patrick held its annual meeting at the London tavern. The duke of Kent, as earl of Dublin, was in the chair . . . After dinner, the children who are educated and supported by the society were brought into the room, and their appearance was such as to afford the most general satisfaction . . . upwards of £2,600 had been subscribed since the last meeting.

It also mentioned that one Father Arthur O'Leary had just died there aged seventy-three. He had set up St Patrick's Chapel in Soho for 'the wretched inhabitants of St Giles . . . mostly catholics and of the lower order . . . immersed in every species of immorality and irreligion'. Despite 'enduring numberless mortifications and disappointments' O'Leary had effected 'the amelioration in the manners and habits of these poor wretches . . . and the very best conse-quences have already arisen'. Although the *Register* reflected the establishment's religious views, it allowed that in a theological debate with a Protestant bishop in 1787 O'Leary's address had 'confounded his antagonist and is a masterpiece of wit and argument'. The Irish poor living in the seat of empire were being helped in different ways, with no adverse comment on their religion and no sense of an alien 'race'. There were perhaps too many London Irish to be helped, some might be inept and too fond of a drink, but there was no law forbidding them from colonizing the imperial city. How they got on in life was up to them. Some would have problems that could only be solved by practical, organized, praiseworthy men.

Arthur had succeeded in business, but was he an entrepreneur? If he had about £500 available by 1760 from his father and Dr Price, and a £1,000 dowry from Olivia in 1761, his estate at his death was sworn at £23,000 –

although probate values are often low. But, like Dr Price's bequest of £100, the much-quoted 1803 estate value was not an exact measure of the wealth he had generated, as we shall see. He had turned an empty brewery into one of Dublin's larger businesses and had rebuilt profitable flour mills; he had two ranges of buildings in Leixlip and his investment in Hibernian Insurance. He had diversified. Luck had played its part, but in networking and by timing his moves well he had also made bad luck less likely. He seems to have planned each step, except for his water dispute, and was not alone in being surprised by the rebellion in 1798.

The truth lies somewhere between the views of two biographers: one an admirer, the other a detractor. Michele Guinness (1999) said Arthur had created 'the biggest business enterprise in Ireland'; not so, as other Dublin brewers, Beamish and Crawford in Cork and various land and linen interests were larger still. Dunne (2003) complains, as we have seen, that modern brewery leaflets 'do not stress Arthur's elite social position but instead describe him as a daring entrepreneur'.[6] In the business world an investment should be well planned and never 'daring', although it must appear daring to those who passed up on the opportunity. Financing for any improvements seems to have come from retained profits and not from loans – a certain, slow, conservative and low-cost method that is rare today.

A true entrepreneur would have sold everything and engaged in shipping and trading, known sources of wealth in northern Europe for centuries, joining Braudel's 'predators', but these involved too many extra risks and unknowns. By the time Arthur could have done so, say after 1780, he was too old to start afresh, he was well established and his businesses and his sons needed oversight if all he had built up was to continue. How could he live away from his beloved Dublin, where he knew so many people, at what must have seemed to be a time of exciting transition? His busy social round did not develop his skills as a hands-on brewer or miller, nor did it lead to greater sales to publicans and bakers, and while he had rubbed shoulders with some of the élite he was not rich enough to become an aristocrat. Nor did he buy acres of farmland to rent out, for reasons that we have examined. Had Arthur II or his brothers married heiresses from the aristocracy with huge dowries and then bought titles, Dunne would have a better argument about an 'elite social position'. The sons had married girls of about equal status to their mother Olivia, given asset inflation between 1761 and the 1790s.

Ultimately, Arthur's real progress had been in developing his businesses and laying a solid foundation. A host of minor elements had helped in the background, however. The growth of Dublin, the bounties for growing corn from 1784, the increased water supply, the boom in the economy of the 1780s, decreasing taxes on Irish beers, increasing taxes on English imports, a lower malt tax, secure shipping of exports, a reliable banking system and a steady currency with low interest rates had all helped at different times. He was lucky to have trained three competent sons who worked well together. Today a business is floated on a strong stock market as soon as possible, and the entrepreneur then sometimes tries to buy it back in a recession, but in Arthur's day such techniques were unavailable. A merchant and his family were all in it together for the long haul, and so the intangible virtue of respectability was much more important than it is today.

In the world of ideas Arthur was not a creative intellectual, nor was he quite the inventive brewer that he has seemed to be – although often credited with inventing porter he had, in fact, copied it very well. His views on politics and business copied others when it made sense to copy, and it is clear that he embraced change successfully. His sense of timing was his most striking skill, and, as luck was also a factor, his caution made bad luck less likely. Within his family he has been hailed as the first of many successful men, the founder, although I argue that he was not exactly the first. He and his siblings were merely the first to show their heads above the parapet in a search for decent earnings, security and civility that had been under way for several generations. Because they were the first to be seen, a sort of hinge between the past and modernity, it has been hard to seek out the earlier life stories and realities, but not without result. In the context of today's Ireland, the overall trend of the story, now shorn of its many legends, will sound familiar to many. The grandson of tenant-farmers and the great-grandson of a barefoot shepherd on a wind-blown Kildare hillside, Arthur simply could not have succeeded as he did without their small steps, their adaptation of new skills, their sacrifices and their cautious choices all designed to improve their lot.

# CHAPTER TWENTY

# Inheritance

*T*WO DAYS AFTER Arthur's death, on 25 January 1803, the *Dublin Evening Post* ran a kindly mention: 'Deaths . . . At his home in Gardiner-street, Mountjoy-square, in the 79th year of his age, Arthur Guinness Esq., long known and respected in the city of Dublin: the worthy and good will regret him because his life has been useful, benevolent and virtuous.' The *Post* had been Valentine O'Connor's main public supporter a decade earlier, and so their comment was heartfelt. The exact cause of Arthur's death is not known.

In the same issue we see that cousins of the Thwaites family, his erstwhile brewing and wholesaling rivals, although colleagues in his guild, were now in the soda-water business:

> Soda Waters &c. &c. In Pint and Half-pint jars [bottles] . . . Augustin Thwaites, sen & jun. [offer] a large stock of the different mineral waters viz. Soda Water . . . Selters [seltzer], Syrment, Rochelle and Cheltenham Waters, which have received the sanction of the Physicians and Medical Gentlemen of this City.

Unlike the Thwaites family, who claimed to have brewed the first porter in Dublin, Guinness porter had survived. Often the originator is copied and improved upon. While George Thwaites had voted against Valentine O'Connor in 1793, Augustin junior was linked to the United Irishmen.[1] Thwaites soda-water is still sold by C&C Group.

On the political front, the brief attempt to start a revolt by Robert Emmet in 1803 was to come, but the *Post*'s editor hoped that the haphazard brigandage would end: 'we have no doubt but the wise and firm measures of Government will restore this country to perfect tranquillity'. However, tension was growing with France, and this would lead to renewed warfare that lasted until 1814.

'Lord Whitworth demanded, that the French should promise, not to send troops to Malta and Egypt under any circumstances, but the French Government refused.'

In the following issue Arthur's much younger cousin Thomas Read – he of the red logo, who was never called Tomas O Riada – placed a notice, still busy and creative: 'Thomas Read, Knife and Sword Cutler, No. 4 Parliament-street, requests his Friends and the Public will give an impartial trial to his new-invented Razor Strops . . . being superior and considerably cheaper than any imported into this kingdom.' As with his cousins Samuel and Arthur, local substitution for English imports was suggested, but 'this kingdom' was by now just a fond memory, only an echo of the patriots' dreams, as Ireland was now to be incorporated for over a century into the United Kingdom.

Under the terms of Arthur's will, which he had signed on 3 May 1802, an equitable but not equal division is apparent. The unequally large shares went to his eldest sons. Hosea, being in the Church and 'not being in any line of life whereby he is likely by Industry to enlarge his Property', was left Beaumont and the investment properties in Leixlip that had been bought and rebuilt in 1756 and 1775. By this stage they must have been worth several thousand pounds. Arthur II already had the title deeds of the still-small brewery as part of his 1793 marriage settlement and was already managing the brewery and flour mills. He was specifically bequeathed a silver salver presented to Arthur by his guild, obviously an object of pride.

The other siblings were well provided for, on an equitable basis that has generally survived in the family until the present day, as they received over half of the value of the estate. By contrast, under the Anglo-Norman practice of primogeniture used in landed families, a wealthy man normally left all his estate to his eldest son and small fixed incomes for other children and his widow. Arthur's overall formula could be described as a hybrid between the English system and the Continental and old Irish methods of partible inheritance, with most of the money going to the older sons but substantial amounts passing to the younger children, including his daughters, allowing for their independence.

The younger brewing sons, Benjamin and William, and John, the youngest, were left £1,500 each. This would allow them to marry well, and John bought a commission in the Indian Army in 1804. Edward the solicitor had had his capital and, sadly, was unsuccessful in his iron-mastering business, requiring further assistance from 1811. Elizabeth Darley, wife of Frederick, was left

£1,000; her dowry had been paid in 1785. Her younger unmarried sisters, Louisa and Mary, still needed a dowry, and so were left rather more, £2,000 each, the same amount as Ann Lee and Margaret Blair. Finally, his widow Olivia, whose life we know little about, was left a fixed annual income of £200, their carriage and their house in Gardiner Street. If this £200 came from gilts that were then yielding 5 per cent annually, it equated to a capital sum of £4,000. These bequests came to a rough value of £13,500 out of an estate of £23,000.

The unwritten reality was that Benjamin and William were also earning something at the brewery, and John was made a sales agent later on. In 1808 Arthur II allowed his brewing brothers full partnerships in the brewery and flour mills, and the firm's name changed to 'Guinness (A., Ben & W.L.) brewers'. As they were then aged thirty-one and twenty-nine the timing reflected their full maturity, in the biblical sense; they must have felt that it had been a long apprenticeship.[2] It seems that Arthur, aged thirty in 1755, and Arthur II, who was thirty in 1798, had also taken on their burdens and opportunities at the same age, then considered the ideal balance of youthful energy with a degree of wisdom and experience.

The probate value of £23,000 has never been analysed and has been taken too literally at face value as Arthur's net financial worth in 1803, rather as Dr Price's £100 is taken as his starting capital. Income from the insurance business and the Leixlip rental properties must have been included. Beaumont had a value. However, the land under the brewery had been passed on to Arthur II in 1793, and the *de facto* partnership of brothers running the brewery and mills in 1803 was largely outside Arthur's estate. Given that the flour mills and the half-rebuilt brewery had made a profit of £8,000 in 1797 and a pro-rata profit of at least £15,000 in 1802, clearly this partnership cash-flow was not included and would itself have had a capital value of about £100,000 at the time.[3] The lack of any relevant accounting paperwork from this period is unhelpful, but luckily the barrelage figures and family letters have survived. We must conclude that the probate value was based only on what Dr Johnson had described as a 'parcel of boilers and vats' and not on the underlying healthy cash-flow. Therefore Arthur's real legacy to his family was considerably more than the £23,000 – in reality perhaps five times higher.

As well as the financial bequests, Arthur's children inherited some strands of his political and social views. These quickly became outdated, and his inherent sense of equality and decency with financial prudence became the exception rather than the rule. Arthur II had stated his views in 1797: emancipation for Catholics and a reform of the franchise were vital, but the financial and trading links to Britain were also essential, at least until Ireland had the skills and capital to stand on its own feet. In a sense, the formula that had worked for the family over a century might be applied to solve the island's many problems. Improve yourself, help to civilize the country and, all going well, Ireland could be ready to govern itself some day. In the meantime the business would allow for the family's independence. The unsustainable doubling of the Irish population to over eight million between 1800 and 1845 swamped this long-term aspiration.

Regarding Daniel O'Connell's campaign to allow Catholic MPs, the family's continuing support was acknowledged on 22 May 1813 by the Dublin Catholic Board, which passed a resolution that the Guinnesses 'were entitled to the confidence, gratitude and thanks of the Catholics of Ireland'.[4] In 1819 Arthur II persuaded the (Protestant) congregation of St Catherine's Church beside the brewery to pledge to support emancipation,[5] and in 1825 he proposed that Catholic directors should be allowed at the Bank of Ireland, of which he was by then Governor. When the Emancipation Act was finally passed in 1829, he spoke at the public celebrations in Dublin:

> although always a sincere advocate for Catholic freedom, I could never look my Catholic neighbour confidently in the face. I felt that I was placed in an unjust, unnatural elevation above him; and I considered how I would have felt if placed in a different position myself. Sorrow was always excited in my mind by such a contemplation, and I longed much to have the cause removed . . . My Catholic brother is a freeman. We shall henceforth meet as equals.[6]

Another view that seems to have been inherited was the family's continuing opposition to overt drunkenness – coming from brewers this must seem unusual or even hypocritical, but it was practical. First concentrating on spirits, advice was given to family members who drank more than they could handle; some were fired from the brewery for over-indulging. Knowing one's limitations is an element in civility and business. One factor in the brewery's success in the nineteenth century was its ability to build upon Father Theobald Mathew's temperance crusade against spirits in the 1830s, with a nourishing beer as the preferred option yet again. If one could down fifteen pints in an evening and enjoy it with no harm done, well and good, but for many Dubliners 'nursing' one pint all evening was the reality.

Arthur II also attended a parliamentary reform meeting in May 1831, although ill, 'lest his absence might be construed into an indifference on this great question in which they were all so vitally interested'. Later that month he seconded the adoption of a County Dublin Reform candidate, and considered that:

> A great change was taking place all over the world. Men were awakening. Reason and intelligence were upon their majestic way, and everywhere the grand principle was beginning to be asserted that Governments were instituted only for the benefit of the people . . . the struggle of popular power had loosened the iron hold of tyranny, and prostrated the oppression that would seek to build itself on the oppression of the human race.[7]

Arthur II's opinion on reform was shared by Daniel O'Connell. Nobody had a right to rule by reason of birth or wealth, the 'benefit of the people' was paramount, and more people should be allowed to vote. The Reform Act became law in 1832.

However, the family disagreed with the 'Great Dan' in his third campaign for repeal of the union with Britain. In 1836 O'Connell's journal *The Pilot* graciously allowed that Arthur II's opposition was based on the financial practicalities, and was not simply reactive and unreasoned. Arthur was a man 'who never committed but this one public error and whose motives for committing this one are unquestioned'. Arthur wrote to the editor explaining his stance 'and repudiated the suggestion that he had associated with the Orange System'. *The Pilot* accepted this, but, in the nature of things, as the unionist–nationalist division became entrenched and emotive in Ireland it became harder for anyone to hold to a reasonable position. The resurgent Catholic hierarchy was unforgiving of past wrongs, and Britain took more interest in its empire and its industrial revolution than in Irish reforms. The family's opinion was that it would probably be many years before it would be sensible and beneficial to end the union; circumstances would reveal the right time. Reform in the 1830s would only benefit O'Connell and his friends, and taxes would increase. In 1839 O'Connell described Arthur in a private letter as 'a miserable old apostate' – some gratitude after decades of support. By the 1850s the brewery was making more profit per barrel from sales into England than on its Irish sales, and naturally Arthur did not want to jeopardize that achievement.[8] It is safe to conclude that the family's publicly stated views on emancipation, liberal social reform, a larger franchise and maintaining a beneficial link with Britain in the nineteenth century were all inherited from Arthur's patriot credo that I trace back to at least the 1770s.

In January 1803 it was clear that the continuity of the brewery and mills businesses, Arthur's opinions, the family origin-legends and the place of his burial at Oughterard were certain, fixed or inevitable matters within his wider family. Yet Michele Guinness considers that his burial was 'a strange last wish, for in his lifetime he never referred to the past, never spoke of his ancestors, not even to his children. He was as much of an enigma the day he died as the day he arrived in Dublin intent on making his fortune.'[9] I beg to differ; the Reads had stopped farming in Oughterard in the 1770s, but all his family knew that Arthur had to make one last round.

As with his Read cousins in Dublin, as with his mother and grandparents, Arthur was borne off to Oughterard church, the symbolic womb of the family. The cortege would have taken a journey of several hours in the freezing weather, with carriages and carts following the hearse. It is also possible that they processed by barge down the Grand Canal.[10] His eldest son Hosea led the service, and, given the season, the family's smart city clothes would have been well covered with layers of hats and greatcoats. The coffin would have been carried the last few steps over the uneven ground towards the Reads' corner of the old church. Finally, beside his mother and all her people, he was set into the ancient ruins, reaching back into the mists of time to those far-off servants of the cult of St Bridget, or Bríd, or Brig, those Ó Maoil Bhríghde. After all the tumults of life, he and the hilltop itself would look down for ever on Celbridge, on Leixlip, on the canal and the plain of the Liffey leading towards Dublin, the scenes of his start in life and of his remarkable worldly success.

To borrow from James Joyce, it had all been a natural 'commodius vicus of recirculation'.

# Abbreviations

| | |
|---|---|
| Ann Reg | Annual Register (using 1759–1803) |
| CAR | Calendar of the Ancient Records of Dublin (series) |
| DHR | Dublin Historical Records (series) |
| GO | Genealogical Office of the National Library of Ireland (NLI) |
| HMSO | Her Majesty's Stationery Office |
| HSG | Henry Seymour Guinness |
| JCKAS: | *Journal of the County Kildare Archaeological Society* (series). |
| KHS | *Kildare History and Society* (Geography Press, Dublin, 2006) |
| MC | Manuscripts Commission (UK) |
| MS/MSS | Manuscript/manuscripts |
| NAD | National Archives, Dublin |
| NLI | National Library of Ireland, Dublin |
| POS | Microfiche file, NLI |
| PRONI | Public Record Office of Northern Ireland, Belfast |
| QUB | Queen's University Belfast |

# *Notes*

For brevity, the author's surname and page number is provided or, in the case of a periodical, its volume and page number (for full details refer to the Bibliography).

### CHAPTER ONE *Origins*

1. CJKAS VIII, p. 222; KHS, p. 176.

2. CJKAS IX, p. 253; CJKAS XVIII, pp. 39ff.

3. CJKAS XI, p. 150; Maginn on the O'Byrnes and O'Tooles; KHS, Chapter 5.

4. Excise Returns 1690; generally, NLI MS GO 3266.

5. Courtesy of the National Gallery of Ireland.

6. Egmont MSS, Historical Manuscripts Commission, HMSO 1905, Vol. 1, Part II, p. 120, 'List of Servants at Castlewarden and Their Wages'.

7. *Lodge's Peerage of Ireland*, 1789, II, p. 252; pp. 1754, passim.

8. Egmont MSS (op. cit.), p. 460.

9. Egmont MSS (op. cit.), p. 575.

10. From *Ap Rhys* meaning 'son of Rhys'.

11. HSG (a), pp. 4–5.

12. Irish Court of Exchequer, Michaelmas 1714.

13. Therefore the four brothers' dates were John 1688–1718; William 1689–1767; George 1690–1731; Richard *c.* 1691–1766. The eldest three were baptized at Monkstown, near Dalkey.

14. Proudfoot (ed.), Chapters 2–8, 'County Down Placenames' series, QUB, passim; Duffy (ed.), maps on pp. 31, 47, 57; Elliott, passim; O'Sullivan text on the Magennis clan; Philip Magennis and Harold O'Sullivan, personal communications. Mac Aonghusa is pronounced 'mac-a-nee-a-sa'.

15. Gillespie (b), passim. Some were regranted other land after the Restoration of 1660.

16. Proudfoot (ed.), p. 190.

17. HSG (a), pp. 15–24. Henry S. Guinness (1858–1945) and his brother Howard (1863–1937) seem to have started their researches in about 1898. Henry was descended from Arthur's brother Samuel and was a financier who became one of the first senators when the Irish Free State was founded in 1922. As a senator, his house at Stillorgan, near Dublin, was nearly burnt by the anti-government forces in the Irish Civil War of 1922–3 (*Freeman's Journal*, 28 March 1923).

18. HSG (a), pp. 3–5; this short but tightly written thirty-page volume examined nine possible origins, all wrong. Colonel W.V. McGuinness (1994) made another useful and very detailed attempt to research his hoped-for descent from the Magennis chiefs, which also proved inconclusive. Sadly, the Colonel died in 1999, just three years before a genetics test would have quickly placed his male lineage amongst other Magennises.

19. Mullally, pp. 227, 232 (appendix).

20. See Bibliography for the relevant literature.

21. McEvoy and Bradley, 'Y-chromosomes and the Extent of Patrilineal Ancestry in Irish Surnames', *Human Genetics*, 2006, Vol. 119, p. 212.

22. Dr Kay Muhr, personal communication.

23. Byrne, F.J., p. 287.

24. Pomery, pp. 90–92.

25. Rosser, Zerjal, Hurley et al. (2000), Semino, Passarino, Oefrer et al. (2000), Y-Chromosome Consortium 2002; this group was called 'haplogroup 1' until 2002 and is currently group 'R1b3'; Stewart, p. 32; Oppenheimer, pp. 99–172; Sykes, pp. 120–46, 156–64.

26. Forde family of Seaforde, County Down, personal communication.

27. O'Sullivan and Gillespie (eds), p. 68.

28. Seán McCartan, personal communication.


**CHAPTER TWO** *Transitions*

1. Gillespie (a); Duffy, Edwards and FitzPatrick (eds), passim.

2. Leerssen (a), p. 203.

3. Nicholls, p. 79.

4. Curtis, p. 264.

5. Gibbons, pp. 174–8.

6. Gillespie (c), passim.

7. Cullen, pp. 70, 80–81.

8. NLI MS GO 8015, Part 11.

9. B. Guinness (ed.), p. 3; Sadleir and Dickinson, pp. 38–9; McCarthy, p. 89. For the Bishopric of Kildare after 1700, see JCKAS XIX, p. 62. Although Celbridge House was its name until the 1780s, there is another Celbridge House today, so for clarity the house is called Oakley Park. In the late 1780s it was the birthplace of the famous generals Napier.

### CHAPTER THREE *Childhood*

1. JCKAS XVI, pp. 396.

2. Dunne (a), p. 1. Price also took a long lease on seventy-one acres at Oldtown, Celbridge, in 1736, and a lease for twenty-nine years on fifty-two acres at Rinawade, Leixlip, in 1717 (JCKA XVIII, p. 340). He had the right to graze on eighteen acres of common land near Celbridge. These disparate holdings would pay rents that Richard probably collected but which are far from the usual definition of an estate, which would at the time have comprised hundreds of acres from which the landlord drew his income. The twenty-one acres at Oakley Park sounds like a home farm, providing for the household. Price's income came from his church, and the 123 acres (at most) away from his home were sublet, not farmed directly by him or any of his 'workers'.

3. HSG (b), p. 2; Kildare Chapter Book 1722, Bundle 4.

4. Price was said to have courted Ester van Homrigh (Vanessa) before Jonathan Swift, without success, on her arrival in Celbridge in 1714; JCKAS XVI, p. 397.

5. HSG (a), p. 1.

6. McCarthy, p. 41; Arnold, pp. 61–73.

7. Conolly Papers, at PRONI, MIC 435 and D2094; at NAD M.6917; KHS, Chapter 11, on Katherine Conolly.

8. Dr Price was the Conollys' tenant under a long lease in Celbridge and acted as their chaplain, so both households at either end of the village would have been in regular contact from 1722. JCKAS XVI, pp. 395–407; Sadleir and Dickinson, p. 38, say that Price 'was largely indebted for his success in life' to the Conollys' support.

9. Donnelly J. and K. Miller (eds), Chapter 5.

10. NLI MS 3266.

11. B. Guinness, pp. 27–8.

12. NLI MS GO 8015, Part 12.

13. James Read *v.* John Farrange and William Guines, Bill of 7 November 1743; the answer by the defendants dated 16 November was, however, signed 'Will

Guinness'. Farrange was a merchant whom James had worked for and who owed him nine months' pay. Possibly William had made an unlucky introduction. NLI MS 3266.

14. Religious Census, 1732–3; commented on in a pamphlet by Rhames and Gunne, Dublin, 1736; Duffy (ed.), pp. 76–7.

15. O'Toole (a), pp. 16–29.

16. NAD M.6917.

### CHAPTER FOUR *Youth*

1. Sadleir and Dickinson, p. 39.

2. Dickson, pp. 41–2, 70–71; McCarthy, pp. 46–7, 128.

3. JCKAS XVIII, pp. 337–47.

4. KHS 189 shows a print of the former church that was burnt in 1798.

5. Donnelly and Miller (eds), Chapter 7.

6. Alex Findlater, personal communication; the specialist Dublin historian on the history of drinks and the director of the Findlater Vaults Museum.

7. Sadleir and Dickinson, pp. 38–9.

8. M. Guinness (b), p. 17.

9. KHS, Chapter 7.

10. Tillyard, passim.

11. A 1999 joint production by the BBC, Irish Screen and WGBH Boston.

12. Part I, p. 101.

13. Downloaded in June 2005 from http://www.heritagetowns.com.

14. Chenevix-Trench, passim.

15. De Landa, pp. 128–9.

### CHAPTER FIVE *The Start*

1. Richard and Arthur were numbers twenty-four and twenty-five on the list, but the first of the servants named in the will.

2. Earsum had also worked for Dr Price since the 1720s. Being Price's butler he may have been senior to Richard in the household. Both witnessed many leases for Price. Earsum lived in the house, and his wife ran a shop in Celbridge. It is easy to imagine competition between these men, but no disagreement is known of. Earsum is often misread and misspelt 'Garson'.

3. Young, Part I, pp. 8, 15; £200 would allow a tenant farmer to start up on 200 acres.

4. By the 1770s the archdiocese of Cashel was worth £4,000 a year, Meath diocese paid £3,400 a year and Price's previous bishoprics were worth between £2,200 and £2,400 a year; Young, Part II, pp. 56–7.

5. JCKAS XVI, p. 398. Finey's lease from the Conollys was dated 28 December 1726. On 1 August 1764 Richard Nelson sold on the sublease 'lately in the possession of Richard Guinness' to Thomas King, a currier of Dublin. It seems likely that Richard and Elizabeth's move to Leixlip was made after Frances was married in June 1763, perhaps in the summer of 1764.

6. St Mary's Register, 19 October 1752: 'licence to Revd W. Fletcher Rector of St Mary's to solemnize matrimony . . .'

7. B. Guinness (ed.), p. 19.

8. In the 1750s and 1760s the London-based French Huguenot cartographer Jean Rocque was commissioned to map Dublin city and county and the Earl of Kildare's estates.

9. The 1752 lease term was 'for and during the natural Lives of said Richard Guinness and Arthur and Samuel Guinness first and second Sons of Richard Guinness and the Survivors of Them paying the yearly Rent of £10'; NLI MS 3266.

10. Garech Browne (often Gaelicized to de Brún), Arthur's four-greats-grandson, founded the Irish-music label Claddagh Records in the 1960s.

11. Such a lease had to be registered at the Registry of Deeds to give it full legal effect.

12. Young, Part II, p. 24.

13. HSG (b), p. 9; B. Guinness (ed.), p. 20.

14. NLI GO MS8015, Part 8, on the Jagos.

15. Ossory Fitzpatrick, Chapter 6, quoting Warburton.

16. Conor O'Brien, personal communication.

17. The signboard was found in about 1958 and some now lost correspondence with my father Desmond ensued, as he had just moved to Leixlip. When followed up it had been burnt by accident; HSG (c), p. 2.

18. Further, the 1755 brewery property was sold in 1803, while the 1756 property lease was extended intact by Arthur's descendants on 13 February 1856; Paul Guinness, archives and personal communication.

19. Dr Ursula Bond, personal communication. On another level, 'uniquely hardy' means well able to adapt and mutate to new circumstances.

20. Dunne (b), p. 1.

21. Drawn and engraved by Jones and King, Dublin, and dedicated to William Conolly, nephew and heir to Speaker Conolly and the father of Tom Conolly.

22. John Colgan has written the first history of the town, published in 2005.

23. 'The Mall' property lease was bought from Tom Conolly on 22 December 1775. This was renewed in 1841 and was converted into a 'fee farm grant' in 1856; Paul Guinness, archives and personal communication.

24. Now the Leixlip House Hotel.

25. Curran, Pegley, Donohoe and Twomey, pp. 29–66; KHS 178.

26. Cullen, p. 74, linked the Dublin banking crisis of 1759 to falling linen sales in 1758. Some considered the cause to be the threat of a French invasion; Ann Reg, 1759, Chronicle 125.

27. See McLynn; Keegan.

28. Dennison and MacDonagh, p. 9.

29. JCKAS XIX, pp. 116–50; Kelly (a), pp. 65–6.

30. Fraser, pp. 34–7, reprints the rules of 1763, which were published in Dublin by Samuel Price.

31. Martelli, pp. 18–19, gave the Knot one sentence.

## CHAPTER SIX *St James's Gate and Marriage*

1. The statue was also mentioned in Ann Reg, 1759, Chronicle 78; Fraser, p. 40.

2. Today the original lease is set into the floor under plate glass at the Storehouse Museum in Dublin. Its text is reprinted in *The Guinness Harp*, pp. 16ff.

3. '. . . little knowing what would sprout from such a small bequest' (M. Guinness, 1999); 'He began business . . . in 1760 with practically no capital' (HSG, 1922); 'Considering his small beginnings . . . with little capital' (Martelli, 1957); '[He] went into business with a £100 inheritance' (*Daily Mail*, 2005).

4. Catherine Boylan, personal communication.

5. *Faulkner's Dublin Journal*, 29 December 1759.

6. *Faulkner's Dublin Journal*, 1 January 1760; No. 3408.

7. Leerssen (a), pp. 295–373 also lists many other examples in the eighteenth century where Anglo-Irish academics studied the former Gaelic culture.

8. HSG (a), p. 22.

9. Wilson, D., p. 17.

10. NLI MS GO 8015, Part 7.

11. NLI MS GO 179, pp. 480–3.

12. Picard, p. 201.

13. Kelly, p. 152.

14. HSG (b), p. 10.

### CHAPTER SEVEN *Beaumont and Dublin*

1. John Deaton, personal communication.
2. Picard, p. 61.
3. B. Guinness (ed.), p. 27; Wilson, p. 20.
4. Walsh, Chapter 4; Harris (1766), Chapter 6; Barrington (a), Chapter 21, 'Procession of the Trades'.
5. Donnelly and Miller (eds), Chapter 8; O'Toole (a), pp. 60–61, on the rural Catholic patterns.

### CHAPTER EIGHT *City Life*

1. HSG (b), p. 5.
2. M. Guinness (b), p. 20–21.
3. B. Guinness (ed.), p. 19.
4. See Laffan (ed.).
5. NLI GO MS 104.
6. M. Guinness (b), p. 20.
7. *Faulkner's Dublin Journal*, 22 March 1760, No. 3431.
8. D. Moore, passim.

### CHAPTER NINE *Problems and Solutions*

1. HSG (b), p. 4.
2. Author's archive.
3. HSG (a), p. 2.
4. Lynch and Vaizey, notes to endnotes.
5. HSG (b), p. 14, quoting *Miscellanea Nova* published by Samuel Whyte in 1801.
6. O'Toole (b), pp. 49–69.
7. O'Toole (b), p. 22; HSG (b), p. 15. Samuel Whyte was a natural cousin of Mrs Sheridan.
8. Barnard (a), pp. 208–78; (b), pp. 330–42.
9. O'Toole (b), p. 45.
10. Paul Guinness, personal communication.
11. B. Guinness (ed.), p. 19.
12. PRONI, D.135, T.910.
13. Journals of the Irish House of Commons, 1773, Vol. 16, pp. 188–90.
14. Journals of the Irish House of Commons, 1773, p. 286.

15. Carwyn Jones in the *Northwest Wales Newsletter*, 16 March 2000; and see Lyn Ebenezer's *The Thirsty Dragon* (2006).

16. The quotations about this water dispute are in the official records, principally the 'Calendar of the Ancient Records of Dublin' (CAR), Vol. 12.

17. Martelli, p. 17.

18. CAR, Vol. 12, pp. 372–4.

19. CAR, Vol. 12, p. 394.

20. M. Guinness (a), p. 5; (b), p. 21; Mullally, p. 6; D. Wilson, p. 20.

21. J.B. Guinness, pp. 5, 10.

22. *Irish Times* supplement, 8 September 2005.

23. D. Moore 1960, passim, on this and the other sources of water available by the 1950s. Modern flow data from a set of plans in the author's archive.

24. Dunne (b), p. 1.

25. See Bibliography, Section B.

### CHAPTER TEN *Porter Comes to Dublin*

1. *The Guinness Harp*, p. 8.

2. Picard, p. 103.

3. *The Guinness Harp*, p. 9.

4. Boswell, p. 430.

5. Quenell, p. 234.

6. HSG (e), letter of 12 December 1925; John Griffiths (descended from John Purser), personal communication.

7. Kelly (a), pp. 165–6.

8. Craig, p. 271, quoting Charles Bowden's 'Tour through Ireland, 1791; Antony Farrell (the famous Dublin publisher, who is descended from James), personal communication.

9. Dennison and McDonagh, pp. 6–7.

10. Schuchard, passim.

11. Lodahl is very knowledgeable on brewing processes and has served on the Beer Style Committee in the USA. See also www.ivo.se/guinness/faq.html, www.bjcp.org and http://hbd.org. The origin of this story may be that some sort of soured pasteurized extract was used in Foreign Export Stout until the 1970s.

12. See Dennison and McDonagh, pp. 161–3, on porter's decline compared with stout after 1914.

13. Bielenberg, p. 114.

**CHAPTER ELEVEN** *Arthur's Patriot Politics*

1. Now available online at Project Gutenberg.

2. Hely Hutchinson was not the first to argue that the Navigation Acts of the 1650s, and subsequent legislation, forbade an Irish merchant to trade directly with the rest of the British Empire, forbade the export of commonly made items such as woollen goods, and a brewer such as Arthur had to buy only English-grown hops, regardless of price and quality. Adam Smith's well-received support for free trade bolstered Hutchinson's arguments.

3. Curtis, p. 258.

4. Glazier (ed.), p. 351. Washington said: 'Patriots of Ireland, your cause is identical with mine.'

5. Tillyard, passim; Leinster MSS at NLI and PRONI; Fitzgerald, passim.

6. Tillyard, p. 309.

7. Article by Professor James Kelly in *History Ireland*, Spring 1994, p. 26.

8. Ingamells, p. 575.

9. Kelly (a), pp. 118–20.

10. Young, Part II, p. 78. He considered that duellers felt 'neglected and despised . . . and unused to good company'. The Friendly Brothers hoped to provide the latter.

11. Kelly (c); W. Flood.

12. Kelly (b); Mansergh; McDowell.

13. On 22 January 1783 the final act was passed by Parliament in London: 'Be it enacted that the right claimed by the people of Ireland to be bound only by laws enacted by his Majesty and the Parliament of that kingdom, in all cases whatever shall be, and is hereby declared to be established and ascertained for ever, and shall at no time be questioned or questionable.'

14. Barrington (a), Chapter 7.

15. Lena Boylan and Patricia Daly, personal communication.

16. But note that up to twenty-seven Volunteer units in Kildare can be identified, some very small. They were often based on the 'array' of the Kildare militia in 1756, officered by some future Knot members; JCKAS XV, pp. 39–43; JCKAS VI, pp. 347–51.

17. JCKAS XII, pp. 102–4. Its preamble included: 'Whereas by the limited state of our Trade and Commerce and by the constant drain of Money out of this kingdom . . . the products of land particularly woolls are greatly diminished in their value . . . the only manner in which these evils can be remedied is by a Free Trade and the only manner in which they can be palliated till such Free Trade shall be obtained is by a

general consumption of domestic commodities and manufactures.'

18. Leerssen (b), p. 20.

19. Young, Part I, p. 101 (Burke's quote was printed in capital letters).

20. Dunne (b), p. 2.

21. See Berlin, I., C. Cruise O'Brien, S. Deane and L. Mitchell (ed.).


### CHAPTER TWELVE *Social Aspects of the Knot*

1. Barrington (a), Chapter 19 (spelling 'Borumborad'); Craig, p. 271; JCKAS XIX, p. 126.

2. Dr Con Costello (historian of the Curragh), personal communication .

3. Sullivan (ed.), p. 236.

4. Dr Con Costello, *Leinster Leader*, 11 November 2004, p. 35.

5. CJKAS XIX, p. 563. The 1781 map of Maynooth showing the ballroom is in Cambridge and has recently been reprinted by the Royal Irish Academy.

6. Young, Part I, pp. 17–18.

7. Young, Part I, pp. 343–4.

8. Barrington (a), Chapter 5, 'Irish Dissipation in 1778'.

9. See also M. Guinness (b), pp. 24–5.

10. Meritocratic in the sense that the Councilmen had to have worked in, and own, a solvent trade important enough to require a guild, while the gentry had usually inherited their land.

11. W.J. Fitzpatrick, Appendix, 'Toping 70 years ago'. Rutland was a popular and social viceroy in the 1780s. Curran was John Philpot Curran, a famous Dublin barrister.

12. Chambers, p. 120.

13. Kelly (a), p. 66.

14. T. Moore, pp. 34–5.


### CHAPTER THIRTEEN *Networks*

1. By a functional but unusual method of filing, Arthur's letter refusing repayment was tacked on to the choir school's Georgian charter. It had been founded in 1432.

2. Today the hospital is said to have been founded in 1753, but the following item clearly states 1756.

3. Journal of the Irish House of Commons 1773, p. 202.

4. The spellings run from 'Twatling' (Brookings map of 1728) to 'tWatling' (Rocque 1756–60) and 'Watling' thereafter.

5. Beckett, p. 183.

6. Dublin almanac, 1778.

7. Today the N4 and R148.

8. JCKAS XVIII, pp .225–46. In 1803 the other turnpike road trustees included his brother Richard and William Donnellan, the son of Nehemiah, who had introduced Arthur into the Kildare Knot back in 1758.

9. Wilson, p. 18.

10. Braudel, pp. 379–81.

11. Ossory Fitzpatrick, Chapter 5.

12. Chart, Section 12.

13. Tillyard, pp. 357–85.

### CHAPTER FOURTEEN *Family Matters in the 1780s*

1. HSG (b), pp. 14, 17–18.

2. HSG (b), pp. 20–21.

3. Barrington (a), Chapter 39.

4. An earlier Darley had worked as a stonemason on the rebuilding of Carton from the 1740s, according to a letter of Emily, Countess of Kildare, dated May 1759, quoted in FitzGerald, p. 71. This may have led to the introduction of the two families. As with Dr Price's help in his career from the Conollys, which benefited Richard Guinness, so also this Darley obligation for work to the FitzGerald earls and dukes just precedes the first of the three Guinness–Darley marriages in 1763. The links have continued, as Desmond Guinness saved Castletown from neglect and ruin in 1967, and his brother Jonathan married a descendant of Lord Edward FitzGerald in 1951.

5. Journal of the Irish House of Commons, 1792.

6. Journal of the Irish House of Commons (King and Bradley), 1791, Vol. 28, pp. 57–8. Twenty tons of wheat would produce about fourteen tons of flour.

7. Braudel, p. 374.

8. Martelli, p. 17–18.

9. Published in serial form in 1860–61.

### CHAPTER FIFTEEN *Turning the Corner*

1. McDowell, p. 130.

2. Donnelly and Miller (eds), Chapter 3.

3. See Appendix B for statistical sources.

4. This top-down paternalism was not recalled nor appreciated. A century later Father Herlihy asked if 'England was responsible for the intemperance of the Irish? Our Celtic ancestors were a very temperate people before the English landed on their shores. In the time of St Patrick drunkenness was unknown among them.' To create a new racial self-image, Mescan, the ancient texts and all those kings drinking *coirm* were being edited out of history. 'Celt above Saxon', Boston, 1904, p. 171.

5. McDowell, passim. Francis Higgins was nicknamed the 'Sham Squire' and was seen by liberals as a journalist who had been 'bought' by the administration.

6. Lynch and Vaizey, p. 58.

### CHAPTER SIXTEEN *Marriages*

1. B. Guinness (ed.), pp. 3, 7, 9.

2. Dublin Registry of Deeds, Vol. 471, No. 299966.

3. NLI GO MS 179; POS 8308. The claimed lineage back to Edward I (reigned 1272–1307) was later annotated just five generations back from Ann Lee with *wrong* and *not so*.

4. For Dorcas Cullen and the Lees, see NLI GO MS 8015, Part 9.

5. Craig, p. 108.

6. Enda Lee, personal communication.

7. Dublin almanac, 1801. The Association for Discountenancing Vice and Promoting the Knowledge and Practice of the Christian Religion was founded in 1792 and incorporated in 1800. By 1822 it was educating 6,200 Protestant and 5,334 Catholic children. This apparent tolerance, educating Catholic and Protestant children together, led on, however, to strong opposition from the Catholic hierarchy, anxious to promote its own schools and fearful of losing numbers by conversion. Catholic schools were technically illegal until 1782, and twenty years later this association was satisfying a demand that the Church was still unable to meet. See also Donnelly and Miller (eds), p. 101, and KHS, Chapter 10.

8. NLI GO MSS 160, 168, 178; microfiches POS 8290, 8302, 8307. MS 178 updated the lineages to 1860.

9. However, when Benjamin Lee Guinness was knighted in 1867, the former Magennis link was again colourfully but wrongly endorsed by Sir Bernard Burke, the editor of *Burke's Peerage*.

10. B. Guinness (ed.), pp. 27–8.

11. CAR, Vol. 12, p. 448.

12. CAR, Vol. 12, p. 517.

13. John Colgan, personal communication.

14. Shown in Mac Leod, pp. 32–3.

15. NLI MS GO 8015 has a section on James Blair. Hornhill is not identifiable in Perthshire today.

16. The marriage was performed by the Reverend Thomas Cradock, perhaps related to Arthur's friend William.


## CHAPTER SEVENTEEN *Politics and Identity*

1. Chambers, p. 26. Others in the group of visitors included Edward Byrne, Dublin brewer and a brother-in-law of James Farrell, and John Keogh, a wealthy merchant who supported and sponsored Tone until 1798.

2. Ann Reg, 1791, Chronicle 3.

3. Ann Reg, 1793, Chronicle 1; Whelan, pp. 40–41.

4. Proceedings of the Irish Parliament, Dublin, 1793, Vol. II, p. 343.

5. CAR, Vol. 14, p. 341.

6. *Dublin Evening Post*, No. 4307, p. 3.

7. Martelli, p. 19.

8. Wilson's Dublin Almanack, 1786, p. 70.

9. Journal of the Irish House of Commons (Grierson), Vol. 15, p. 403. The report was published in June 1793. The committee was formed to investigate profiteering by coal merchants and the effects on the poor, after pressure from Henry Grattan; McDowell, p. 110.

10. 'Emancipation' usually means a release from slavery. While this was not literally the case, its use up to 1829 reflects the strength of the feeling by Irish Catholics about the remaining restrictions.

11. *Dublin Evening Post*, No. 4312, p. 2.

12. If Arthur generally supported Burke, the latter had by now divided views with Fox and R.B. Sheridan on the evolution of the French Revolution. See Ann Reg, 1791, 'History of Europe', pp. 105–15. For Burke's support of Catholic emancipation see Whelan, pp. 111–12.

13. Grattan had campaigned against the tithe laws from the late 1780s; Kelly (b), p. 24.

14. Chambers, p. 27; Mansergh, pp. 147–9. The Association's secretary was Richard Griffith, who was a retired Indian 'nabob' and the neighbour and frequent sponsor of Theobald Wolfe Tone. See KHS, p. 389.

15. Moody and Martin (eds.), p. 234.

16. McDowell, pp. 114–18; Mansergh, pp. 153–76.

17. *Freeman's Journal*, No. 5197, p. 4.

18. Four of these wax seals on leases dated 1795 were owned by Henry Guinness; HSG (a), p. 23.

19. Dunne (a), p. 1; (b), p. 2. I asked Mr Dunne in 2004 for his references, hoping for new and unexpected proof of how Arthur was directly opposed to the views of the liberal patriots, but the eminent lecturer has remained silent. On today's conflicting views about Irishness by other sociologists, see Negra (ed.), pp. 11, 130–60.

### CHAPTER EIGHTEEN *Rebellion*

1. Schama (b), pp. 204–7, 280.

2. Cooper, p. 83.

3. Martelli, p. 23.

4. NAD; RP 620/10/121/146; Whelan, p. 90–92, on the many United Irish meetings held in pubs, particularly in the Liberties area of Dublin, and the warnings against such meetings.

5. *The Report from the Secret Committee of the House of Commons*, Dublin, 1798, Appendix XXVII, p. 259.

6. Some have argued that the pensionary Mr Cox was a different person but have not gone on to identify who the pensionary was nor to compare the outspoken styles of the Union Star and the later *Irish Magazine*.

7. *The Report from the Secret Committee of the House of Commons*, Dublin, 1798, Appendix XXV, pp. 243–7.

8. Boylan (ed.) 1999.

9. By now the United States had also debated heatedly the very different economic and financial policies of Jefferson and Hamilton, but without resorting to violence. The French paper money 'assignats','mandats' and 'rescriptions' had already proved to be a disaster, yet such a system was promised if the United Irish took power; Ann Reg, 1796, 'History of Europe', pp. 154–6.

10. For Santerre, see Schama (a), pp. 668–70; for Sweetman, Mansergh, p. 235.

11. Costello, p. 98; KHS, pp. 394–5.

12. In contrast, the Duke of Leinster spoke out strongly against the military abuses in the English House of Lords on 15 June; Ann Reg, 1798, 'History', p. 225.

13. Ann Reg, 1798, Chronicle 29.

14. Martelli, p. 19.

15. *Freeman's Journal*, 29 November 1793. The case was titled R. (Scully) v. Kairin.

16. HSG (b), pp. 18–19.

17. Barrington (a), Chapter 41.

18. HSG (b), pp. 19–20.

19. Barrington (a), Chapter 22.

20. While the Duke of Leinster was in touch with T.A. Emmet in 1793 (see above, Chambers, p. 27), it is also interesting that Richard Guinness's barrister friend Peter Burrowes went on to defend Robert Emmet on his trial for treason in 1803.

21. For example, Richard Madden secured notes on secret service expenditure in 1841 on a sale of Lord Mulgrave's books and papers. W.J. Fitzpatrick, passim.

22. W.J. Fitzpatrick, appendix on Walter Cox; letter dated 18 December 1819.

23. KHS, Chapter 14.

24. Plunder followed the subsequent French conquests elsewhere in Italy and those of Egypt (1798–99), Haiti (1802), Germany (1805–7) and Spain (1808–13).

25. Schama (a), pp. 854–5, argues that the richer peasants prospered in the French Revolution but not the poor.

26. Madden, Part II, p. 334.

27. M. Guinness, p. 30.

28. *The Tree of Liberty*, particularly Part 4, ''98 after '98'.

29. Foster (b), p. 222. The statue of Tone was never finished.

30. Schama (a), p. xiii.

### CHAPTER NINETEEN *Revolution*

1. The two books examined in this chapter have no reference numbers, not least because they are the treasures of the Storehouse Museum Archives. There is debate on whether the barrels are of thirty-two or thirty-six gallons. Dennison and McDonagh say that Guinness used thirty-two-gallon barrels in the following century, but this does not alter my findings that production nearly quadrupled pro rata in 1797–9.

2. Ann Reg, 1796, Chronicle, pp. 48–9.

3. Jonathan Guinness, personal communication.

4. JCKAS XVI, p. 373. The Forenaughts Cavalry included Mathew Tone, a cousin of Theobald; KHS, p. 391.

5. Ann Reg, 1802, passim, for these miscellaneous items; Barrington (a), Chapter 43, on Father O'Leary.

6. M. Guinness (b), p. 33; Dunne (a), p. 1; (b), p. 1.

### CHAPTER TWENTY *Inheritance*

1. William Dick, personal communication.

2. I say 'biblical', as it was inspired by the start of Jesus Christ's ministry at the age of thirty. This was a fairly common practice at that time. The partnership of the three brothers was not legally formalized in 1803, but clearly it was already an agreed family policy.

3. Gilts (British government debt) yielded 5 per cent per annum in 1803, so capital of £300,000 in gilts would have yielded £15,000 per annum free of effort and risk. The value of the cash-flow at a private Dublin brewery would have been heavily discounted to this. The future success of the brewery and flour mills was not inevitable in 1803; any discounting today must be arbitrary, and so I suggest £100,000. Certainly the brewing brothers had the means to create much more wealth if they played their cards right.

4. This resolution was proposed by Edward Byrne, a rival Dublin brewer. We have crossed his path before, as Byrne was the brother-in-law of James Farrell and was one of the group that persuaded Tom Conolly to support Catholic Relief in 1792; the others including John Keogh and T.W. Tone (see Chambers, p. 26).

5. D. Wilson, p. 38.

6. D. Wilson, p. 41.

7. D. Wilson, p. 41–2.

8. Bielenberg, pp. 114–15.

9. M. Guinness (b), p. 16.

10. Since 1786 a Mr McCreevy was employed as the local lock-keeper. He was the ancestor of Dr Charlie McCreevy, who was born there and who is currently a European Commissioner and who was the Minister of Finance who enabled the 'Celtic Tiger' boom in the Irish economy in the 1990s.

# Appendix A: Measures and Currency

Easy comparison is complicated by the differences between Irish, English (imperial) and metric measures, some of which were not standardized until after 1800. The measures here are given for beer aficionados and younger readers.

*Source:* Dennison and McDonagh, 1998, pp.154, 163 and 272.

### Distance
1 foot = 30.48 centimetres
3 feet = 1 yard = 91.4 centimetres
1 perch = 5½ yards = 5.027 metres
1 mile = 1.609 kilometres
1 old Irish mile = 2.57 kilometres

### Area
1 acre = 4,840 square feet = 0.405 hectares

### Money
It would be impossible to try to equate the relative values of today's money with currencies in the late eighteenth and early nineteenth centuries; however, the pre-decimal system was as follows:
12 pennies (12d.) = 1 shilling (1s.) = 5p
20 shillings = 1 pound (£1)
21 shillings = 1 guinea

### Volume

1 imperial gallon = 8 pints = 4.546 litres = 1.2 US gallons

1 barrel = 36 imperial gallons, which was standard in the brewing industry; it was 32 imperial gallons at the Guinness brewery until 1881

1 Irish barrel = 42 Irish gallons = 32.96 imperial gallons

1 barrel of barley = 224 pounds = 101.696 kilograms

1 barrel of malt = 168 pounds

1 bushel of wheat = 56 pounds (that is, 4 bushels per barrel)

1 bushel of malt = 42 pounds

If the Guinness mills were selling 7,500 barrels of flour in 1798 (750 imperial tons), this was a small percentage of the 300 tons of flour that Dublin consumed every week.

### Guinness barrel sizes in the 1800s

1 firkin = 8 imperial gallons (often 9 gallons elsewhere in the industry)

1 kilderkin = 16 gallons (18 gallons elsewhere in the industry)

1 hogshead = 52 gallons (54 gallons elsewhere in the industry)

### A later comparison of porter and stout beers

Beer historians can compare the specific gravity strengths of Guinness porter and stouts in the early 1900s. If porter was revolutionary in Dublin in the 1770s, it became the more affordable poor cousin of stout in the 1800s and was reduced in strength by law during the First World War. Thus:

1914 porter: 1058 s.g.

1920s porter: 1036–41 s.g.

1920s stout: 1073 s.g.

# Appendix B: The Tax on Beer, 1791–1792: The Underlying Statistics

*Sources:* Irish Parliamentary Journals published by King and Bradley (K&B) and Grierson.

Beer and ale brewed in Ireland (in barrels of 32 imperial gallons) (K&B, Vol. 28, 1791, pp. 120, 121, 164):

1761: 588,217 barrels
1765: 578,068 barrels
1770: 439,863 barrels
1775: 465,207 barrels
1780: 429,200 barrels
1785: 361,903 barrels
1790: 434,397 barrels

This explains the brewers' problems in 1760–90; sales had dropped over the long term, despite a rise in population. The increase in 1785–90 was less than the increase in English imports.

Irish malt and barley sent to Dublin (in imperial tons) (K&B, Vol. 28, p. 74):

1761: 341 tons
1765: 557 tons
1770: 382 tons
1775: 8 tons
1780: 258 tons
1785: 265 tons
1790: 10 tons

Erratic supply; the brewers had to import much of their malt from England.

Imported beer (K&B, Vol. 28, p. 176):
1761: 17,348 barrels[NB]
1765: 25,116 barrels
1770: 39,121 barrels
1775: 52,910 barrels
1780: 39, 594 barrels
1785: 47,685 barrels
1790: 106,965 barrels

By 1790 beer sales had increased; imported beer more so. Recalling the brewers' complaint made in 1773, it seems that the competition around 1790 was greater.

Licences granted for retailers:

|  | *Beers* | *Spirits* |
|---|---|---|
| 1788 | 9,327 | 8,735 |
| 1789 | 8,927 | 8,389 |
| 1790 | 8,795 | 8,496 |

Beer outlets were declining faster (Grierson, Vol.15, p. 76).

In 1792 Parliament published the sales of alcohol in the nine months to Michaelmas:

|  | *1790* | *1791* |
|---|---|---|
| Imported beers | 70,601 | 88,456 imperial barrels |
| Irish beers | 346,838 | 386,517 imperial barrels |
| Imported spirits | 888,063 | 661,464 imperial gallons |
| Irish spirits | 2,297,786 | 2,202,082 imperial gallons |

5 March 1792: 'Resolved; . . . the Use of spirituous Liquors has decreased and the Use of Malt Liquors has increased.'

# Appendix C: Family Trees

## Selective Family Tree

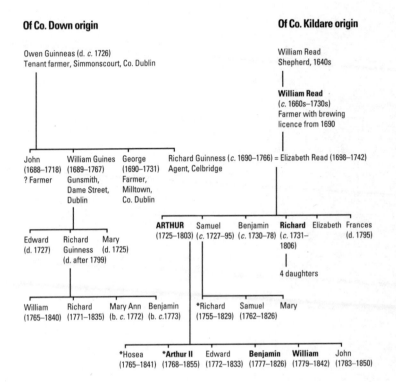

**Of Co. Down origin**

Owen Guinneas (d. *c.* 1726)
Tenant farmer, Simmonscourt, Co. Dublin

**Of Co. Kildare origin**

William Read
Shepherd, 1640s

**William Read**
(*c.* 1660s–1730s)
Farmer with brewing
licence from 1690

John
(1688–1718)
? Farmer

William Guines
(1689–1767)
Gunsmith,
Dame Street,
Dublin

George
(1690–1731)
Farmer,
Milltown,
Co. Dublin

Richard Guinness (*c.* 1690–1766) = Elizabeth Read (1698–1742)
Agent, Celbridge

Edward
(d. 1727)

Richard
Guinness
(d. after 1799)

Mary
(d. 1725)

**ARTHUR**
(1725–1803)

Samuel
(*c.* 1727–95)

Benjamin
(*c.* 1730–78)

**Richard**
(*c.* 1731–
1806)

Elizabeth

Frances
(d. 1795)

4 daughters

William
(1765–1840)

Richard
(1771–1835)

Mary Ann
(b. *c.* 1772)

Benjamin
(b. *c.*1773)

*Richard
(1755–1829)

Samuel
(1762–1826)

Mary

*Hosea
(1765–1841)

**\*Arthur II**
(1768–1855)

Edward
(1772–1833)

**Benjamin**
(1777–1826)

**William**
(1779–1842)

John
(1783–1850)

Brewers marked in **bold**

\* Three male-DNA samples tested in 2001 from
descendants of these men

# *Reads of Oughterard in the 1700s*

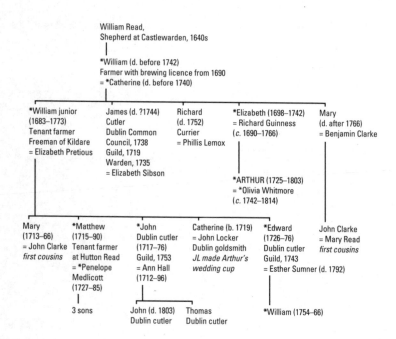

William Read,
Shepherd at Castlewarden, 1640s

\*William (d. before 1742)
Farmer with brewing licence from 1690
= \*Catherine (d. before 1740)

\*William junior
(1683–1773)
Tenant farmer
Freeman of Kildare
= Elizabeth Pretious

James (d. ?1744)
Cutler
Dublin Common
Council, 1738
Guild, 1719
Warden, 1735
= Elizabeth Sibson

Richard
(d. 1752)
Currier
= Phillis Lemox

\*Elizabeth (1698–1742)
= Richard Guinness
(*c.* 1690–1766)

Mary
(d. after 1766)
= Benjamin Clarke

\*ARTHUR (1725–1803)
= \*Olivia Whitmore
(*c.* 1742–1814)

Mary
(1713–66)
= John Clarke
*first cousins*

\*Matthew
(1715–90)
Tenant farmer
at Hutton Read
= \*Penelope
Medlicott
(1727–85)

3 sons

\*John
Dublin cutler
(1717–76)
Guild, 1753
= Ann Hall
(1712–96)

John (d. 1803)
Dublin cutler

Thomas
Dublin cutler

Catherine (b. 1719)
= John Locker
Dublin goldsmith
*JL made Arthur's
wedding cup*

\*Edward
(1726–76)
Dublin cutler
Guild, 1743
= Esther Sumner (d. 1792)

\*William (1754–66)

John Clarke
= Mary Read
*first cousins*

\* Those buried at Oughterard

# Guinness Cousin Marriages in the 1800s in the Brewing Line

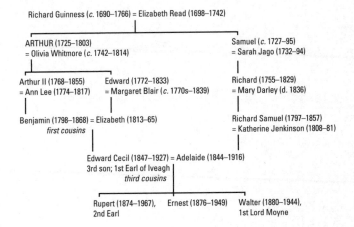

Richard Guinness (*c.* 1690–1766) = Elizabeth Read (1698–1742)

ARTHUR (1725–1803)
= Olivia Whitmore (*c.* 1742–1814)

Samuel (*c.* 1727–95)
= Sarah Jago (1732–94)

Arthur II (1768–1855)
= Ann Lee (1774–1817)

Edward (1772–1833)
= Margaret Blair (*c.* 1770s–1839)

Richard (1755–1829)
= Mary Darley (d. 1836)

Benjamin (1798–1868) = Elizabeth (1813–65)
        *first cousins*

Richard Samuel (1797–1857)
= Katherine Jenkinson (1808–81)

Edward Cecil (1847–1927) = Adelaide (1844–1916)
3rd son; 1st Earl of Iveagh
        *third cousins*

Rupert (1874–1967),
2nd Earl

Ernest (1876–1949)

Walter (1880–1944),
1st Lord Moyne

# Bibliography

This divides for ease into: Guinness-related sources (A); Dublin or city-related books (B); books on Ireland (C); other background sources (D); and books and articles on genetics (E).

## A: The Guinness Family and the Dublin Brewery

Aalen, F., *The Iveagh Trust 1890–1990*, Iveagh Trust, Dublin, 1990

Anon, *Guinness Dublin* (brewery guidebook), Guinness, Dublin, 1955

Bielenberg, A., 'The Irish Brewing Industry and the Rise of Guinness, 1790–1914', in *The Dynamics of the International Brewing Industry Since 1800* by R.G. Wilson and T.R. Gourvish (eds), Routledge, London, 1998

Byrne, A., *Guinness Times*, Town House, Dublin, 1999

Corcoran, T., *The Goodness of Guinness*, Liberties Press, Dublin, 2005

Dennison, S.R. and O. MacDonagh, *Guinness 1886–1939*, Cork University Press, Cork, 1998

Derrington, M., *Journey*, Diageo, Dublin, 2005

Dunne, S. (a), 'Guinness Is Not Irish', http://www.zmag.org, 2003

— (b), 'Guinness Stout: From English to Corporate Colonialism', http://www.indymedia.ie, July 2003

Guinness, B. (ed.) and M. Galwey, *The Guinness Family* (family trees) (3rd edn), privately printed, 1985

Guinness, J.B., *Requiem for a Family Business*, Macmillan, London, 1997

Guinness, H.S. (a), *The Family of Guinness*, privately printed, 1924

— (b), *Notes on the Family of Guinness of Dublin*, privately printed, 1924

— (c), *James's Gate Brewery*, PRONI D3031/3/1, typed notes, undated

— (d), 'Purser Family of Dublin', letter dated 12 December 1925

— (e), *Richard Guinness of Celbridge Co. Kildare*, privately printed, 1934

Guinness, M., *The Guinness Legend*, Hodder and Stoughton, London 1990

— *The Guinness Spirit*, Hodder and Stoughton, London, 1999

Lynch, P. and J. Vaizey, *Guinness's Brewery in the Irish Economy, 1759–1876*, Cambridge University Press, Cambridge, 1960

Martelli, G., *Man of His Time*, privately printed, London, 1957 (about Arthur's great-grandson Lord Iveagh)

Moore, D., 'The Guinness Saga', DHR, Vol. 16, No. 2, October 1960

Mullally, F., *The Silver Salver*, Granada, London, 1981

Murphy, B., 'Pure Genius: Guinness Consumption and Irish Identity', *New Hibernia Review*, Winter 2003

Walsh, P., *Guinness*, Eason and Co., Dublin, 1980 (illustrated booklet in a series on Irish heritage)

Wilson, D., *Dark and Light*, Weidenfeld and Nicholson, London, 1998

### B: Kildare and Dublin, 1600–1800

Annual Register, 1759–1803

Barrington, J. (a), *Personal Sketches and Recollections of His Own Times*, Colburn and Bentley, London, 1828

— (b), *Memoirs of Ireland*, Richard Bentley, London, 1833

Barnard, T. (a), *The Irish Protestants 1649–1770*, Yale University Press, New Haven, 2003

— (b), *Irish Protestant Ascents and Descents 1641–1770*, Four Courts Press, Dublin, 2004

Calendar of the Ancient Records of Dublin

Chambers, L., *Rebellion in Kildare 1790–1803*, Four Corners Press, Dublin, 1998

Chart, D.A., *The Story of Dublin*, Dent, London, 1907

Colgan, J., *Leixlip, County Kildare, Vol. I*, Tyrconnell Press, Leixlip, 2005

Costello, C., *A Class Apart: The Gentry Families of County Kildare*, Nonsuch Publishing, Dublin, 2005

Craig, M., *Dublin 1660–1860*, Cresset Press, Dublin, 1952

Curran, L., S. Pegley, P. Donohoe, V. Twomey, *Aspects of Leixlip*, LPSV Publishers, Dublin, 2001

Dickson, D., *Arctic Ireland*, White Row Press, Belfast, 1997

Dublin Historical Records series

FitzGerald, B., *Emily, Duchess of Leinster*, Staples Press, London, 1949

Fitzpatrick, W.J., *The Sham Squire and the Informers of '98*, Kelly, Dublin, 1866

Flood, W., *Memoirs of Henry Flood, MP*, Cumming, Dublin, 1838

Fraser, A.M., *The Friendly Brothers of St Patrick*, DHR, Vol. 14, pp. 34–40

*The Guinness Harp* (in-house magazine bicentenary edition), Dublin, May/June 1959

Harris, W., *The History and Antiquities of the City of Dublin Compiled from Authentick Memoirs, Offices of Record, Manuscript Collections, and Other Unexceptionable Vouchers*, Flinn and Williams, Dublin, 1766

Joyce, W., *The Neighbourhood of Dublin*, M.H. Gill, Dublin, 1912

Johnson-Liik, E.M., *MPs in Dublin 1692–1800*, Ulster Historical Foundation, Belfast, 2006

*Journal of the County Kildare Archaeological Society* (1891–2005)

Kelly, J. (a), '*That Damn'd Thing Called Honour': Duelling in Ireland 1570–1860*, Cork University Press, Cork, 1995

— (b), *Henry Grattan*, Dunalgan Press, Dundalk, 1993

— (c), *Henry Flood*, University of Notre Dame Press, Notre Dame, Indiana, 1998

Laffan, W. (ed.), *The Cries of Dublin*, Irish Georgian Society, Dublin, 2003

McCarthy, G., *The Forgotten Heritage of Kildare*, Nonsuch Publishing, Dublin, 2006

McDowell, R.B., *Grattan: A Life*, Lilliput Press, Dublin, 2001

MacLeod, C., *Irish Volunteer Glass*, National Museum of Ireland booklet, Dublin, undated

Maginn, C., *Civilising Gaelic Leinster: The Extension of Tudor Rule in the O'Byrne and O'Toole Lordships*, Four Courts Press, Dublin, 2005

Malcolmson, A., *Nathaniel Clements*, Four Courts Press, Dublin, 2005

Mansergh, D., *Grattan's Failure: Parliamentary Opposition and the People in Ireland 1779–1800*, Irish Academic Press, Dublin, 2005

Ossory Fitzpatrick, S.A., *Dublin: A Historical and Topographical Account of the City*, Methuen, London, 1907

Sadleir, T.U. and P.L. Dickinson, *Georgian Mansions in Ireland*, Ponsonby and Gibbs, Dublin, 1915

Semple, G., *A Treatise on Building in Water*, Husband, Dublin, 1776

Sullivan, E. (ed.), *Buck Whaley's Memoirs*, Alexander Moring, London, 1906

Small, S., *Political Thought in Ireland 1776–98*, Oxford University Press, Oxford, 2002

Tillyard, S., *Aristocrats*, Chatto and Windus, London, 1994

Walsh, J.E., *Ireland 120 Years Ago*, M.H. Gill and Son, Dublin, 1911

Warburton J. (with J. Whitelaw and R. Walsh), *History of the City of Dublin*, 2 vols, W. Bulmer and Co., London, 1818

S. Watson, *The Gentleman's and Citizen's Almanack* (principally for the years 1778, 1786, 1787, 1788, 1801)

W. Wilson, *Wilson's Dublin Directory* (principally for the years 1778, 1786, 1787, 1788, 1801)

Young, A., *A Tour in Ireland*, Cadell and Dodsley, London, 1780

### C: County Down/Ireland, 1000–1800

Arnold, B., *Swift: An Illustrated Life*, Lilliput Press, Dublin, 2001

Beckett, J.C., *The Making of Modern Ireland*, Faber, London, 1966

Boylan, H. (ed.), *A Dictionary of Irish Biography* (3rd edn), Gill and Macmillan, Dublin, 1999

Byrne, F.J., *Irish Kings and High-Kings*, Four Courts Press, Dublin, 1973

Chenevix-Trench, C., *Grace's Card Irish Catholic Landlords 1690–1800*, Mercier Press, Cork, 1997

Cullen, L., *An Economic History of Ireland*, Batsford, London, 1972

Curtis, E., *A History of Ireland*, Methuen, London, 1936

Deane, S., *Foreign Affections: Essays on Edmund Burke*, Cork University Press, Cork, 2005

Donnelly, J. and K. Miller (eds.), *Irish Popular Culture 1650–1850*, Irish Academic Press, Dublin, 1999

Duffy, Patrick, David Edwards and Elizabeth FitzPatrick (eds.), *Gaelic Ireland*, Four Courts Press, Dublin, 2001

Duffy, S. (ed.), *Atlas of Irish History*, Gill and Macmillan, Dublin, 1997

Elliott, M., *The Catholics of Ulster*, Penguin, London, 2001

Foster, R. (a), *Modern Ireland 1600–1972*, Penguin, London, 1988

— (b), *The Irish Story*, Allen Lane, London, 2001

Fothergill, B., *The Mitred Earl*, Faber and Faber, London, 1974

Geoghegan, P., *The Irish Act of Union: A Study in High Politics 1798–1801*, Gill and Macmillan, Dublin, 1999

Gibbons, L., *Transformations in Irish Culture*, Cork University Press, Cork, 1996

Gillespie, R. (a), *The Transformation of the Irish Economy 1550–1700*, Dundalgan Press, Dundalk, 1998

— (ed.) (b), *Colonial Ulster*, Cork University Press, Cork, 1985

— (c), *Seventeenth-Century Ireland: Making Ireland Modern*, Gill and Macmillan, Dublin, 2006

Glazier, M. (ed.), *Encyclopedia of the Irish in America*, University of Notre Dame Press, Notre Dame, Indiana, 1999

Ingamells, J., *British and Irish Travellers in Italy 1701–1800*, New Haven: Yale, 1997

Keogh, D. and K. Whelan, *Acts of Union*, Four Courts Press, Dublin, 2001

Leerssen, J. (a), *Mere Irish and Fíor-Ghael*, Cork University Press, Cork, 1986

— (b), *Remembrance and Imagination*, Cork University Press, Cork, 1996

Lodge, J. (ed.), *The Peerage of Ireland*, Dublin, 1754

McGuinness, W.V., *Our Ancestors and Relatives, Vol. I: The McGuinness Family*, privately printed, Avon, Connecticut, 1994

Madden, R.R., *The United Irishmen*, 7 vols, Madden and Co., London, 1843–60

Mitchell, L. (ed.), *Edmund Burke: Reflections on the Revolution in France*, Oxford University Press, Oxford, 1993

Moody, T.W. (ed.), *The Course of Irish History*, Mercier Press, Cork, 1967

Moore, T., *The Life and Death of Lord Edward FitzGerald*, 2 vols, Davison, Simmons and Co., London, 1831

Nicholls, K.W., *Gaelic and Gaelicised Ireland in the Middle Ages*, Lilliput Press, Dublin, 2003

O'Brien, C. Cruise, *The Great Melody*, Minerva Press, London, 1992

O'Sullivan, H. and R. Gillespie (eds.), *The Borderlands*, Queen's University, Belfast, 1989

— *The Magennises, Lords of Iveagh*, unpublished draft, 2004

O'Toole, F. (a), *White Savage*, Faber and Faber, London, 2005

— (b), *A Traitor's Kiss: The Life of Richard Brinsley Sheridan*, Granta, London, 1998

Proudfoot, L. (ed.), *Down History and Society*, Geography Press, Dublin, 1997

Stewart, A.T.Q., *The Shape of Irish History*, Blackstaff Press, Belfast, 2001

Stockman, G. (ed.), *Place Names of Northern Ireland* (the County Down volumes), Queen's University, Belfast, 1992–6

Whelan, K., *The Tree of Liberty*, Cork University Press, Cork, 1996

Wolfe Tone, W., *Life of Theobald Wolfe Tone*, 2 vols, Gale and Seaton, Washington, DC, 1826

### D: Background/General

Berlin, I., *Political Ideas in the Romantic Age*, Pimlico, London, 2006

Boswell, J., *The Life of Samuel Johnson*, ed. A. Calder, Wordsworth Press, London, 1999

Braudel, F., *The Perspective of the World: Civilization and Capitalism 15th–18th Centuries, Vol. 3*, Phoenix, London, 2003

Cooper, D., *Talleyrand*, Harper and Brothers, London, 1932

De Landa, M., *A Thousand Years of Nonlinear History*, Zone Books, New York, 2000

Keegan, Sir J., *The Price of Admiralty*, Arrow, London, 1988

Lowenthal, D., *The Heritage Crusade and the Spoils of History*, Cambridge University Press, Cambridge, 1998

McLynn, F., *1759: The Year Britain Became Master of the World*, Pimlico, London, 2004

Mathias, P., *The Brewing Industry in England 1700–1830*, Cambridge University Press, Cambridge, 1959

Negra, D. (ed.), *The Irish in Us: Irishness, Performativity and Popular Culture*, Duke, London, 2006

Picard, L., *Dr Johnson's London*, Phoenix, London, 2000

Quennell, P., *Samuel Johnson, His Friends and Enemies*, Weidenfeld, London, 1972

Schama, S. (a), *Citizens: A Chronicle of the French Revolution*, Penguin, London, 1989

— (b), *Patriots and Liberators: Revolution in the Netherlands 1780–1813* (2nd edn), Fontana, London, 1992

Schuchard, M., *Why Mrs Blake Cried: William Blake and the Sexual Basis of Spiritual Vision*, Century, London, 2006

### E: Books and Articles on Genetics

Butler, J., *Forensic DNA Typing*, Academic Press, San Diego, 2001

Cavalli-Sforza, L., *Genes, Peoples and Languages*, Allen Lane, London, 2000

Hill, E.W., M.A. Jobling and D.G. Bradley, 'Y-chromosome Variation and Irish Origins: A Pre-neolithic Gene Gradation Starts in the Near East and Culminates in Western Ireland', *Nature*, 2000, Vol. 404, p. 351

Jobling, M.A. and C. Tyler-Smith, 'The Human Y-chromosome: An Evolutionary Marker Comes of Age', *Nature*, 2003, Vol. 4, p. 598

Jones, S., *In the Blood: God, Genes and Destiny*, Flamingo, London, 1997

McEvoy, B., M. Richards, P. Forster and D.G. Bradley, 'The Longue Durée of Genetic Ancestry: Multiple Genetic Marker Systems and Celtic Origins on the Atlantic Facade of Europe', *American Journal of Human Genetics*, 2004, Vol. 75, p. 693

McEvoy, B. and D.G. Bradley, 'Y-chromosomes and the Extent of Patrilineal Ancestry in Irish Surnames', *Human Genetics*, 2006, Vol. 119, p. 212

Moore, L.T., B. McEvoy, E. Cape et al., 'A Y-chromosome Signature of Hegemony in Gaelic Ireland', *American Journal of Human Genetics*, 2006, Vol. 78, p. 334

Olson, S., *Mapping Human History: Discovering the Past Through Our Genes*, Bloomsbury, London, 2002

Oppenheimer, S., *The Origins of the British: A Genetic Detective Story*, Constable, London, 2006

Passarge, E., *Color Atlas of Genetics*, Thieme, New York, 2001

Pomery, C., *DNA and Family History*, National Archives: London, 2004

Rosser, Z.T., T. Zerjal, M.E. Hurley et al., 'Y-chromosomal Diversity in Europe Is Clinal and Influenced Primarily by Geography Rather Than by Language', *American Journal of Human Genetics*, 2000, Vol. 67, p. 1526

Semino , O., G. Passarino, P. Oefner et al., 'The Genetic Legacy of Paleolithic *Homo Sapiens Sapiens* in Extant Europeans: A Y-chromosome Perspective', *Science*, 2000, Vol. 290, p. 1155

Sykes, B., *Blood of the Isles: Exploring the Genetic Roots of Our Tribal History*, Bantam, London, 2006

# Index